Thai

lonely planet

phrasebooks
and
Bruce Evans

Thai phrasebook
5th edition – September 2004

Published by
Lonely Planet Publications Pty Ltd ABN 36 005 607 983
90 Maribyrnong St, Footscray, Victoria 3011, Australia

Lonely Planet Offices
Australia Locked Bag 1, Footscray, Victoria 3011
USA 150 Linden St, Oakland CA 94607
UK 72-82 Rosebery Ave, London, EC1R 4RW
France 1 rue du Dahomey, 75011 Paris

Cover illustration
Tuk-tuk'n Around in Bangers by Patrick Marris

ISBN 1 74059 231 X

  10 9 8 7 6 5 4 3 2

Printed by The Bookmaker International Ltd
Printed in China

acknowledgments

Editor Piers Kelly would like to acknowledge the following people for their contributions to this phrasebook:

Bruce Evans for his meticulous translations, cultural insight and assistance in overcoming technical difficulties. Bruce lived in Thailand for more than 20 years and has translated a number of books from Thai to English. Bruce would like to thank Annie Main for helping with some of the more obscure terms, his wife Lek for help with Thai idioms, and Thai proofers Benjawan and Mike Golding for valuable suggestions.

Joe Cummings who wrote much of the original grammar material.

Nicholas Stebbing, Ben Handicott and Mark Germanchis who surmounted baffling script difficulties, esoteric fonts and arcane unicode enigmas.

Project manager Glenn van-der-Knijff who filled in while Fabrice was away.

Fellow editor Francesca Coles for her proofing prowess.

Lonely Planet Language Products

Publishing Manager: Karin Vidstrup Monk

Commissioning Editor: Karina Coates

Editors: Piers Kelly, Francesca Coles and
Annelies Mertens

Layout Designer: David Kemp

Project Manager: Fabrice Rocher

Managing Editor: Karin Vidstrup Monk

Layout Manager: Sally Darmody

Series Designer: Yukiyoshi Kamimura

Cartographer: Wayne Murphy

make the most of this phrasebook ...

Anyone can speak another language! It's all about confidence. Don't worry if you can't remember your school language lessons or if you've never learnt a language before. Even if you learn the very basics (on the inside covers of this book), your travel experience will be the better for it. You have nothing to lose and everything to gain when the locals hear you making an effort.

finding things in this book

For easy navigation, this book is in sections. The Tools chapters are the ones you'll thumb through time and again. The Practical section covers basic travel situations like catching transport and finding a bed. The Social section gives you conversational phrases, pick-up lines, the ability to express opinions – so you can get to know people. Food has a section all of its own: gourmets and vegetarians are covered and local dishes feature. Safe Travel equips you with health and police phrases, just in case. Remember the colours of each section and you'll find everything easily; or use the comprehensive Index. Otherwise, check the two-way traveller's Dictionary for the word you need.

being understood

Throughout this book you'll see coloured phrases on each page. They're phonetic guides to help you pronounce the language. You don't even need to look at the language itself, but you'll get used to the way we've represented particular sounds. The pronunciation chapter in Tools will explain more, but you can feel confident that if you read the coloured phrase slowly, you'll be understood.

communication tips

Body language, ways of doing things, sense of humour – all have a role to play in every culture. 'Local talk' boxes show you common ways of saying things, or everyday language to drop into conversation. 'Listen for ...' boxes supply the phrases you may hear. They start with the phonetic guide (because you'll hear it before you know what's being said) and then lead in to the language and the English translation.

social 101

thai

spoken as 1st language   spoken as 2nd language

For more details see the **introduction**.

Cradled between Cambodia, Laos, Malaysia, and Myanmar, the Kingdom of Thailand is something of a Tower of Babel, with numerous dialects spoken from north to south. What has come to be known as Standard Thai is actually a dialect spoken in Bangkok and the surrounding provinces. Standard Thai is the official language of administration, education and the media, and most Thais understand it even if they speak another dialect. For this reason all the words and phrases in this book are translated into Standard Thai.

Thai belongs to the Tai language group meaning that it is closely related to a number of languages spoken outside the borders of present-day Thailand. Some of these are Lao (Laos), Khampti (India) and Lue (China). The Isaan dialect, spoken in the northeast of Thailand, is linguistically identical to Lao. Thai has borrowed a number of words from languages such as Mon (Myanmar) and Khmer (Cambodia). Ancient languages also continue to influence Thai. Just as English relies on Latin and ancient Greek for coining new words or formalising rules of grammar, Thai has adopted Sanskrit and Pali as linguistic models. More recently, English has become a major influence on Thai, particularly in words related to technology or business.

The elegant characters of the Thai script are a source of fascination for those experiencing the language for the first time. The curved symbols seem to

---

at a glance ...

language name:
Thai, Siamese

name in language:
ภาษาไทย pah-săh tai

language family:
Tai

approximate number of speakers:
25–37 million

close relatives:
Khampti, Khmer, Lao, Lue, Mon, Nhang, Shan, Zhuang

---

introduction

run together but they are all divisible into distinct alphabetical units. There are 44 consonants which are classified into three categories depending on the kinds of vowels they are associated with. Vowels are indicated by symbols, or combinations of symbols, that may appear before, after or even around the consonant. The Thai government has instituted the Royal Thai General Transcription System (or RTGS) as a standard method of writing Thai using a Roman 26-letter alphabet. You'll notice its use in official documents, road signs and on maps. The system is convenient for writing but not comprehensive enough to account for all the sounds in Thai. In this book we have devised a phonetic system based on how the language sounds when it's spoken.

The social structure of Thai society demands different registers of speech depending on who you're talking to. To make things simple we've chosen the correct form of speech appropriate to the context of each phrase. Thai is a logical language and despite some challenges, rattling off a meaningful phrase is easier than you might think. This phrasebook includes the script next to the pronunciation so that when all else fails you can open the book and point at what you want to say.

This book contains the useful words you'll need to get by as well as fun, spontaneous phrases that lead to a better understanding of Thailand and its people. The contact you make using Thai will make your travels unique. Local knowledge, new relationships and a sense of satisfaction are on the tip of your tongue, so don't just stand there – say something!

abbreviations used in this book

f	feminine
inf	informal
m	masculine
pl	plural
pol	polite

Just about all of the sounds in Thai exist in English. While some people may find it difficult to pronounce Thai words, persistence is the key. Locals will appreciate your efforts and often help you along. Smile, point and try again. You'll be surprised how much sense you can convey with just a few useful words.

vowel sounds

Thai vowel sounds are similar to those in the English words listed in this table. Accents above vowels (like à, é and ò) relate to the tones (see next page).

symbol	english equivalent	example
a	run	bàt
aa	bad	gàa
ah	father	gah
ai	aisle	jài
air	flair	wair-lah
e	bed	pen
i	bit	bìt
ee	see	bee
eu	her or french bleu	beu
ew	new with rounded lips	néw
o	hot	bòt
oh	note	đoh
or	for	pôr

u	put	sùk
oo	moon	kôo
ou	o plus u, similar to the the **o** in old	láa·ou
ow	cow	bow
oy	boy	soy

tones

If you listen to someone speaking Thai you'll notice that some vowels are pronounced at a high or low pitch while others swoop or glide in a sing-song manner. This is because Thai, like a number of other Asian languages, uses a system of care-fully-pitched tones to make distinctions between words. There are five distinct tones in Thai: mid, low, falling, high and rising. The accent marks above the vowel remind you which to use. The mid tone has no accent.

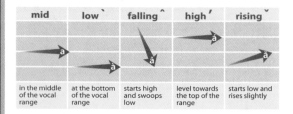

mid	low ``	falling ^	high ´	rising ˇ
in the middle of the vocal range	at the bottom of the vocal range	starts high and swoops low	level towards the top of the range	starts low and rises slightly

consonant sounds

Most consonants in our phonetic system are pronounced the same as in English but Thai does has a few tricky consonants. Watch out for the ъ sound which is halfway between a 'b' and a 'p', and the đ sound which is halfway between a 'd' and a 't'.

symbol	english equivalent	example
b	**big**	bòr
b̃	ri**b-p**unch	b̃lah
ch	**ch**art	chìng
d	**d**og	dèk
đ	har**d-t**imes	đòw
f	**f**ull	fäh
g	**g**et	gài
h	**h**at	hèep
j	**j**unk	jahn
k	**k**ite	kài
l	**l**ike	ling
m	**m**at	máh
n	**n**ut	nŏo
ng	si**ng**	ngoo
p	**p**ush	pahn
r	**r**at	reu·a
s	**s**it	säh-lah
t	**t**ap	tów
w	**w**atch	wat
y	**y**es	yàhk

syllables

In this book we have used hyphens to separate syllables from each another. So the word ang-grìt (English) is made up of two distinct syllables ang and grìt.

In some words we have divided the syllables further with a dot · in order to help you separate vowel sounds and avoid mispronunciation. So the word kĕe·an is actually pronounced as one syllable with two separate vowel sounds.

You'll also occasionally come across commas in our phonetic guides. This just means you need to pause slightly to prevent a misinterpretation of the phrase.

plunge in!

Don't be discouraged if Thai seems difficult at first – this is only because we aren't used to pronouncing certain Thai sounds the way we do in English. Speak slowly and follow the coloured phonetic guides next to each phrase. If you absolutely can't make yourself understood, simply point to the Thai phrase and show it to the person you're speaking to. The most important thing is to laugh at your mistakes and keep trying. Remember, communicating in a foreign language is, above all, great fun.

This chapter contains a basic grammar of Thai explained in simple terms. It's arranged alphabetically to help you make your own sentences. We hope it will encourage you to explore beyond the territory of the phrases given in this phrasebook and to create your own adventures in communication. You should be encouraged by the fact that Thai grammar is really quite a simple and logical system.

a/an & the

In Thai there are no equivalents to the English articles a, an or the. Simply say the noun by itself. For example:

The radio doesn't work.

วิทยุเสีย
           wí-tá-yú sĕe·a
           (lit: radio ruined)

See also **nouns**.

adjectives & adverbs see describing things

be

The verb ben เป็น is the closest Thai equivalent to the English verb 'be' but with some important differences. It's used to join nouns or pronouns.

I am a teacher.
ผม/ดิฉันเป็นครู

pŏm/dì-chăn ben kroo m/f
(lit: I ben teacher)

This dog is a ridgeback.
หมานี้เป็นหมาหลังอาน

măh née ben măh lăng ahn
(lit: dog this ben dog ridgeback)

However, it can't be used to join pronouns and adjectives – the adjective simply follows the noun directly, with no verb:

tall person
คนสูง

kon sŏong
(lit: person tall)

The word ben also has other meanings, such as 'have' when describing a person's condition:

I have a fever.
ผม/ดิฉันเป็นไข้

pŏm/dì-chăn ben kâi m/f
(lit: I ben fever)

She has a cold.
เขาเป็นหวัด

kŏw ben wàt
(lit: she ben cold)

It can even be used to show ability:

She knows how to play guitar.
เขาเล่นกีตาร์เป็น

kŏw lên gee-đah ben
(lit: she play guitar ben)

One question you'll hear quite often in Thailand is:

Can you eat Thai food?
คุณทานอาหารไทยเป็นไหม

kun tahn ah-hăhn tai ben măi
(lit: you eat food Thai ben măi)

This ultimately means, 'Can you tolerate spicy food?' (see **questions and answers** for a description of măi).

See also **pointing something out** and **verbs**.

classifiers see counting things

commands & requests

The word kŏr is used to make polite requests. Depending on the context, it's roughly equivalent to 'Please give me a …' or 'May I ask for a …'. Note that kŏr always comes at the beginning of a sentence and is often used in conjunction with the added 'polite' word nòy (a little), spoken with a low tone at the end of the sentence:

Can I have some rice?
ขอข้าวหน่อย

kŏr kôw nòy
(lit: kŏr rice nòy)

To ask someone to do something, preface the sentence with chôo·ay ช่วย. To invite someone to do something, use cheun เชิญ. The closest English equivalent is 'please':

Please close the window.
ช่วยปิดหน้าต่าง

chôo·ay bìt nâh-đàhng
(lit: chôo·ay close window)

Please sit down.
เชิญนั่ง

cheun nâng
(lit: cheun sit)

To express a greater sense of urgency, use sì สิ at the end of the sentence:

Close the door!
ปิดประตูสิ

bìt brà-đoo sì
(lit: close door sì)

comparing things

Just about any adjective in Thai can be used to make comparisons by adding gwàh กว่า to it (a bit like English '-er').

good	ดี	dee
better	ดีกว่า	dee-gwàh

cheap	ถูก	tòok
cheaper	ถูกกว่า	tòok-gwàh

To say something is the best of its kind, add têe-sùt ที่สุด :

delicious	อร่อย	a-ròy
the most delicious	อร่อยที่สุด	a-ròy têe-sùt

expensive	แพง	paang
the most expensive	แพงที่สุด	paang têe-sùt

To say that two things are the same use either měu·an gan เหมือนกัน which means 'is/are the same', or měu·an gàp เหมือนกับ which means 'is/are the same as':

Thai customs are the same.
ประเพณีไทยเหมือนกัน   ŧrà-peh-nee tai měu·an gan
(lit: custom Thai are-the-same)

That kind is the same as this kind.
อย่างนั้นเหมือนกับอย่างนี้   yàhng nán měu·an gàp yàhng née
(lit: kind that is-the-same-as kind this)

counting things

Occasionally in English you can't just put a number with a noun – you use an extra word which 'classifies' the noun. These are also known as counters. For example, we would say 'three pairs of pants' instead of 'three pants'. The word 'pairs' not only classifies pants but also shoes, sunglasses, socks and so on. In Thai, you always need to use a classifier whenever you specify a number of objects in a given category. The classifier always goes after the noun and the number. For example:

Four houses.

บ้านสี่หลัง   bâhn sèe lăng
(lit: house four lang)

Here are some examples of classifiers in Thai:

animals, furniture, clothing	ตัว	đoo·a
books, candles	เล่ม	lêm
eggs	ฟอง	forng
glasses (of water, tea)	แก้ว	gâa·ou
houses	หลัง	lăng
letters, newspapers	ฉบับ	chà·bàp
monks, Buddha images	รูป	rôop
pieces, slices (cakes, cloth)	ชิ้น	chín
pills, seeds, small gems	เม็ด	mét
plates, glasses, pages	ใบ	bai
plates of food	จาน	jahn
rolls (toilet paper, film)	ม้วน	móo·an
royalty, stupas	องค์	ong
stamps, planets, stars	ดวง	doo·ang
small objects	อัน	an
trains	ขบวน	kà·boo·an
vehicles (bikes, cars, train carriages)	คัน	kan

If you don't know (or forget) the relevant classifier, the word an อัน may be used for almost any small object. Alternatively, Thais sometimes repeat the noun rather than use a classifier.

For more on classifiers see **numbers & amounts**, page 35.

describing things

To describe something in Thai, all you need to do is place the adjective after the thing you wish to describe:

big house	บ้านใหญ่	bâhn yài (lit: house big)
small room	ห้องเล็ก	hôrng lék (lit: room small)
delicious food	อาหารอร่อย	ah-hăhn à-ròy (lit: food delicious)

Adjectives that can logically be used to modify action may also function as adverbs in Thai. An adjective used adverbially is most often doubled, and always follows the verb:

| slow horse | ม้าช้า | máh cháh
(lit: horse slow) |

and

| drive slowly | ขับช้าๆ | kàp cháh-cháh
(lit: drive slow-slow) |

See also **comparing things**.

future see verbs

gender

The pronoun 'I' will change depending on the gender of the speaker – so a man will refer to himself as pŏm ผม (I, me) while a woman will refer to herself as dì-chăn คิฉัน (I, me). When being polite to others, it's customary to add the word kráp ครับ (if you're a man) or kâ ค่ะ (if you're a woman) as a kind of a 'softener' to the end of questions and statements.

Often you'll see the symbol m/f in this book which stands for male/female. Whenever a sentence is marked with m/f you have to make a choice between pŏm and dì-chăn or kráp and kâ depending on your gender. For example in the sentence:

I don't understand.
ผม/คิฉันไม่เข้าใจ   pŏm/dì-chăn mâi kôw jai m/f

A man would say 'pŏm mâi kôw jai' but a woman would say 'dì-chăn mâi kôw jai'. Thai also has a neutral form of I, chăn นัน, although we don't use it in this book.

have

The verb 'have' is expressed by simply placing the word mee มี before the object:

I have a bicycle.
ผม/คิฉันมีรถจักรยาน   pŏm/dì-chăn mee
                                          rót-jàk-gà-yahn m/f
                                          (lit: I have bicycle)

Do you have fried noodles?
มีก๋วยเตี๋ยวผัดไหม   mee gŏo·ay-đĕe·o pàt măi
                                          (lit: have noodle fry not)

See also **possession**.

joining words

Use these conjunctions to join two phrases together:

and	และ	láa
because	เพราะว่า	pró wâh
but	แต่	đàa
or	หรือ	rěu
so that	เพื่อ	pêu·a
therefore	เพราะฉะนั้น	pró chà-nán
with	กับ	gàp (also 'and', as in 'rice and curry')

location

Location is indicated by using prepositions. These are words that show relationships between objects or people. Instead of just pointing, try using some of these useful terms:

adjacent to	ติดกับ	đit gàp
around	รอบ	rôrp
at	ที่	têe
at the edge of	ริมกับ	rim gàp
from	จาก	jàhk
in	ใน	nai
inside	ภายใน	pai nai
under	ใต้	đâi
with	กับ	gàp

See also the section **directions**, page 61.

more than one see also **numbers & amounts**

Words in Thai do not change when they become plural:

The house is large.
The houses are large.

บ้านใหญ่   bâhn yài
         (lit: house large)

A 'classifier' or number before the object will help you determine whether or not a word is plural.

For more about numbers see **classifiers** and the section **numbers & amounts**, page 35.

my & your see **possession**

negative

The most common negative marker in Thai is mâi ไม่ (not). Any verb or adjective may be negated by the insertion of mâi immediately before it. You can also use ปเล่า เปล่า but only in conjunction with questions that use the ปเล่า tag (see questions and answers).

He/She isn't thirsty.

เขาไม่หิวน้ำ   kŏw mâi hĕw nám
         (lit: he/she not thirsty)

I don't have any cash.

ผม/ดิฉันไม่มีตางค์   pŏm/dì-chăn mâi mee đahng m/f
         (lit: I not have cash)

We're not French.

เราไม่เป็นคนฝรั่งเศษ   row mâi ben kon fà-rang-sèt
         (lit: we not be person France)

John has never gone to Chiang Mai.

จอนไม่เคยไปเชียงใหม่ jon mâi keu·i bai chee·ang mài
(lit: John not ever go Chiang Mai)

We won't go to Ubon tomorrrow.

พรุ่งนี้เราจะไม่ไปอุบล prûng-née row jà mâi bai ù-bon
(lit: tomorrow we will not go Ubon)

nouns

Nouns always remain the same whether or not they're singular or plural. They don't need to be introduced with articles such as 'a' or 'the'.

I'm a soldier.

ผม/ดิฉันเป็นทหาร pŏm/dì-chăn ben tá-hăhn m/f
(lit: I be soldier)

We're soldiers.

เราเป็นทหาร row ben tá-hăhn
(lit: we be soldier)

You can form nouns from verbs of physical action by adding gahn การ before the verb:

to travel	เดินทาง	deun tahng
travel	การเดินทาง	gahn deun tahng

You can form nouns from adjectives by adding kwahm ความ before the adjective:

hot	ร้อน	rórn
heat	ความร้อน	kwahm rórn

past see verbs

plural see more than one

pointing something out

If you want to say 'there is' or 'there are', to describe the existence of something somewhere else, the verb mee มี (have) is used instead of ben เป็น (see also **be**):

In Bangkok there are many cars.
ที่กรุงเทพฯมีรถยนต์มาก   têe grung têp mee rót-yon mâhk
                       (lit: in Bangkok mee car many)

At Wat Pho there is a large Buddha image.
ที่วัดโพธิ์มีพระพุทธรูปใหญ่   têe wát poh mee
                       prá-pút-tá-rôop yài
                       (lit: in Wat Pho mee Buddha
                       image large)

See also **have** and **this & that**.

polite forms see pronouns

possession

The word kŏrng ของ is used to denote possession and is roughly the same as 'of' or 'belongs to' in English:

| my bag | กระเป๋าของผม | grà-bŏw kŏrng pŏm
(lit: bag kŏrng me) |
| his/her seat | ที่นั่งของเขา | têe nâng kŏrng kŏw
(lit: seat kŏrng him/her) |

Does this belong to you?
นี่ของคุณหรือเปล่า   nêe kŏrng kun rĕu blòw
                   (lit: this kŏrng you or not)

present see **verbs**

pronouns

Personal pronouns (I, you, she, he etc) aren't used as frequently as they are in English, as the subject of a sentence is frequently omitted after the first reference, or when it's clear from the context. There's no distinction between subject and object pronouns – the word pŏm ผม means both 'I' and 'me' (for a man), and kŏw เขา means 'he/she/they' and 'him/her/them'.

I, me (m)	ผม	pŏm
I, me (f)	ดิฉัน	dì-chăn
I, me (m&f)	ฉัน	chăn
you	คุณ	kun
he, she	เขา	kŏw
they	เขา	kŏw

In Thai there are additional words for the personal pronoun 'you' depending on the level of politeness or informality required:

you (very polite – to monks, royalty)	ท่าน	tâhn
you (informal – to a child or lover)	เธอ	teu
you (very informal – to a small child)	หนู	nŏo
you (vulgar – to a close friend)	มึง	meung

Don't worry if you're not sure which one to choose. In this phrasebook we have always provided the appropriate form of 'you' demanded by the context of the phrase.

See also **gender**.

questions & answers

Thai has two ways of forming questions – through the use of question words like 'who', 'how' and 'what', or through the addition of a tag like 'isn't it?' to the end of a sentence.

To form a yes-or-no question in Thai, all you need to do is place mǎi ไหม (no literal translation) at the end of a statement:

Is the weather hot?

อากาศร้อนไหม　　　　　　　ah-gàht rórn mǎi
　　　　　　　　　　　　　　(lit: weather hot mǎi)

To say 'aren't you?' use châi mǎi ใช่ไหม:

You're a student, aren't you?

คุณเป็นนักเรียนใช่ไหม　　　　kun ben nák ree·an châi mǎi
　　　　　　　　　　　　　　(lit: you be student châi mǎi)

The tag châi mǎi is also used to mean 'isn't it?'.

To answer a question, just repeat the verb, with or without the negative particle. The negative particles are mâi, châi mǎi, b̀lòw and yang. The word rěu means 'or', and with a negative particle it means 'or not' – however often the negative isn't stated and the question simply ends with rěu. Informally, a negative particle alone will do for a negative reply.

Do you want a beer? เอาเบียร์ไหม		ow bee·a mǎi (lit: want beer mǎi)
Yes.	เอา	ow (lit: want)
No.	ไม่เอา	mâi ow (lit: not want)
Are you angry? โกรธหรือเปล่า		gròht rěu b̀lòw (lit: angry rěu b̀lòw)
Yes.	โกรธ	gròht (lit: angry)
No.	เปล่า	b̀lòw (lit: not)

question words

Many English speakers instinctively place a raised inflection to the end of a Thai question. Try to avoid doing this as it will usually interfere with the tones (see the section **pronunciation**, page 11). In Thai a question is formed by using 'question tags' at the beginning or end of a phrase:

what	อะไร	à-rai
What do you need?	คุณต้องการอะไร	kun đôrng gahn à-rai (lit: you want what)
how	อย่างไร	yàhng rai
How do you do it?	ทำอย่างไร	tam yàhng rai (lit: do how)
who	ใคร	krai
Who is sitting there?	ใครนั่งที่นั่น	krai nâng têe nán (lit: who sit there)
when	เมื่อไร	mêu·a·rai
When will you go to Chiang Mai?	เมื่อไรจะไปเชียงใหม่	mêu·a·rai jà bai chee·ang mài (lit: when will go Chiang Mai)
why	ทำไม	tam-mai
Why are you quiet?	ทำไมเงียบ	tam-mai ngêe·ap (lit: why quiet)
where	ที่ไหน	têe năi
Where is the bathroom?	ห้องน้ำอยู่ที่ไหน	hôrng nám yòo têe năi (lit: bathroom is where)
which	ไหน	năi
Which one do you like?	ชอบอันไหน	chôrp an năi (lit: like one which)

the see a/an & the

this & that

The words nêe นี้ (this) and nân นั้น (that) are spoken with a fall-ing tone when used alone as pronouns:

What's this?
นี่อะไร　　　　nêe à-rai
　　　　　　　(lit: this what)

How much is that?
นั่นเท่าไร　　　nân tôw rai
　　　　　　　(lit: that how much)

However, when used with a noun, they're spoken with a high tone (nán นั้น, née นี้) and like Thai adjectives, they follow the noun they refer to:

| this bus | รถนี้ | rót née
(lit: bus this) |
| that plane | จานนั้น | jahn nán
(lit: plane that) |

To say 'these' and 'those' add the word lòw เหล่า before née and nán and use a high tone:

| these | เหล่านี้ | lòw née |
| those | เหล่านั้น | lòw nán |
| these chickens | ไก่เหล่านี้ | gài lòw née
(lit: chicken these) |

verbs

Thai verbs don't change according to tense. Thus the sentence kǒw gin gài เขากินไก่ can mean 'He/She **eats** chicken', 'He/She **ate** chicken' or 'He/She **has eaten** chicken'. Context will often tell you what time is being referred to. Otherwise you can do one of the following:

• specify the time with a word like wan-née วันนี้ (today) or mêu·a wahn née เมื่อวานนี้ (yesterday):

He/She ate chicken yesterday.
เมื่อวานนี้เขากินไก่
mêu·a wahn née kǒw gin gài
(lit: yesterday he/she eat chicken)

• add one of the words explained below to indicate whether an action is **ongoing**, **completed** or **to-be-completed**:

ongoing action

The word gam-lang กำลัง is used before the verb to mark ongoing or progressive action, a bit like the English 'am/are/is doing'. However, it's not used unless the speaker feels it's absolutely necessary to express the continuity of an action:

I'm washing the clothes.
กำลังซักเสื้อผ้า
gam-lang sák sêu·a pâh
(lit: gam-lang wash clothes)

completed action

A common way of expressing completed action in Thai is by using the word láa·ou แล้ว (already) at the end of the sentence:

We have been to Bangkok.
เราไปกรุงเทพฯแล้ว
row bai grung têp láa·ou
(lit: we go Bangkok láa·ou)

I have spent the money.
ผม/ดิฉันจ่ายเงินแล้ว
pǒm/dì-chǎn jài ngeun láa·ou m/f
(lit: I spend money láa·ou)

The word láa·ou can also refer to a current condition that began a short time ago:

I'm hungry already.

ผม/ดิฉันหิวแล้ว   pŏm/dì-chăn hĕw kôw láa·ou m/f
(lit: I hungry rice láa·ou)

The marker dâi ได้ shows past tense, but unlike láa·ou, never refers to a current condition. It immediately precedes the verb, and is often used in conjunction with láa·ou. It's more commonly used in negative statements than in the affirmative:

Our friends didn't go to Chiang Mai.

เพื่อนเราไม่ได้ไป   pêu·an row mâi dâi bai
เชียงใหม่   chee·ang mài
(lit: friend us not dâi go
Chiang Mai)

to-be-completed action

The word ja จะ is used to mark an action to be completed in the future. It always appears directly before the verb:

He/She will buy rice.

เขาจะซื้อข้าว   kŏw jà séu kôw
(lit: he/she ja buy rice)

word order

Generally speaking the word order follows the pattern of subject-verb-object like in English:

We eat rice.

เรากินข้าว   row gin kôw
(lit: we eat rice)

You study Thai.

คุณเรียนภาษาไทย   kun ree·an pah-săh tai
(lit: you study language Thai)

Sometimes the object is placed first to add emphasis:

I don't like that bowl

ชามนั้นผม/ดิฉันไม่ชอบ   chahm nán pŏm/dì-chăn
mâi chôrp m/f
(lit: bowl that I not like)

yes/no questions see questions

language difficulties

Do you speak English?
คุณพูดภาษาอังกฤษได้ไหม

kun pôot pah·săh ang·grìt dâi măi

Does anyone speak English?
มีใครพูดภาษาอังกฤษ
ได้บ้างไหม

mee krai pôot pah·săh ang·grìt dâi bâhng măi

Do you understand?
คุณเข้าใจไหม

kun kôw jai măi

Yes, I do.
ครับ/ค่ะ เข้าใจ

kráp/kâ, kôw jai m/f

No, I don't.
ไม่เข้าใจ

mâi kôw jai

I speak a little.
พูดได้นิดหน่อย

pôot dâi nít nòy

I (don't) understand.
ผม/ดิฉัน (ไม่) เข้าใจ

pŏm/dì·chăn (mâi) kôw jai m/f

How do you ...? ... อย่างไร ... yàhng rai
pronounce this ออกเสียง òrk sĕe·ang
write 'Saraburi' เขียนสระบุรี kĕe·an sà·rà·bù·ree

What does 'anahkot' mean?
อนาคต แปลว่าอะไร

à·nah·kót blaa wâh à·rai

---

listen for ...

kun pôot pah·săh tai dâi măi
คุณพูดภาษาไทยได้ไหม **Can you speak Thai?**

Could you please ...?	... ได้ไหม	... dâi măi
repeat that	พูดอีกที	pôot èek tee
speak more slowly	พูดช้าๆ	pôot cháa cháa
write it down	เขียนลงให้	kĕe·an long hâi

thai with a twist

Thai people love to use colourful language to express themselves. Here are a couple of common sayings you could try out for effect:

To ride an elephant to catch a grasshopper.
(to go overboard)

ขี่ช้างจับตั๊กแตน   kèe cháhng jàp đák-gà-đaan

When you're fat, you smell good. When you're thin, you stink.
(Nobody loves you when you're down-and-out.)

เมื่อพีเนื้อหอม   mêu·a pee néu·a hŏrm
เมื่อผอมเนื้อเหม็น   mêu·a pŏrm néu·a mĕn

Feeling confident? See if you can impress a local with this Thai tongue twister:

tá-hăhn tĕu ɓeun bàak ɓoon ɓai bòhk đèuk
ทหารถือปืนแบกปูน   **(A soldier with his gun**
ไปโบกตึก   **carries cement to render**
         the building.)

cardinal numbers

เลขนับจำนวน

1	หนึ่ง	nèung
2	สอง	sŏrng
3	สาม	săhm
4	สี่	sèe
5	ห้า	hâh
6	หก	hòk
7	เจ็ด	jèt
8	แปด	฿àat
9	เก้า	gôw
10	สิบ	sìp
11	สิบเอ็ด	sìp-èt
12	สิบสอง	sìp-sŏrng
13	สิบสาม	sìp-săhm
14	สิบสี่	sìp-sèe
15	สิบห้า	sìp-hâh
16	สิบหก	sìp-hòk
17	สิบเจ็ด	sìp-jèt
18	สิบแปด	sìp-฿àat
19	สิบเก้า	sìp-gôw
20	ยี่สิบ	yêe-sìp
21	ยี่สิบเอ็ด	yêe-sìp-èt
22	ยี่สิบสอง	yêe-sìp-sŏrng
30	สามสิบ	săhm-sìp
40	สี่สิบ	sèe-sìp
50	ห้าสิบ	hâh-sìp
100	หนึ่งร้อย	nèung róy
200	สองร้อย	sŏrng róy
1,000	หนึ่งพัน	nèung pan
1,000,000	หนึ่งล้าน	nèung láhn

ordinal numbers

1st	ที่หนึ่ง	têe nèung
2nd	ที่สอง	têe sŏrng
3rd	ที่สาม	têe săhm
4th	ที่สี่	têe sèe
5th	ที่ห้า	têe hâh

classifiers

ลักษณนาม

Words of measure, or classifiers, are sometimes used in English with phrases such as 'three loaves of bread' (not 'three breads') and 'three sheets of paper' (and not 'three papers'). In Thai, whenever you specify a particular number of any noun, you must use a classifier.

For example, the question 'Can I have a bottle of beer?' (kŏr bee·a kòo·at nèung ขอเบียร์ขวดหนึ่ง) is literally 'Can I have beer one bottle?'.

For examples of classifiers and how to use them, see the **phrasebuilder**, page 15.

go figure

Just as in English we can use a figure, eg '7', instead of writing out the whole word, Thai also has a basic system for writing numbers. Use this chart to decipher numbers on street signs, shop doors and price tags:

1	๐	6	๖	11	๐๐	16	๐๖
2	๒	7	๗	12	๐๒	17	๐๗
3	๓	8	๘	13	๐๓	18	๐๘
4	๔	9	๙	14	๐๔	19	๐๙
5	๕	10	๐๐	15	๐๕	20	๒๐

telling the time

การบอกเวลา

Telling the time in Thai can be very challenging for an outsider to master. While the Western twelve-hour clock divides the day between two time periods, am and pm, the Thai system has four periods. The 24-hour clock is also commonly used by government and media. If you plan to stay in Thailand for a long time it's worth learning how to tell the time. Otherwise simply refer to the list below where each hour of the twelve-hour clock has been translated into the Thai system.

What time is it?	กี่โมงแล้ว	gèe mohng láa·ou
12 midnight	หกทุ่ม/เที่ยงคืน	hòk tûm/têe·ang keun
1am	ตีหนึ่ง	đee nèung
2am	ตีสอง	đee sŏrng
3am	ตีสาม	đee săhm
4am	ตีสี่	đee sèe
5am	ตีห้า	đee hâh
6am	หกโมงเช้า	hòk mohng chów
7am	หนึ่งโมงเช้า	nèung mohng chów
11am	ห้าโมงเช้า	hâh mohng chów
12 noon	เที่ยง	têe·ang
1pm	บ่ายโมง	bài mohng
2pm	บ่ายสองโมง	bài sŏrng mohng
4pm	บ่ายสี่โมง	bài sèe mohng
4pm	สี่โมงเย็น	sèe mohng yen
6pm	หกโมงเย็น	hòk mohng yen
7pm	หนึ่งทุ่ม	nèung tûm
8pm	สองทุ่ม	sŏrng tûm
9pm	สามทุ่ม	săhm tûm
10pm	สี่ทุ่ม	sèe tûm
11pm	ห้าทุ่ม	hâh tûm

To give times after the hour, just add the number of minutes following the hour.

4.30pm
ป่ายสี่โมงครึ่ง
bài sèe mohng krêung
(lit: four afternoon hours half)

4.15pm
ป่ายสี่โมงสิบห้านาที
bài sèe mohng sìp-hâh nah-tee
(lit: four afternoon hours fifteen)

To give times before the hour, add the number of minutes beforehand.

3.45pm
อีกสิบห้านาทีป่ายสี่โมง
èek sìp-hâh nah-tee bài sèe mohng
(lit: another fifteen minutes four afternoon hoùrs)

Thai time

In Thailand you may hear a person who arrives late for an appointment joke about being on 'Thai time' as punctuality is generally a more fluid concept than some Westerners are used to. But there is a specifically Thai way of telling the time which you'll need to learn if you want to avoid being late yourself.

The day is broken up into four periods. From midnight to six in the morning times begin with the word đee ต (strike), from six in the morning until midday they end with the word chów เช้า (morning), from midday to six in the evening they begin with the word bai ป่าย (afternoon) and from six in the evening until midnight they end with the word tûm ทุ่ม (thump).

So 3am is đee sǎhm ตีสาม (lit: strike three) and 9pm is sǎhm tûm สามทุ่ม (lit: three thumps).

days of the week

Monday	วันจันทร์	wan jan
Tuesday	วันอังคาร	wan ang-kahn
Wednesday	วันพุธ	wan pút
Thursday	วันพฤหัสบดี	wan pá-réu-hàt
Friday	วันศุกร์	wan sùk
Saturday	วันเสาร์	wan sŏw
Sunday	วันอาทิตย์	wan ah-tít

the calendar

เดือน

months

January	เดือนมกราคม	deu·an má-gà-rah-kom
February	เดือนกุมภาพันธ์	deu·an gum-pah-pan
March	เดือนมีนาคม	deu·an mee-nah-kom
April	เดือนเมษายน	deu·an mair-săh-yon
May	เดือนพฤษภาคม	deu·an préut-sà-pah-kom
June	เดือนมิถุนายน	deu·an mí-tù-nah-yon
July	เดือนกรกฎาคม	deu·an gà-rák-gà-dah-kom
August	เดือนสิงหาคม	deu·an sĭng-hăh-kom
September	เดือนกันยายน	deu·an gan-yah-yon
October	เดือนตุลาคม	deu·an đù-lah-kom
November	เดือนพฤศจิกายน	deu·an préut-sà-jì-gah-yon
December	เดือนธันวาคม	deu·an tan-wah-kom

time & dates

39

dates

What date is it today?
วันนี้วันที่เท่าไร   wan née wan têe tôw-rai

It's (27 September).
วันที่ (ยี่สิบเจ็ดเดือนกันยายน)   wan têe (yêe-sìp-jèt deu·an gan-yah-yon)

seasons

dry season (November to March)	หน้าแล้ง	nâh láang
rainy season (June to September)	หน้าฝน	nâh fŏn
cool season (winter)	หน้าหนาว	nâh nŏw
hot season (summer)	หน้าร้อน	nâh rórn
moonsoon	หน้ามรสุม	nâh mor-rá-sŭm

For more on the weather, see **outdoors**, page 147.

present

ปัจจุบัน

now	เดี๋ยวนี้	dĕe·o née
this ...	... นี้	... née
afternoon	บ่าย	bài
month	เดือน	deu·an
morning	เช้า	chów
week	อาทิตย์	ah-tít
year	ปี	bee
today	วันนี้	wan née
tonight	คืนนี้	keun née

past

(three days) ago	(สามวัน) ทีแล้ว	(săhm wan) tee láa·ou
day before yesterday	เมื่อวานซืน	mêu·a wahn seun
last ...	... ทีแล้ว	... tee láa·ou
month	เดือน	deu·an
week	อาทิตย์	ah-tít
year	ปี	bee
last night	เมื่อคืนนี้	mêu·a keun née
since (May)	ตั้งแต่ (พฤษภาคม)	đâng đàa (préut-sà-pah-kom)
yesterday ...	... เมื่อวาน	... mêu·a wahn
afternoon	บ่าย	bài
evening	เย็น	yen
morning	เช้า	chów

future

day after tomorrow	วันมะรืน	wan má-reun
in (six days)	อีก (หกวัน)	èek (hòk wan)
next ...	... หน้า	... nâh
month	เดือน	deu·an
week	อาทีตย์	ah-tít
year	ปี	bee
tomorrow ...	พรุ่งนี้ ...	prûng née ...
afternoon	บ่าย	bài
evening	เย็น	yen
morning	เช้า	chów
until (June)	จนถึง (มิถุนายน)	jon tĕung (mí-tù-nah-yon)

during the day

afternoon	บ่าย	bài
dawn	อรุณ	à-run
day	วัน	wan
evening	เย็น	yen
midday	เที่ยงวัน	têe·ang wan
midnight	เที่ยงคืน	têe·ang keun
morning	เช้า	chów
night	ตอนคืน	đorn keun
sunrise	ตะวันขึ้น	đà-wan kêun
sunset	ตะวันตก	đà-wan đòk

42

How much is it?
ราคาเท่าไร — rah-kah tôw rai

Can you write down the price?
เขียนราคาลงให้ได้ไหม — kĕe·an rah-kah long hâi dâi măi

Can you count it out for me?
นับให้ดูได้ไหม — náp hâi doo dâi măi

Can I have smaller notes?
ขอใบย่อยได้ไหม — kŏr bai yôy dâi măi

Do you accept …?	รับ … ไหม	ráp … măi
credit cards	บัตรเครดิต	bàt krair-dìt
debit cards	บัตรธนาคาร	bàt tá-nah-kahn
travellers cheques	เช็คเดินทาง	chék deun tahng
I'd like …, please.	ขอ … หน่อย	kŏr … nòy
my change	เงินทอน	ngeun torn
a refund	เงินคืน	ngeun keun
a receipt	ใบเสร็จ	bai sèt
to return this	เอามาคืน	ow mah keun
I'd like to …	ผม/ดิฉัน อยากจะ …	pŏm/dì-chăn yàhk jà … m/f
cash a cheque	ขึ้นเช็ค	kêun chék
change a travellers cheque	แลกเช็คเดินทาง	lâak chék deun tahng
change money	แลกเงิน	lâak ngeun
get a cash advance	รูดเงินจากบัตรเครดิต	rôot ngeun jàhk bàt krair-dìt
withdraw money	ถอนเงิน	tŏrn ngeun

Where's ...?	... อยู่ที่ไหน	... yòo têe năi
an ATM	ตู้เอทีเอ็ม	đôo air tee em
a foreign	ที่แลกเงินต่าง	têe lâak ngeun
exchange office	ประเทศ	đàhng brà-têt

What's the ...?	... เท่าไร	... tôw rai
charge	ค่าธรรมเนียม	kâh tam-nee·am
exchange rate	อัตราแลกเปลี่ยน	àt-đrah lâak
		blèe·an

It's ...		
free	ไม่มีค่าธรรมเนียม	mâi mee kâh
		tam-nee·am
(12) baht	(สิบสอง) บาท	(sìp sŏrng) baht

talking *kráp*

Adopting the proper niceties in Thailand is a good practical habit to get into. You'll notice that some of the phrases in this book end with the word kráp ครับ for a male speaker or kâ ค่ะ for a female speaker.

These are used at the end of a sentence in situations that require a verbal softener. For instance, the question kun bai năi คุณไปไหน (Where are you going?) could sound very abrupt. A more polite way to say it would be kun bai năi kráp คุณไปไหนครับ if you are a man or kun bai năi kâ คุณไปไหนค่ะ if you are a woman.

การขนส่ง

getting around

การเดินทาง

Which boat goes to (Ayuthaya)?
เรือลำไหนไป
(อยุธยา)

reu·a lam năi bai
(à-yút-tá-yah)

Which bus/*songthaew* goes to (Ayuthaya)?
รถเมล์/สองแถว คัน
ไหนไป (อยุธยา)

rót mair/sŏrng-tăa·ou kan
năi bai (à-yút-tá-yah)

Which train goes to (Ayuthaya)?
รถไฟ ขบวนไหนไป
(อยุธยา)

rót fai kà-buan năi bai
(à-yút-tá-yah)

Is this the ... to	อันนี้เป็น ...ไป	an née ben ... bai
(Chiang Mai)?	(เชียงใหม่)	(chee·ang mài)
	ใช่ไหม	châi măi
boat	เรือ	reu·a
bus	รถเมล์	rót mair
train	รถไฟ	rót fai

When's	รถเมล์ คัน ...	rót mair kan ...
the ... bus?	มาเมื่อไร	mah mêu·a rai
first	แรก	râak
last	สุดท้าย	sùt tái
next	ต่อไป	dòr bai

What time does it leave?
ออกกี่โมง

òrk gèe mohng

What time does it get to (Chiang Mai)?
ถึง (เชียงใหม่) กี่โมง

tĕung (chee·ang mài)
gèe mohng

How long will it be delayed?
จะเสียเวลานานเท่าไร

jà sĕe·a wair-lah nahn tôw-rai

Excuse me, is this seat free?
ขอโทษ ครับ/ค่ะ ที่นั่งนี้ว่างไหม

kŏr tôht kráp/kâ têe
nâng née wâhng măi m/f

That's my seat.
นั่นที่นั่งของ ผม/ดิฉัน

nân têe nâng kŏrng
pŏm/dì-chăn m/f

Please tell me when we get to (Chiang Mai).
เมื่อถึง (เชียงใหม่)
กรุณาบอกด้วย

mêu·a tĕung (chee·ang mài)
gà-rú-nah bòrk dôo·ay

Please stop here.
ขอจอดที่นี่

kŏr jòrt têe née

How long do we stop here?
เราจะหยุดที่นี่นานเท่าไร

row jà yùt têe née
nahn tôw-rai

tickets

ตั๋ว

Where do I buy a ticket?
ต้องซื้อตั๋วที่ไหน

đôrng séu đŏo·a têe năi

Do I need to book?
ต้องจองล่วงหน้าหรือเปล่า

đôrng jorng lôo·ang nâh
rĕu ฺblòw

Can I have a ... ticket (to Chiang Mai)?	ขอตั๋ว ...ไป (เชียงใหม่)	kŏr đŏo·a ...ฺbai (chee·ang mài)
1st-class	ชั้นหนึ่ง	chán nèung
2nd-class	ชั้นสอง	chán sŏrng
3rd-class	ชั้นสาม	chán săhm
child's	สำหรับเด็ก	săm-ràp dèk
one-way	เที่ยวเดียว	têe·o dee·o
return	ไปกลับ	ฺbai glàp
student's	สำหรับนักศึกษา	săm-ràp nák sèuk-săh

PRACTICAL

an nán	อันนั้น	that one
an née	อันนี้	this one
bor-rí-sàt tôrng têe·o	บริษัทท่องเที่ยว	travel agent
cháh wair-lah	ช้าเวลา	delayed
chan-chah-lah	ชานชาลา	platform
chôrng kǎi đǒo·a	ช่องขายตั๋ว	ticket window
đah-rahng wair-lah	ตารางเวลา	timetable
đem	เต็ม	full
yók lêrk	ยกเลิก	cancelled

I'd like a/an ... seat.	ต้องการที่นั่ง ...	đôrng gahn têe nâng ...
aisle	ติดทางเดิน	đìt tahng deun
nonsmoking	ในเขตห้ามสูบบุหรี่	nai kèt hâhm sòop bù-rèe
smoking	ในเขตสูบบุหรี่ได้	nai kèt sòop bù-rèe dâi
window	ติดหน้าต่าง	đìt nâh đàhng

Is there (a) ...?	มี ... ไหม	mee ... mǎi
air-conditioning	ปรับอากาศ	bràp ah-gàht
blanket	ผ้าห่ม	pâh hòm
sick bag	ถุงขยะ	tǔng kà-yà
toilet	ส้วม	sôo·am

How much is it?
ราคาเท่าไร
rah-kah tôw-rai

How long does the trip take?
การเดินทางใช้เวลานานเท่าไร
gahn deun tahng chái wair-lah nahn tôw-rai

Is it a direct route?
เป็นทางตรงไหม
ben tahng đrong mǎi

Can I get a stand-by ticket?
จะซื้อที่นั่งสำรองได้ไหม
jà séu têe nâng sǎm-rorng dâi mǎi

Can I get a sleeping berth?
จะจองที่นอนได้ไหม   jà jorng têe norn dâi măi

What time should I check in?
จะต้องมากี่โมง   jà đôrng mah gèe mohng

I'd like to … my ticket, please.	ผม/ดิฉัน อยาก จะขอ … ตั๋ว	pŏm/dì-chăn yàhk jà kŏr … đŏo·a m/f
cancel	ยกเลิก	yók lêuk
change	เปลี่ยน	ʼblèe·an
confirm	ยืนยัน	yeun yan

luggage

สัมภาระ

Where can I find …?	จะหา … ได้ที่ไหน	jà hăh … dâi têe năi
the baggage claim	ที่รับกระเป๋า	têe ráp grà-ʼbŏw
the left-luggage office	ห้องฝากกระเป๋า	hôrng fàhk grà-ʼbŏw
a luggage locker	ตู้ฝากกระเป๋า	đôo fàhk grà-ʼbŏw
a trolley	รถเข็น	rót kĕn

My luggage has been …	กระเป๋าของ ผม/ดิฉัน โดน … แล้ว	grà-ʼbŏw kŏrng pŏm/dì-chăn dohn … láa·ou m/f
damaged	เสียหาย	sĕe·a hăi
lost	หายไป	hăi ʼbai
stolen	ขโมย	kà-moy

That's (not) mine.
นั่น (ไม่) ใช่ของ ผม/ดิฉัน   nân (mâi) châi kŏrng pŏm/dì-chăn m/f

PRACTICAL

48

plane

เครื่องบิน

Where does flight (TG 132) arrive/depart?
เที่ยวบิน (ทีจี หนึ่งสามสอง)　　têe·o bin (tee jee nèung
เข้า/ออก ที่ไหน　　　　　　　　săhm sŏrng) kôw/òrk têe năi

Where's …?	… อยู่ที่ไหน	… yòo têe năi
the airport shuttle	รถบัสสนามบิน	rót bàt sà-năhm bin
arrivals	เที่ยวบินขาเข้า	têe·o bin kăh kôw
departures	เที่ยวบินขาออก	têe·o bin kăh òrk
the duty-free	ที่ขายของปลอดภาษี	têe kăi kŏrng ฿lòrt pah-sĕe
gate (12)	ประตูที่ (สิบสอง)	฿rà-đoo têe (sìp-sŏrng)

listen for ...

bàt kêun krêu·ang bin	บัตรขึ้นเครื่องบิน	**boarding pass**
gahn ohn	การโอน	**transfer**
năng-sĕu deun tahng	หนังสือเดินทาง	**passport**
tahng pàhn	ทางผ่าน	**transit**

bus, coach & train

รถเมล์รถทัวร์ และรถไฟ

How often do buses come?
รถบัสมาบ่อยเท่าไร　　　　　　rót bàt mah bòy tôw-rai

Does it stop at (Saraburi)?
รถจอดที่ (สระบุรี) ไหม　　　　rót jòrt têe (sà-rà-bù-ree) măi

What's the next stop?
ที่จอดต่อไปคือที่ไหน　　　　　têe jòrt đòr pai keu têe năi

I'd like to get off at (Saraburi).
ขอลงที่ (สระบุรี) kŏr long têe (sà-rà-bù-ree)
ครับ/ค่ะ kráp/kâ m/f

air-conditioned bus	รถปรับอากาศ	rót bràp ah-gàat
city bus	รถเมล์	rót mair
1st-class bus	รถชั้นหนึ่ง	rót chán nèung
government bus	รถ บ.ข.ส.	rót bor kŏr sŏr
intercity bus	รถบัส	rót bàt
ordinary bus	รถธรรมดา	rót tam-má-dah
VIP bus	รถวีไอพี	rót wee ai pee

What station is this?
ที่นี่สถานีไหน têe née sà-tăh-nee năi

What's the next station?
สถานีต่อไปคือสถานีไหน sà-tăh-nee đòr bai keu
sà-tăh-nee năi

Does it stop at (Kaeng Koi)?
จอดอยู่ที่ (แก่งคอย) jòrt yòo têe (gàang koy)
ไหม măi

Do I need to change?
ต้องเปลี่ยนรถไหม đôrng plèe·an rót măi

Is it …?	… หรือเปล่า	… rĕu plòw
direct	สายตรง	săi đrong
express	รถด่วน	rót dòo·an

Which carriage is (for) …?	ตู้ไหนสำหรับ …	đôo năi săm-ràp …
(Kaeng Koi)	(แก่งคอย)	(gàang koy)
1st class	ชั้นหนึ่ง	chán nèung
the dining car	ตู้ทานอาหาร	đôo tahn ah-hăhn
the sleeping car	ตู้นอน	đôo norn

I'd like a/an ...	ต้องการ ...	đôrng gahn ...
upper berth	ที่นอนชั้นบน	têe norn chán bon
lower berth	ที่นอนชั้นล่าง	têe norn chán lâhng

train	รถไฟ	rót fai
express train	รถไฟด่วน	rót fai dòo·an
sky train	รถไฟฟ้า	rót fai fáh
ordinary train	รถธรรมดา	rót tam·má·dah
rapid train	รถเร็ว	rót re·ou

boat

เรือ

What's the sea like today?
วันนี้สภาพน้ำเป็นอย่างไร

wan née sà·pâhp nám
ben yàhng rai

Are there life jackets?
มีเสื้อชูชีพไหม

mee sêu·a choo chêep măi

What island is this?
นี่คือเกาะไหน

nêe keu gò năi

What beach is this?
นี่คือชายหาดไหน

nêe keu chai hàht năi

I feel seasick.
รู้สึกเมาคลื่น

róo·sèuk mow klêun

cabin	ห้องนอน	hôrng norn
canal	คลอง	klorng
captain	นายเรือ	nai reu·a
car deck	ดาดฟ้าสำหรับรถ	dàht fáh săm·ràp rót
Chinese junk	เรือสำเภา	reu·a săm·pow
cross-river ferry	เรือข้ามฟาก	reu·a kâhm fâhk
deck	ดาดฟ้า	dàht fáh
express boat	เรือด่วน	reu·a dòo·an
ferry	เรือข้ามฟาก	reu·a kâhm fâhk
hammock	เปลญวน	blair yoo·an

hire boat	เรือรับจ้าง	reu·a ráp jâhng
life jacket	เสื้อชูชีพ	sêu·a choo chêep
lifeboat	เรือชูชีพ	reu·a choo chêep
longtail boat	เรือหางยาว	reu·a hăhng yow
sampan	เรือสำปั้น	reu·a săm-bân
yacht	เรือยอชต์	reu·a yôrt

taxi, *samlor* & *túk-túk*

แท็กซี่สามล้อและตุ๊กๆ

A fun way to travel short distances in Thailand is by *samlor* (săhm lór สามล้อ) which are three-wheeled bicycle-rickshaws powered by an energetic chauffeur. In city districts that are too congested or chaotic for a săhm lór get a ride with a mor-đeu-sai ráp jâhng มอเตอร์ไซค์รับจ้าง or motorcycle taxi. Almost emblematic of Thailand's cities is the *túk-túk* (đúk đúk ตุ๊กๆ), a name suggestive of the sound these three-wheeled taxis make as they buzz through the traffic. Bargain hard for all of these transport options, but be sure to offer a tip to any *samlor* driver who works up a worthy sweat .

I'd like a taxi ...	ต้องการรถแท็กซี่ ...	đôrng gahn rót-táak sêe ...
at (9am)	เมื่อ (สามโมงเช้า)	mêu·a (săhm mohng chów)
now	เดี๋ยวนี้	děe·o née
tomorrow	พรุ่งนี้	prûng née
Is this ... free?	... อันนี้ฟรีหรือเปล่า	... an née free rěu blòw
motorcycle	มอเตอร์ไซค์	mor-đeu-sai
taxi	รับจ้าง	ráp jâhng
samlor	สามล้อ	săhm lór
taxi	แท็กซี่	táak-sêe
túk-túk	ตุ๊กๆ	đúk đúk

Please ...   ขอ ...   kŏr ...
  slow down   ให้ช้าลง   hâi cháh long
  stop here   หยุดตรง นี้   yùt đrong née
  wait here   คอยอยู่ที่นี้   koy yòo têe née

Where's the taxi rank?
ที่ขึ้นรถแท็กซี่อยู่ที่ไหน
tÊe kêun rót táak-sêe
yòo têe năi

Is this a metered taxi?
แท็กซี่คันนี้มีมิเตอร์ไหม
táak-sêe kan née mee
mí-đeu măi

Please put the meter on.
ขอเปิดมิเตอร์ด้วย
kŏr bèut mí-đeu dôo·ay

How much is it to ...?
ไป ... เท่าไร
pai ... tôw-rai

Please take me to (this address).
ขอพาไป (ที่นี้)
kŏr pah bai (têe née)

How much is it?
ราคาเท่าไร
rah-kah tôw-rai

That's too expensive. How about ... baht?
แพงไป ... บาทได้ไหม
paang bai ... bàht dâi măi

car & motorbike

รถยนต์และรถมอเตอร์ไซค์

car & motorbike hire

How much   ค่าเช่า ...   kâh chôw ...
for ... hire?   ละเท่าไร   lá tôw-rai
  daily   วัน   wan
  weekly   อาทิตย์   ah-tít

Do I need to leave a deposit?
จะต้องมีเงินฝากด้วยไหม
jà đông mee ngeun fàhk
dôo·ay măi

I'd like to hire a/an ...	อยากจะเช่า ...	yàhk jà chôw ...
4WD	รถโฟร์วีล	rót foh ween
automatic	รถเกียร์ออโต	rót gee·a or-đoh
car	รถเก๋ง	rót gĕng
jeep	รถจี๊ป	rót jéep
manual	รถเกียร์ธรรมดา	rót gee·a tam-má-dah
motorbike	รถมอเตอร์ไซค์	rót mor-đeu-sai
motorbike with driver	รถมอเตอร์ไซค์ รับจ้าง	mor-đeu-sai ráp jâhng
scooter	รถสกู๊ตเตอร์	rót sa-góot-đeu
van	รถตู้	rót đôo

With ...	กับ ...	gàp ...
air-conditioning	แอร์	aa
a driver	คนขับ	kon kàp

Does that include insurance?
รวมประกันด้วยไหม
roo·am brà-gan dôo·ay măi

Does that include mileage?
รวมระยะทางด้วยไหม
roo·am rá-yá tahng dôo·ay măi

Do you have a road map?
มีแผนที่ถนนไหม
mee păan têe tà-nŏn măi

Can I have a helmet?
ขอหมวกกันน็อกด้วย
kŏr mòo·ak gan nórk dôo·ay

How many cc's is it?
เครื่องขนาดกี่ซีซี
krêu·ang kà-nàht gèe see-see

When do I need to return it?
จะต้องเอามาคืนเมื่อไร
jà đôrng ow mah keun mêu·a rai

on the road

What's the speed limit?
กฎหมายกำหนดความเร็วเท่าไร · gòt-măi gam-nòt kwahm
re·ou tôw-rai

Is this the road to (Ban Bung Wai)?
ทางนี้ไป (บ้านบุ่งหวาย) ไหม · tahng née bai (bâhn
bùng wăi) măi

Where's a petrol station?
ปั๊มน้ำมันอยู่ที่ไหน · bâm nám man yòo têe năi

Please fill it up.
เติมให้เต็ม · đeum hâi đem

I'd like ... litres.
เอา ... ลิตร · ow ... lít

diesel	น้ำมันโซล่าร์	nám man soh-lâh
LPG	ก๊าช	gáht
premium unleaded	ชนิดพิเศษ	chá-nít pí-sèt
regular unleaded	ชนิดธรรมดา	chá-nít tam-má-dah

Can you check the ...?	ตรวจ ... ด้วยหน่อย	đròo·at ... dôo·ay nòy
oil	น้ำมันเครื่อง	nám man krêu·ang
tyre pressure	ลม	lom
water	น้ำ	nám

Can I park here?
จอดที่นี่ได้ไหม · jòrt têe née dâi măi

road signs

ทางเข้า	tahng kôw	Entrance
ทางออก	tahng òrk	Exit Freeway
ให้ทาง	hâi tahng	Give Way
ห้ามเข้า	hâhm kôw	No Entry
ทางเดียว	tahng dee·o	One-way
หยุด	yùt	Stop
ค่าผ่าน	kâh pàhn	Toll

transport

55

How long can I park here?
จอดที่นี่ได้นานเท่าไร   jòrt têe née dâi nahn tôw-rai

Do I have to pay?
ต้องเสียเงินไหม   đôrng sĕe·a ngeun măi

drivers licence	ใบขับขี่	bai kàp kèe
kilometres	กิโลเมตร	gì-loh-mét
parking meter	มิเตอร์จอดรถ	mí-đeu jòrt rot
petrol (gasoline)	เบนซิน	ben-sin

problems

I need a mechanic.
ต้องการช่างรถ   đôrng gahn châhng rót

I've had an accident.
มีอุบัติเหตุ   mee ù-bàt-đì-hèt

The vehicle has broken down (at Kaeng Koi).
รถเสียแล้ว (ที่แก่งคอย)   rót sĕe·a láa·ou
                                       (têe gàang koy)

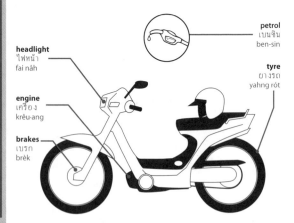

petrol
เบนซิน
ben-sin

headlight
ไฟหน้า
fai năh

tyre
ยางรถ
yahng rót

engine
เครื่อง
krêu·ang

brakes
เบรก
brèk

The vehicle won't start.
รถสตาร์ตไม่ติด

rót sà-đáht mâi đìt

I have a flat tyre.
ยางแบน

yahng baan

I've lost my car keys.
ทำกุญแจรถหาย

tam gun-jaa rót hăi

I've locked the keys inside.
ปิดกุญแจรถข้างในรถ

ɓìt gun-jaa rót kâhng nai rót

I've run out of petrol.
หมดน้ำมัน

mòt nám man

Can you fix it (today)?
ซ่อม(วันนี้)ได้ไหม

sôrm (wan née) dâi măi

How long will it take?
จะใช้เวลานานเท่าไร

jà chái wair-lah nahn tôw-rai

bicycle

I'd like …	ต้องการ …	đôrng gahn …
my bicycle repaired	ซ่อมรถจักรยาน	sôrm rót jàk-gà-yahn
to buy a bicycle	ซื้อรถจักรยาน	séu rót jàk-gà-yahn
to hire a bicycle	เช่ารถจักรยาน	chôw rót jàk-gà-yahn
I'd like a … bike.	ต้องการรถจักรยาน …	đôrng gahn rót jàk-gà-yahn …
mountain	ภูเขา	poo kŏw
racing	แข่ง	kàang
second-hand	มือสอง	meu sŏrng

How much is
it per …?   ... ละเท่าไร   ... lá tôw-rai
   day   วัน   wan
   hour   ชั่วโมง   chôo·a mohng

Do I need a helmet?
   ต้องใช้หมวกกันน็อกไหม   đôrng chái mòo·ak
                   gan nórk măi

I have a puncture.
   ยางแตกแล้ว   yahng đàak láa·ou

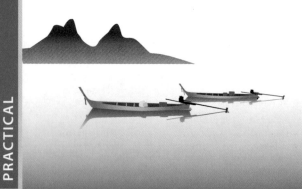

border crossing
การข้ามชายแดน

I'm ... ผม/ดิฉัน ... pŏm/dì-chăn ... **m/f**
   in transit เดินทางผ่าน deun tahng pàhn
   on business มาธุระ mah tú-rá
   on holiday มาพักผ่อน mah pák pòrn

I'm here for ... ผม/ดิฉัน pŏm/dì-chăn mah
     มาพักที่นี่ ... pák têe née ... **m/f**
   (10) days (สิบ) วัน (sìp) wan
   (two) months (สอง) เดือน (sŏrng) deu·an
   (three) weeks (สาม) อาทิตย์ (săhm) ah-tít

I'm going to (Ayuthaya).
ผม/ดิฉัน กำลังไป (อยุธยา) pŏm/dì-chăn gam-lang bai
     (à-yút-tá-yah) **m/f**

I'm staying at the (Bik Hotel).
พักอยู่ที่ (โรงแรมบิ๊ก) pák yòo têe (rohng raam bík)

The children are on this passport.
ลูกอยู่ในหนังสือเดินทางเล่มนี้ lôok yòo nai năng-sĕu
     deun tahng lêm née

listen for ...		
kon dee·o	คนเดียว	**alone**
krôrp kroo·a	ครอบครัว	**family**
ká-ná	คณะ	**group**
năng-sĕu deun tahng	หนังสือเดินทาง	**passport**
wee-sâh	วีซ่า	**visa**

I have nothing to declare.
ไม่มีอะไรที่จะแจ้ง

mâi mee à-rai têe jà jâang

I have something to declare.
มีอะไรที่จะต้องแจ้ง

mee à-rai têe jà đôrng jâang

Do I have to declare this?
อันนี้ต้องแจ้งไหม

an née đôrng jâang măi

That's (not) mine.
นั่น (ไม่ใช่) ของ ผม/ดิฉัน

nân (mâi châi) kŏrng pŏm/dì-chăn m/f

I didn't know I had to declare it.
ไม่รู้ว่าต้องแจ้งอันนี้ด้วย

mâi róo wâh đôrng jâang an née dôo·ay

I have an export permit for this.
ผม/ดิฉัน มีใบอนุญาตส่งออก

pŏm/dì-chăn mee bai à-nú-yâht sòng òrk m/f

These are for personal use, not resale.
สิ่งเหล่านี้สำหรับการใช้ ส่วนตัว ไม่ใช่เพื่อขาย

sìng lòw née săm-ràp gahn chái sòo·an đoo·a, mâi châi pêu·a kăi

signs		
ศุลกากร	sŭn-lá-gah-gorn	**Customs**
ปลอดภาษี	blòrt pah-sĕe	**Duty-Free**
กองตรวจคนเข้าเมือง	gorng đròo·at kon kôw meu·ang	**Immigration**
ด่านตรวจหนังสือเดินทาง	dàhn đròo·at năng-sĕu deun tahng	**Passport Control**
ด่านกักโรค	dàhn gàk rôhk	**Quarantine**

Where's (the tourist office)?
(สำนักงานท่องเที่ยว) อยู่ที่ไหน

(săm-nák ngahn tôrng têe·o) yòo têe năi

How far is it?
อยู่ไกลเท่าไร

yòo glai tôw-rai

It's ...	อยู่ ...	yòo ...
behind ...	ที่หลัง ...	têe lăng ...
diagonally opposite	เยื้อง	yéu·ang
in front of ...	ตรงหน้า ...	đrong nâh ...
near ...	ใกล้ ๆ ...	glâi glâi ...
next to ...	ข้าง ๆ ...	kâhng kâhng ...
on the corner	ตรงหัวมุม	đrong hŏo·a mum
opposite ...	ตรงกันข้าม ...	đrong gan kâhm ...
straight ahead	ตรงไป	đrong bai

north	ทิศเหนือ	tít nĕu·a
south	ทิศใต้	tít đâi
east	ทิศตะวันออก	tít đà-wan òrk
west	ทิศตะวันตก	tít đà-wan đòk

Turn ...	เลี้ยว ...	lée·o ...
at the corner	ตรงหัวมุม	đrong hŏo·a mum
left	ซ้าย	sái
right	ขวา	kwăh

listen for ...		
... gì-loh-mét	... กิโลเมตร	... kilometres
... mét	... เมตร	... metres
... nah-tee	... นาที	... minutes

By ...	โดย ...	doy ...
bus	รถเมล์	rót mair
samlor	สามล้อ	săhm lór
taxi	แท็กซี่	táak-sêe
túk-túk	ตุ๊กๆ	đúk đúk
On foot.	เดินไป	deun bai

typical addresses

What's the address?	ที่อยู่คืออะไร	têe yòo keu à-rai
city	เมือง	meu·ang
district	อำเภอ	am-peu
hamlet	ตำบล	đam-bon
lane	ซอย	soy
stream	ห้วย	hôo·ay
street	ถนน	tà-nŏn
village	หมู่บ้าน	mòo bâhn

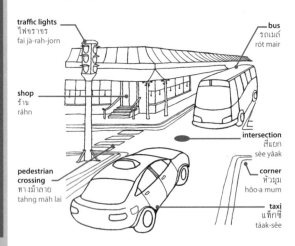

traffic lights
ไฟจราจร
fai jà-rah-jorn

shop
ร้าน
ráhn

pedestrian crossing
ทางม้าลาย
tahng máh lai

bus
รถเมล์
rót mair

intersection
สี่แยก
sèe yâak

corner
หัวมุม
hŏo·a mum

taxi
แท็กซี่
táak-sêe

finding accommodation

Where's a …?	… อยู่ที่ไหน	… yòo têe năi
camping ground	ค่ายพักแรม	kâi pák raam
beach hut	กระท่อมชายหาด	grà-tôrm chai hàht
bungalow	บังกะโล	bang-gà-loh
guesthouse	บ้านพัก	bâhn pák
hotel	โรงแรม	rohng raam
temple lodge	วัด	wát
youth hostel	บ้านเยาวชน	bâhn yow-wá-chon

Can you recommend somewhere …?	แนะนำที่ … ได้ ไหม	náa nam têe … dâi măi
cheap	ราคาถูก	rah-kah tòok
good	ดี ๆ	dee dee
luxurious	หรูหรา	rŏo-răh
nearby	ใกล้ ๆ	glâi glâi
romantic	โรแมนติก	roh-maan-đìk

What's the address?

ที่อยู่คืออะไร · têe yòo keu à-rai

Do you offer homestay accommodation?

มีการพักในบ้านคนไหม · mee gahn pák nai bâhn kon măi

For phrases on how to get there, see **directions**, page 61.

local talk		
dive	ที่เลว	têe le-ou
rat-infested	ที่สกปรก	têe sòk-gà-ฺbròk
top spot	ที่ที่เยี่ยม	têe têe yêe-am

booking ahead & checking in

I'd like to book a room, please.
ขอจองห้องหน่อย
kŏr jorng hôrng nòy

I have a reservation.
จองห้องมาแล้ว
jorng hôrng mah láa·ou

My name's …
ชื่อ …
chêu …

---

listen for ...

đem láa·ou	เต็มแล้ว	**full**
gèe keun	กี่คืน	**How many nights?**
năng·sĕu deun tahng	หนังสือเดินทาง	**passport**

For (three) nights/weeks.
เป็นเวลา (สาม) คืน/อาทิตย์
ben wair·lah (săhm) keun/ah·tít

From … to ….
จากวันที่ … ถึงวันที่ …
jàhk wan têe … tĕung wan têe …

Do I need to pay upfront?
ต้องจ่ายเงินล่วงหน้าไหม
đôrng jài ngeun lôo·ang nâh măi

How much is it per …?	… ละเท่าไร	…lá tôw·rai
night	คืน	keun
person	คน	kon
week	อาทิตย์	ah·tít

Can I pay by …?	จ่ายเป็น … ได้ไหม	jài ben … dâi măi
credit card	บัตรเครดิต	bàt krair·dìt
travellers cheque	เช็คเดินทาง	chék deun tahng

Do you have a/an … room? มีห้อง … ไหม   mee hôrng … măi

air-conditioned	แอร์	aa
double	เตียงคู่	đee·ang kôo
single	เดี่ยว	dèe·o
twin	สองเตียง	sŏrng đee·ang

Do you have a room with a fan?
มีห้องพัดลมไหม   mee hôrng pát lom măi

Does the price include breakfast?
ราคาห้องรวมค่า   rah-kâh hôrng roo·am kâh
อาหารเช้าด้วยไหม   ah-hăhn chów dôo·ay măi

That's too expensive.
แพงไป   paang bai

Can you lower the price?
ลดราคาได้ไหม   lót rah-kah dâi măi

Can I see it?
ดูได้ไหม   doo dâi măi

I'll take it.
เอา   ow

signs

มีห้องว่าง	mee hôrng wâhng	**vacancy**
ไม่มีห้องว่าง	mâi mee hôrng wâhng	**no vacancy**

requests & queries

การขอและสอบถาม

When is breakfast served?
อาหารเช้าจัด กี่โมง   ah-hăhn chów jàt gèe mohng

Where is breakfast served?
อาหารเช้าจัด ที่ไหน   ah-hăhn chów jàt têe năi

Please wake me at (seven).

กรุณาปลุกให้เวลา	gà-rú-nah blùk hâi wair-lah
(เจ็ด) นาฬิกา	(jèt) nah-lí-gah

For time expressions see **times & dates**, page 37.

Can I use the ...?	ใช้ ... ได้ไหม	chái ... dâi măi
kitchen	ห้องครัว	hôrng kroo·a
laundry	ห้องซักผ้า	hôrng sák pâh
telephone	โทรศัพท์	toh-rá-sàp

Do you have a/an ...?	มี ... ไหม	mee ... măi
elevator	ลิฟท์	líp
laundry service	บริการซักผ้า	bor-rí-gahn sák pâh
safe	ตู้เซฟ	đôo sép
swimming pool	สระว่ายน้ำ	sà wâi nám

Do you ... here?	ที่นี้ ... ไหม	têe née ... măi
arrange tours	จัดนำเที่ยว	jàt nam têe·o
change money	แลกเงิน	lâak ngeun

Could I have ..., please?	ขอ ... หน่อย	kŏr ... nòy
an extra blanket	ผ้าห่มอีกผืนหนึ่ง	pâh hòm èek pĕun nèung
the key	กุญแจห้อง	gun-jaa hôrng
a mosquito coil	ยาจุดกันยุง	yah jùt gan yung
a mosquito net	มุ้ง	múng
a receipt	ใบเสร็จ	bai sèt
some soap	สบู่ก้อนหนึ่ง	sà-bòo gôrn nèung
a towel	ผ้าเช็ดตัว	pâh chét đoo·a

Is there a message for me?
มีข้อความฝากให้ ผม/ดิฉัน ไหม

mee kôr kwahm fàhk hâi
pŏm/dì-chăn măi m/f

Can I leave a message for someone?
ฝากข้อความให้คนได้ไหม

fàhk kôr kwahm hâi kon
dâi măi

I'm locked out of my room.
ห้อง ผม/ดิฉัน ปิดกุญแจ
ไว้ เข้าไม่ได้

hôrng pŏm/dì-chăn ʰìt
gun-jaa wái, kôw mâi dâi m/f

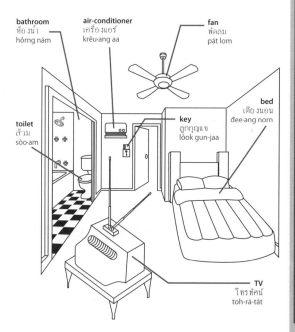

bathroom
ห้องน้ำ
hôrng nám

air-conditioner
เครื่องแอร์
krêu·ang aa

fan
พัดลม
pát lom

toilet
ส้วม
sôo·am

key
ลูกกุญแจ
lôok gun-jaa

bed
เตียงนอน
đee·ang norn

TV
โทรทัศน์
toh-rá-tát

complaints

It's too ...	... เกินไป	... geun bai
bright	สว่าง	sà-wàhng
cold	หนาว	nŏw
dark	มืด	mêut
expensive	แพง	paang
noisy	เสียงดัง	sĕe·ang dang
small	เล็ก	lék

The ... doesn't work.	... เสีย	... sĕe·a
air-conditioning	แอร์	aa
fan	พัดลม	pát lom
toilet	ส้วม	sôo·am

Can I get another (blanket)?
ขอ (ผ้าห่ม) อีกผืนได้ไหม
kŏr (pâh hòm) èek pĕun dâi măi

This (pillow) isn't clean.
(หมอนใบ) นี้ไม่สะอาด
(mŏrn bai) née mâi sà-àht

There's no hot water.
ไม่มีน้ำร้อน
mâi mee nám rórn

a knock at the door ...

Who is it?	ใคร ครับ/คะ	krai kráp/kâ m/f
Just a moment.	รอเดี๋ยว	ror dĕe·o
Come in.	เข้ามาได้	kôw mah dâi
Come back later, please.	กลับมาทีหลังได้ไหม	glàp mah tee lăng dâi măi

checking out

What time is checkout?
ต้องออกห้องกี่โมง
đôrng òrk hôrng gèe mohng

Can I have a late checkout?
ออกห้องสายหน่อยได้ไหม
òrk hôrng săi nòy dâi măi

Can you call a taxi for me (for 11 am)?
เรียกแท็กซี่ให้ (เวลา
สิบเอ็ดโมง) ได้ไหม
rêe·ak táak·sêe hâi (wair-lah sìp-èt mohng) dâi măi

I'm leaving now.
จะออกห้องเดี๋ยวนี้
jà òrk hôrng dĕe·o née

Can I leave my bags here?
ฝากกระเป๋าไว้ที่นี่ได้ไหม
fàhk grà-฿ŏw wái têe née dâi măi

There's a mistake in the bill.
บิลใบนี้ผิดนะ ครับ/ค่ะ
bin bai née pìt ná kráp/kâ m/f

Could I have my …, please?	ขอ … หน่อย	kŏr … nòy
deposit	เงินมัดจำ	ngeun mát jam
passport	หนังสือเดินทาง	năng-sĕu deun tahng
valuables	ของมีค่า	kŏrng mee kâh

I had a great stay, thank you.
พักที่นี่สนุกมาก ขอบคุณ
pák têe née sà-nùk mâhk kòrp kun

I'll recommend it to my friends.
จะแนะนำที่นี่ให้เพื่อนด้วย   jà náa-nam têe née hâi
                              pêu·an dôo·ay

I'll be back ...   จะกลับมา ...   jà glàp mah ...
  in (three) days   อีก (สาม) วัน   èek (săhm) wan
  on (Tuesday)   เมื่อ(วันอังคาร)   mêu·a (wan
                                                   ang-kahn)

camping

Do you have ...?	มี ... ไหม	mee ... măi
electricity	ไฟฟ้า	fai fáh
a laundry	ห้องซักผ้า	hôrng sák pâh
shower facilities	ที่อาบน้ำฝักบัว	têe àhp nám fàk boo·a
a site	ที่ปักเต็นท์	têe bàk đen
tents for hire	เต็นท์ให้เช่า	đen hâi chôw

How much is it per ...?	... ละเท่าไร	... lá tôw-rai
person	คน	kon
tent	เต็นท์ที่	đen
vehicle	รถคัน	rót kan

Is the water drinkable?
น้ำดื่มได้ไหม   nám dèum dâi măi

Is it coin-operated?
ต้องหยอดเหรียญไหม   đôrng yòrt rĕe·an măi

Can I ...?	... ได้ไหม	... dâi măi
camp here	พักแรมที่นี่	pák raam têe née
park next to my tent	จอดรถข้างๆ เต็นท์	jòrt rót kâhng kâhng đen

Who do I ask to stay here?
ถ้าจะพักที่นี่จะต้องถามใคร   tâh jà pák têe née jà đôrng
                                 tăhm krai

renting

Do you have a/an … for rent?	มี … ให้เช่าไหม	mee … hâi chôw măi
apartment	ห้องชุด	hôrng chút
cabin	บ้านพัก	bâhn pák
house	บ้าน	bâhn
room	ห้อง	hôrng

staying with locals

Can I stay at your place?
พักที่บ้านคุณได้ไหม   pák têe bâhn kun dâi măi

Is there anything I can do to help?
มีอะไรที่จะให้ช่วยไหม   mee à-rai têe jà hâi
chôo·ay măi

I have my own …	ผม/ดิฉัน มี …	pŏm/dì-chăn mee …
	ของตัวเอง	kŏrng đoo·a eng m/f
mattress	ฟูก	fôok
sleeping bag	ถุงนอน	tŭng norn
Can I …?	จะให้ฉัน … ไหม	ja hâi chăn … măi
bring anything for the meal	เอาอาหาร อะไรมาช่วย	ow ah-hăhn à-rai mah chôo·ay
do the dishes	ช่วยล้างจาน	chôo·ay láhng jahn
set/clear the table	ช่วย ตั้ง/เก็บ โต๊ะ	chôo·ay đâng/gèp dó
take out the rubbish	ช่วยเก็บขยะ ออกไป	chôo·ay gèp kà-yà òrk bai

Thanks for your (warm) hospitality.

ขอบคุณมากสำหรับ   kòrp kun mâhk săm-ràp
การต้อนรับ(ที่อบอุ่น)   gahn đôrn ráp (têe òp-ùn)

For dining-related expressions, see **food**, page 153.

body language

In Thailand it's important to be aware of your body. Close physical proximity, except in special circumstances such as a crowded Bangkok bus, can be discomforting to Thai people. Thus, you should avoid standing over people or encroaching too much on their personal space.

The head is considered the most sacred part of the body, while the feet are seen as vulgar. Never point at things with your feet nor intentionally touch another person with your feet. Neither should you sit with your feet pointing at someone or at an object of worship, such as a shrine, a picture of the king or Buddha statue. Equally, you should never touch or reach over another person's head. If it's necessary to reach over someone, such as when getting something from a luggage compartment on a bus or train, it's customary to say kŏr tôht ขอโทษ ('Excuse me') first.

looking for ...

การดูของ ...

Where's ...?	... อยู่ที่ไหน	... yòo têe nǎi
a department store	ห้างสรรพสินค้า	hâhng sàp-pá-sĭn-káh
a floating market	ตลาดน้ำ	đà-làht nám
a market	ตลาด	đà-làht
a supermarket	ซูเปอร์มาร์เก็ต	soo-ɓeu-mah-gèt

Where can I buy (a padlock)?
จะซื้อ (แม่กุญแจ) ได้ที่ไหน   jà séu (mâa gun-jaa) dâi têe nǎi

For phrases on directions, see **directions**, page 61.

making a purchase

การลงมือซื้อ

I'm just looking.
ดูเฉย ๆ   doo chěu·i chěu·i

I'd like to buy (an adaptor plug).
อยากจะซื้อ (ปลั๊กต่อ)   yàhk jà séu (ɓlák đòr)

How much is it?
เท่าไรครับ/คะ   tôw-rai kráp/ká m/f

Can you write down the price?
เขียนราคาให้หน่อยได้ไหม   kěe·an rah-kah hâi nòy dâi mǎi

Do you have any others?
มีอีกไหม   mee èek mǎi

Can I look at it?
ขอดูได้ไหม   kŏr doo dâi mǎi

Do you accept …?	รับ … ไหม	ráp … măi
credit cards	บัตรเครดิต	bàt krair-dìt
debit cards	บัตรธนาคาร	bàt tá-nah-kahn
travellers cheques	เช็คเดินทาง	chék deun tahng

Could I have a …, please?	ขอ … ด้วย	kŏr … dôo·ay
bag	ถุง	tŭng
receipt	ใบเสร็จ	bai sèt

Could I have it wrapped?
ห่อให้ได้ไหม   hòr hâi dâi măi

Does it have a guarantee?
มีรับประกันด้วยไหม   mee ráp brà·gan dôo·ay măi

Can I have it sent overseas?
จะส่งเมืองนอกให้ได้ไหม   jà sòng meu·ang nôrk hâi dâi măi

Can you order it for me?
สั่งให้ได้ไหม   sàng hâi dâi măi

Can I pick it up later?
จะกลับมารับทีหลังได้ไหม   jà glàp mah ráp tee lăng dâi măi

It's faulty.
มันบกพร่อง   man bòk prôrng

It's a fake.
เป็นของปลอม   ben kŏrng blorm

I'd like …, please.	อยากจะ … ครับ/ค่ะ	yàhk jà … kráp/kâ m/f
a refund	ได้เงินคืน	dâi ngeun keun
my change	ได้เงินทอน	dâi ngeun torn
to return this	เอามาคืน	ow mah keun

signs

bargain	ราคาย่อมเยา	rah-kah yôrm yow
rip-off	ราคาขี้โกง	rah-kah kêe gohng
specials	ของลดราคา	kŏrng lót rah-kah
sale	ขายลดราคา	kăi lót rah-kah

bargaining

That's too expensive.
แพงไป — paang bai

Can you lower the price?
ลดราคาได้ไหม — lót rah-kah dâi măi

I don't have much money.
มีเงินไม่มากเท่าไร — mee ngeun mâi mâhk tôw-rai

Do you have something cheaper?
มีถูกกว่านี้ไหม — mee tòok gwàh née măi

I'll give you (five baht).
จะให้ (ห้าบาท) — jà hâi (hâh bàht)

I won't give more than … baht.
จะให้ไม่เกิน … บาท — jà hâi mâi geun … bàht

What's your lowest price?
เท่าไรราคาต่ำสุด — tôw-rai rah-kah đàm sùt

The quality isn't very good.
คุณภาพไม่ดีเท่าไร — kun-ná-pâhp mâi dee tôw-rai

little gems

diamond	เพชร	pét
emerald	แก้วมรกต	gâa·ou mor-rá-gòt
gems	เพชรพลอย	pét ploy
gold	ทอง	torng
gold-plated	เคลือบทอง	klêu·ap torng
jade	หยก	yòk
necklace	สร้อยคอ	sôy kor
ring	แหวน	wăn
ruby	ทับทิม	táp-tim
sapphire	นิล	nin
silver	เงิน	ngeun

clothes

My size is …	ฉันใช้ขนาด … เบอร์	chăn chái kà-nàht …
(32)	(สามสิบสอง)	beu (săhm sìp sŏrng)
large	ใหญ่	yài
medium	กลาง	glahng
small	เล็ก	lék

Can I try it on?
ลองได้ไหม   lorng dâi măi

It doesn't fit.
ไม่ถูกขนาด   mâi tòok kà-nàht

I'm looking for fisherman's pants.
มกๆเก็ๆกวยไหม   mee gahng geng kăh goo·ay
     măi

Can you make …?
ทำ … ได้ไหม   tam … dâi măi

The arms/legs are too …	แขน/ขา … เกินไป	kăan/kăh … geun bai
short	สั้น	sân
long	ยาว	yow

For clothing items, see the **dictionary**.

hairdressing

I'd like (a) …	ต้องการ …	đôrng gahn …
blow wave	เป่าผมสลวย	bòw pŏm sà-lŏo·ay
colour	ย้อมผม	yórm pŏm
haircut	ตัดผม	đàt pŏm
my beard trimmed	ตกแต่งหนวด	đòk đàang nòo·at
shave	โกนหนวด	gohn nòo·at
trim	เล็ม	lem

Don't cut it too short.
อย่าตัดให้สั้นเกินไป   yàh đàt hâi sân geun ɓai

Is this a new blade?
ใบมีดนี้ใหม่หรือเปล่า   bai mêet née mài rěu ɓlòw

Shave it all off!
โกนให้หมดเลย   gohn hâi mòt leu·i

I should never have let you near me!
ไม่น่าจะให้คุณแตะต้องฉันเลย   mâi nâh jà hâi kun đàa
                             đôrng chǎn leu·i

For colours, see the **dictionary**.

repairs

Can I have my ...	ที่นี้ซ่อม ... ได้ไหม	têe née sôrm ...
repaired here?		dâi mǎi
When will	จะซ่อม...เสร็จ	jà sôrm ... sèt
my ... be ready?	เมื่อไร	mêu·a rai
backpack	เป้	ɓâir
camera	กล้องถ่ายรูป	glôrng tài rôop
(sun)glasses	แว่นตา (กันแดด)	wâan đah (gan dàat)
shoes	รองเท้า	rorng tów

books & reading

Do you have a book by (Sulak Sivarak)?
มีหนังสือโดย (อาจารย์   mee nǎng-sěu doy (ah-jahn
สุลักษณ์ ศิวรักษ์) ไหม   sù-lák sì-wá-rák) mǎi

Do you have an entertainment guide?
มีคู่มือการบันเทิง ไหม   mee kôo meu gahn
                             ban-teung mǎi

Is there an English-language ...?	มี ... ภาษาอังกฤษ ไหม	mee ... pah-săh ang-grìt măi
bookshop	ร้านขายหนังสือ	ráhn kăi năng-sĕu
section	แผนก	pà-nàak
I'd like a ...	ต้องการ ...	dôrng gahn ...
dictionary	พจนานุกรม	pót-jà-nah-nú-grom
newspaper (in English)	หนังสือพิมพ์ (ภาษาอังกฤษ)	năng-sĕu pim (pah-săh ang-grìt)
notepad	สมุดบันทึก	sà-mùt ban-téuk

Can you recommend a book to me?

แนะนำหนังสือดีๆ ได้ไหม
náa-nam năng-sĕu dee dee dâi măi

Do you have Lonely Planet guidebooks?

มีคู่มือท่องเที่ยว โลน ลี พลาเนต ไหม
mee kôo meu tôrng têe·o lohn-lee plah-nét măi

> ### listen for ...
>
> jà ow à-rai èek măi
> จะเอาอะไรอีกไหม
> **Anything else?**
>
> mâi mee kráp/kâ m/f
> ไม่มี ครับ/ค่ะ
> **No, we don't have any.**
>
> mee à-rai jà hâi chôo·ay măi
> มีอะไรจะให้ช่วยไหม
> **Can I help you?**

music

คนตรี

I'd like a ...	ต้องการ ...	dôrng gahn ...
blank tape	ม้วนเทปเปล่า	móo·an tép Ьlòw
CD	แผ่นซีดี	pàan see-dee
DVD	แผ่นดีวีดี	pàan dee-wee-dee
VCD	แผ่นวีซีดี	pàan wee-see-dee

I'm looking for something by (Carabao).

กำลังหาชุดเพลง   gam-lang hăh chút pleng
(วงคาราบาว)   (wong kah-rah-bow)

What's their best recording?

เพลงชุดไหนเป็นชุด   pleng chút năi ɓen chút
ที่ดีที่สุดของเขา   têe dee têe sùt kŏrng kŏw

Can I listen to this?

ฟังได้ไหม   fang dâi măi

photography

การถ่ายรูป

Can you …?	… ได้ไหม	… dâi măi
develop this film	ล้างฟิล์มนี้	láhng fim née
load my film	ใส่ฟิล์มให้	sài fim hâi

When will it be ready?

จะเสร็จเมื่อไร   jà sèt mêu·a-rai

How much is it?

ราคาเท่าไร   rah-kah tôw-rai

I need … film	ต้องการฟิล์ม …	đôrng gahn fim …
for this camera.	สำหรับกล้องนี้	săm-ràp glôrng née
APS	เอพีเอ็ส	air-pee-ét
B&W	ขาวดำ	kŏw dam
colour	สี	sĕe
slide	สไลด์	sà-lai
(200) speed	มีความไว	mee kwahm wai
	(๒๐๐)	(sŏrng róy)

I need a passport photo taken.

ต้องการถ่ายภาพ   đôrng gahn tài pâhp săm-
สำหรับหนังสือเดินทาง   ràp năng-sěu deun tahng

I'm not happy with these photos.

ผม/ดิฉันไม่พอใจภาพนี้เลย   pŏm/dì-chăn mâi por jai
                        pâhp née leu·i **m/f**

I don't want to pay the full price.

ไม่อยากจ่ายราคาเต็ม   mâi yàhk jài rah-kah đem

---

gender benders

There are two word for the pronoun 'I' in Thai. Male speakers refer to themselves as pŏm ผม and female speakers refer to themselves as dì-chăn ดิฉัน. Wherever you see an **m/f** symbol in this book it means you have to make a choice depending on your gender. This also goes for the polite softeners kráp ครับ (for a man) and kâ ค่ะ (for a woman). See page 21 for an explanation of softeners.

post office

ที่ทำการไปรษณีย์

I want to send a ...	ผม/ดิฉัน อยาก จะส่ง ...	pŏm/dì-chăn yàhk jà sòng ... m/f
fax	แฟกซ์	fàak
letter	จดหมาย	jòt-măi
parcel	พัสดุ	pát-sà-dù
postcard	ไปรษณียบัตร	Ƀrai-sà-nee-yá-bàt
I want to buy ...	ผม/ดิฉัน ยากจะซื้อ ...	pŏm/dì-chăn yàhk jà séu ... m/f
an aerogramme	จดหมายอากาศ	jòt-măi ah-gàht
an envelope	ของจดหมาย	sorng jòt-măi
a stamp	แสตมป์	sà-đaam

May I have a registered receipt?
ขอใบเสร็จการลงทะเบียนด้วย   kŏr bai sèt gahn long tá-bee·an dôo·ay

customs declaration	ใบแจ้งศุลกากร	bai jâang sŭn-lá-gah-gorn
domestic	ภายในประเทศ	pai nai Ƀrà-têt
fragile	ระวังแตก	rá-wang đàak
international	ระหว่างประเทศ	rá-wàhng Ƀrà-têt
mail	ไปรษณีย์	Ƀrai-sà-nee
mailbox	ตู้ไปรษณีย์	đôo Ƀrai-sà-nee
postcode	รหัสไปรษณีย์	rá-hàt Ƀrai-sà-nee

snail mail

airmail	ไปรษณีย์อากาศ	ฅrai-sà-nee ah-gàht
express mail	ไปรษณีย์ด่วน	ฅrai-sà-nee dòo·an
registered mail	ลงทะเบียน	long tá-bee·an
sea mail	ไปรษณีย์ทางทะเล	ฅrai-sà-nee tahng tá-lair
surface mail	ไปรษณีย์ทางธรรมดา	tahng tam-má-dah

Please send it by airmail to (Australia).
ขอส่งทาง อากาศ
ไปประเทศ (ออสเตรเลีย)
kŏr sòng tahng ah-gàht ฅai ฅrà-têt (or-sà-đrair-lee·a)

Please send it by surface mail to (Australia).
ขอส่งทาง ธรรมดา
ไปประเทศ (ออสเตรเลีย)
kŏr sòng tahng tam-má-dah ฅai ฅrà-têt (or-sà-đrair-lee·a)

It contains (souvenirs).
ข้างในมี (ของที่ระลึก)
kâhng nai mee (kŏrng têe rá-léuk)

Is there any mail for me?
มีจดหมายของผม/ดิฉัน ด้วยไหม
mee jòt-măi kŏrng pŏm/ dì-chăn dôo·ay măi m/f

phone

What's your phone number?
เบอร์โทรของคุณคืออะไร
beu toh kŏrng kun keu à-rai

Where's the nearest public phone?
ตู้โทรศัพท์ที่ใกล้เคียง อยู่ที่ไหน
đôo toh-rá-sàp têe glâi kee·ang yòo têe năi

Can I look at a phone book?
ขอดูสมุดโทรศัพท์ได้ไหม
kŏr doo sà-mùt toh-rá-sàp dâi măi

Can you help me find the number for …?
ช่วยหาเบอร์ของ … ให้หน่อย

chôo·ay hăh beu
kŏrng … hâi nòy

I'd like to speak for (10) minutes.
อยากจะพูดเป็นเวลา
(สิบ) นาที

yàhk jà pôot ben wair-lah
(sìp) nah-tee

I want to …   อยากจะ …   yàhk jà …

buy a phonecard	ซื้อบัตรโทรศัพท์	séu bàt toh-rá-sàp
call (Singapore)	โทรไปประเทศ (สิงคโปร์)	toh bai brà-têt (sĭng-ká-boh)
make a (local) call	โทร(ภายใน จังหวัดเดียวกัน)	toh (pai nai jang-wàt dee·o gan)
reverse the charges	โทรเก็บปลายทาง	toh gèp blai tahng
speak for (three) minutes	พูดเป็นเวลา (สาม) นาที	pôot ben wair-lah (săhm) nah-tee

How much does … cost?   … คิดเงินเท่าไร   … kít ngeun tôw-rai

a (three)-minute call	โทร (สาม) นาที	toh (săhm) nah-tee
each extra minute	ทุกนาทีต่อไป	túk nah-tee dòr bai

The number is …
เบอร์ก็คือ …

beu gôr keu …

What's the country code for (New Zealand)?
รหัสประเทศ
(นิวซีแลนด์) คืออะไร

rá-hàt brà-têt
(new see-laan) keu à-rai

It's engaged.
โทรศัพท์ไม่ว่าง

toh-rá-sàp mâi wâhng

I've been cut off.
สายขาดแล้ว

săi kàht láa·ou

The connection's bad.
สายไม่ดี

săi mâi dee

Hello.
ฮัลโหล

han-lŏh

Can I speak to …?
ขอเรียนสาย … หน่อยนะ
ครับ/ค่ะ

kŏr ree·an săi … nòy ná
kráp/ká m/f

It's ...	นี่คือ ...	nêe keu ...
Is ... there?	... อยู่ไหม	... yòo măi

Please say I called.
กรุณาบอกเขาด้วย gà-rú-nah bòrk kŏw dôo·ay
ว่าผม/ดิฉันโทรมา wâh pŏm/dì-chăn toh mah m/f

Can I leave a message?
ฝากข้อความได้ไหม fàhk kôr kwahm dâi măi

My number is ...
เบอร์ของ ผม/ดิฉันคือ ... beu kŏrng pŏm/dì-chăn keu ... m/f

I don't have a contact number.
ผม/ดิฉันไม่มีเบอร์ติดต่อ pŏm/dì-chăn mâi mee beu
đìt-đòr m/f

I'll call back later.
จะโทรอีกทีทีหลัง jà toh èek tee têe lăng

mobile/cell phone

โทรศัพท์มือถือ

I'd like a ...	ต้องการ ...	đôrng gahn ...
charger for	เครื่องชาร์จ	krêu·ang cháht
my phone	โทรศัพท์	toh-rá-sàp
mobile/cell phone	เช่าโทรศัพท์	chôw toh-rá-sàp
for hire	มือถือ	meu tĕu
prepaid mobile/	โทรศัพท์มือถือ	toh-rá-sàp meu tĕu
cell phone	แบบจ่ายล่วงหน้า	bàap jài lôo·ang nâh
SIM card	บัตรซิม	bàt sim

What are the rates?
อัตราการใช้เท่าไร   àt-đrah gahn chái tôw-rai

(Three baht) per minute.
(สามบาท) ต่อหนึ่งนาที   (săhm bàht) đòr nèung
nah-tee

the internet

Where's the local Internet café?
ที่ไหนร้านอินเตอร์เนต   têe năi ráhn in-đeu-nét
ที่ใกล้เคียง   têe glâi kee·ang

I'd like to ...	อยากจะ ...	yàhk jà ...
check my email	ตรวจอีเมล	đròo·at ee-mairn
get Internet access	ติดต่อทางอินเตอร์เนต	đìt đòr tahng in-đeu-nét
use a printer	ใช้เครื่องพิมพ์	chái krêu·ang pim
use a scanner	ใช้เครื่องสแกน	chái krêu·ang sà-gaan

Do you have ...?	มี ... ไหม	mee ... măi
Macs	เครื่องแม็ก	krêu·ang máak
PCs	เครื่องพีซี	krêu·ang pee-see
a Zip drive	ซิบไดรว์	síp drai

How much per ...?	คิด ... ละเท่าไร	kít ... lá tôw-rai
hour	ชั่วโมง	chôo·a mohng
(five)-minutes	(ห้า) นาที	(hâh) nah-tee
page	หน้า	nâh

How do I log on?
ต้องล็อกอินอย่างไร   đôrng lórk-in yàhng rai

Please change it to the English-language setting.
ช่วยเปลี่ยนเป็นระบบ   chôo·ay ɓlèe·an ɓen rá·bòp
ภาษาอังกฤษหน่อย   pah·săh ang·grìt nòy

This computer is too slow.
เครื่องนี้ช้าไป   krêu·ang née cháh ɓai

Can I change computers?
เปลี่ยนเครื่องได้ไหม   ɓlèe·an krêu·ang dâi mǎi

It's crashed.
เครื่องแฮ้งแล้ว   krêu·ang háang láa·ou

I've finished.
เสร็จแล้ว   sèt láa·ou

bank

ธนาคาร

Automated teller machines – ATMs – (đôo air-tee-em ตู้เอทีเอ็ม) are widely available in regional towns, even small ones, as long as they have a bank, but you won't find them in villages. Credit cards (bàt krair-dìt บัตรเครดิต) are generally used in large towns, but don't count on them being accepted in small towns. Travellers cheques (chék deun tahng เช็คเดินทาง) can be changed in banks that have a Foreign Exchange (lâak ngeun đàhng ɓrà-têt แลกเงินต่างประเทศ) sign on them.

What time does the bank open?

ธนาคารเปิดกี่โมง

tá-nah-kahn ɓèut gèe mohng

Where can I …?	… ได้ที่ไหน	… dâi têe nǎi
I'd like to …	อยากจะ …	yàhk jà …
cash a cheque	ขึ้นเช็ค	kêun chék
change a travellers cheque	แลกเช็คเดินทาง	lâak chék deun tahng
change money	แลกเงิน	lâak ngeun
get a cash advance	รูดเงินจาก บัตรเครดิต	rôot ngeun jàhk bàt krair-dìt
withdraw money	ถอนเงิน	tǒrn ngeun
Where's …?	… อยู่ที่ไหน	… yòo têe nǎi
an ATM	ตู้เอทีเอ็ม	đôo air-tee-em
a foreign exchange office	ที่แลกเงินต่างประเทศ	têe lâak ngeun đàhng ɓrà-têt

The ATM took my card.

ตู้เอทีเอ็มกินบัตรของผม/ดิฉัน

đôo air-tee-em gin bàt kǒrng pǒm/dì-chǎn m/f

I've forgotten my PIN.
ผม/ดิฉัน ลืมรหัสบัตรเอทีเอม

pŏm/dì-chǎn leum rá-hàt bàt air-tee-em **m/f**

Can I use my credit card to withdraw money?
ใช้บัตรเครดิตถอนเงินได้ไหม

chái bàt krair-dìt tŏrn ngeun dâi mǎi

Can I have smaller notes?
เอาเป็นใบย่อยกว่านี้ได้ไหม

ow ben bai yôy gwàh née dâi mǎi

Has my money arrived yet?
เงินของ ผม/ดิฉัน มาถึงหรือยัง

ngeun kŏrng pŏm/dì-chǎn mah tĕung rĕu yang **m/f**

How long will it take to arrive?
อีกนานเท่าไรจึงจะมา

èek nahn tôw-rai jeung jà mah

What's the …? … เท่าไร … tôw-rai
  charge for that ค่าธรรมเนียม kâh tam-nee·am
  exchange rate อัตราแลกเปลี่ยน àt-đrah lâak blèe·an

listen for …		
làk tǎhn	หลักฐานส่วนตัว	**identification**
nǎng-sĕu deun tahng	หนังสือเดินทาง	**passport**
long chêu têe née	ลงชื่อที่นี้	**Sign here.**
mee ban-hǎh	มีปัญหา	**There's a problem.**
mâi mee ngeun	ไม่มีเงินเหลือแล้ว	**You have no**
lĕu·a láa·ou		**funds left.**
tam mâi dâi	ทำไม่ได้	**We can't do that.**

I'd like ...	ผม/ดิฉัน ต้องการ ...	pŏm/dì-chăn đôrng gahn m/f
an audio set	ชุดเทปนำเที่ยว	chút tép nam têe·o
a catalogue	คู่มือแนะนำ	kôo meu náa nam
a guide	ไกด์	gai
a guidebook in English	คู่มือนำเที่ยว เป็นภาษาอังกฤษ	kôo meu nam têe·o ɓen pah-săh ang-grìt
a (local) map	แผนที่ (ท้องถิ่น)	păan têe (tórng tìn)

Do you have information on ... sights?	มีข้อมูลเกี่ยว กับแหล่งท่อง เที่ยว ... ไหม	mee kôr moon gèe·o gàp làang tôrng têe·o ... măi
cultural	ทางวัฒนธรรม	tahng wát-tá-ná-tam
historical	ทางประวัติศาสตร์	tahng ɓrà-wàt-đì-sàht
religious	ทางศาสนา	tahng sàht-sà-năh

I'd like to see ...
ผม/ดิฉัน อยากจะดู ...
pŏm/dì-chăn yàhk jà doo ... m/f

What's that?
นั่นคืออะไร
nân keu à-rai

Who made it?
ใครสร้าง
krai sâhng

How old is it?
เก่าเท่าไร
gòw tôw-rai

Can we take photos?
ถ่ายรูปได้ไหม · tài rôop dâi măi

Could you take a photo of me?
ถ่ายรูปให้ผม/ดิฉันหน่อยได้ไหม · tài rôop hâi pŏm/dì-chăn nòy dâi măi **m/f**

Can I take a photo (of you)?
ถ่ายรูป (คุณ) ได้ไหม · tài rôop (kun) dâi măi

I'll send you the photo.
จะส่งภาพมาให้ · jà sòng pâhp ma hâi

Buddhist temple	วัด	wát
statue	รูปหล่อ	rôop lòr
temple ruins	ซากวัดโบราณ	sâhk wát boh-rahn

getting in

Is there a	ลดราคาสำหรับ ...	lót rah-kah
discount for ...?	ไหม	săm-ràp ... măi
children	เด็ก	dèk
families	ครอบครัว	krôrp kroo·a
groups	คณะ	ká-ná
older people	คนสูงอายุ	kon sŏong ah-yú
pensioners	คนกินเงินบำนาญ	kon gin ngeun bam-nahn
students	นักศึกษา	nák sèuk-săh

What time does it open/close?
เปิด/ปิด กี่โมง · bèut/bìt gèe mohng

What's the admission charge?
ค่าเข้าเท่าไร · kâh kôw tôw-rai

tours

ทัวร์

Can you recommend a ...?	แนะนำ ... ได้ไหม	náa-nam ... dâi măi
When's the next ...?	... ต่อไปออกกี่โมง	... đòr bai òrk gèe mohng
boat-trip	เที่ยวเรือ	têe·o reu·a
day trip	เที่ยวรายวัน	têe·o rai wan
tour	ทัวร์	too·a
Is ... included?	รวม ... ด้วยไหม	roo·am ... dôo·ay măi
accommodation	ค่าพัก	kâh pák
food	ค่าอาหาร	kâh ah-hăhn
transport	ค่าการขนส่ง	kâh gahn kŏn sòng

The guide will pay.
ไกด์จะจ่ายให้   gai jà jài hâi

The guide has paid.
ไกด์จ่ายไปแล้ว   gai jài bai láa·ou

How long is the tour?
การเที่ยวใช้เวลานานเท่าไร   gahn têe·o chái wair-lah
                              nahn tôw-rai

What time should we be back?
ควรจะกลับมากี่โมง

koo·an jà glàp mah gèe mohng

I'm with them.
ผม/ดิฉัน อยู่กับเขา

pŏm/dì-chăn yòo gàp kŏw m/f

I've lost my group.
ผม/ดิฉัน หลงคณะอยู่

pŏm/dì-chăn lŏng ká-ná yòo m/f

who's who in the zoo

Ever wonder how a rooster says 'cock-a-doodle-do' in a foreign land? If you find yourself face-to-face with a friendly-looking creature, make sure you adopt the correct forms of address. Accidently greeting a dog as a cat can have embarrassing consequences so refer to the chart below if you are unsure:

bird	จิ๊บๆ	jíp jíp	*tweet-tweet*
cat	เหมียว	mĕe·o	*miao*
chick	เจี๊ยบ ๆ	jée·ap jée·ap	*cheep-cheep*
cow	มอ	mor	*moo*
dog	โฮ่งๆ	hôhng hôhng	*woof woof*
duck	ก้าบๆ	gáhp gáhp	*quack quack*
elephant	แปร้นแปร๊	brâan brăa	*trumpet*
frog	อบ ๆ	òp	*croak*
monkey	เจี๊ยก	jée·ak	*squeal*
rooster	เอ้กอี้เอ้กเอ้ก	ék-ee-êk-êk	*cock-a-doodle-doo*

I'm attending a ...	ผม/ดิฉัน กำลังอยู่ใน ...	pŏm/dì-chăn gam- lang yòo nai ... m/f
conference	ที่ประชุม	têe ʔrà-chum
course	ที่อบรม	têe òp-rom
meeting	ที่ประชุม	têe ʔrà-chum
trade fair	งานแสดงสินค้า	ngahn sa-daang sĭn káh

I'm with ...	ผม/ดิฉัน อยู่กับ ...	pŏm/dì-chăn yòo gàp ... m/f
(Sahaviriya Company)	(บริษัทสหวิริยา)	(bor-rí-sàt sà-hà- wí-rí-yah)
my colleague(s)	เพื่อนงาน	pêu·an ngahn
(two) others	อีก (สอง) คน	èek (sŏrng) kon

I'm alone.
อยู่คนเดียว
yòo kon dee·o

I have an appointment with ...
ผม/ดิฉัน มีนัดกับ ...
pŏm/dì-chăn mee nát
gàp ... m/f

I'm staying at ..., room ...
พักอยู่ที่ ... ที่ห้อง ...
pák yòo têe ... têe
hôrng ...

I'm here for (two) days/weeks.
อยู่ที่นี่ (สอง) วัน/อาทิตย์
yòo têe née (sŏrng) wan/
ah-tít

Here's my ...
นี่คือ ... ของผม/ดิฉัน
nêe keu ... kŏrng
pŏm/dì-chăn m/f

What's your ...?	... ของคุณคืออะไร	... kŏng kun keu à-rai
address	ที่อยู่	têe yòo
email address	ที่อยู่อีเมล	têe yòo ee-mairn
fax number	เบอร์แฟกซ์	beu fàak
mobile number	เบอร์มือถือ	beu meu tĕu
pager number	เบอร์เครื่องเพจ	beu krêu·ang pét
work number	เบอร์ที่ทำงาน	beu têe tam ngahn

Where's the ...?	... อยู่ที่ไหน	... yòo têe năi
business centre	ศูนย์ธุรกิจ	sŏon tú-rá-gìt
conference	การประชุม	gahn brà-chum
meeting	การประชุม	gahn brà-chum

I need ...	ต้องการ ...	đôrng gahn ...
a computer	เครื่องคอมพิวเตอร์	krêu·ang korm-pew-đeu
an Internet connection	ที่ต่ออินเตอร์เนต	têe đòr in-đeu-nét
an interpreter	ล่าม	lâhm
more business cards	นามบัตรอีก	nahm bàt èek
to send a fax	ส่งแฟกซ์	sòng fàak

That went very well.
ก็ล่วงไปด้วยดีนะ
gôr lôo·ang bai dôo·ay dee ná

Thank you for your time.
ขอบคุณที่ให้เวลา
kòrp kun têe hâi wair-lah

Shall we go for a drink?
จะไปดื่มกันไหม
jà bai dèum gan măi

Shall we go for a meal?
จะไปทานอาหารกันไหม
jà bai tahn ah-hăhn gan măi

It's on me.
ผม/ดิฉันเลี้ยงนะ
pŏm/dì-chăn lée·ang ná m/f

senior & disabled travellers

คนเดินทางพิการและคนเดินทางสูงอายุ

Services for senior and disabled travellers are very limited in Thailand, but these phrases should help you with your needs.

Should you require special assistance make sure you get up-to-date information on facilities before you leave. The elderly are treated with great respect and older travellers will find that Thai people often go out of their way to accommodate their needs.

I have a disability.
ผม/ดิฉัน พิการ

pŏm/dì-chăn pí-gahn m/f

I need assistance.
ผม/ดิฉัน ต้องการความ
ช่วยเหลือ

pŏm/dì-chăn đôrng gahn
kwahm chôo·ay lěu·a m/f

What services do you have for people with a disability?
มีบริการอะไรบ้างสำหรับ
คนพิการ

mee bor·rí·gahn à-rai bâhng
săm-ràp kon pí-gahn

Is there wheelchair access?
รถเข็นคนพิการเข้าได้ไหม

rót kĕn kon pí-gahn kôw
dâi măi

How wide is the entrance?
ทางเข้ากว้างเท่าไร

tahng kôw gwâhng tôw rai

I'm deaf.
ผม/ดิฉัน หูหนวก

pŏm/dì-chăn hŏo nòo·ak m/f

I have a hearing aid.
ผม/ดิฉัน ใช้หูเทียม

pŏm/dì-chăn chái hŏo
tee·am m/f

How many steps are there?
มีบันไดกี่ขั้น

mee ban-dai gèe kân

Is there a lift?

มีลิฟท์ไหม · mee líp măi

Are there rails in the bathroom?

ในห้องน้ำมีราวจับไหม · nai hôrng nám mee row jàp măi

Could you help me cross the street safely?

ช่วย ผม/ดิฉัน ข้าม ถนนได้ไหม · chôo·ay pŏm/dì-chăn kâhm tà-nŏn dâi măi m/f

Is there somewhere I can sit down?

มีที่ไหนที่จะนั่งได้ไหม · mee têe năi têe jà nâng dâi măi

person with a disability	คนพิการ	kon pí-gahn
older person	คนสูงอายุ	kon sŏong ah-yú
ramp	ทางลาด	tahng lâht
walking frame	กรอบเหล็กช่วยเดิน	gròrp lèk chôo·ay deun
walking stick	ไม้เท้า	mái tów
wheelchair	รถเข็น	rót kĕn

travelling with children

Is there a ...?	มี ... ไหม	mee ... măi
baby change room	ห้องเปลี่ยนผ้าอ้อม	hôrng ɓlèe·an pâh ôrm
child discount	ลดราคาสำหรับเด็ก	lót rah·kah săm·ràp dèk
child-minding service	บริการดูแลเด็ก	bor·rí·gahn doo laa dèk
child's portion	อาหารขนาดของเด็ก	ah·hăhn kà·nàht kŏrng dèk
crèche	ที่ฝากเลี้ยงเด็ก	têe fàhk lée·ang dèk

I need a/an ...	ต้องการ ...	đôrng gahn ...
(English-speaking) babysitter	พี่เลี้ยงเด็ก (ที่พูดภาษาอังกฤษได้)	pêe lée·ang dèk (têe pôot pah·săh ang·grìt dâi)
child car seat	เบาะนั่งสำหรับเด็ก	bò nâng săm·ràp dèk
cot	เปล	ɓlair
highchair	เก้าอี้เด็ก	gôw·êe dèk
potty	กระโถน	grà·tŏhn
pram	รถเข็นเด็ก	rót kĕn dèk
sick bag	ถุงอ้วก	tŭng ôo·ak

Where's the nearest ...?	... ที่ใกล้เคียงอยู่ที่ไหน	... têe glâi kee·ang yòo têe năi
playground	สนามเด็กเล่น	sà·năhm dèk lên
swimming pool	สระว่ายน้ำ	sà wâi nám
tap	ก็อกน้ำ	górk nám
toyshop	ร้านขายของเล่น	ráhn kăi kŏrng lên

Do you sell ...?	ที่นี่ขาย ... ไหม	têe née kăi ... măi
baby painkillers	ยาแก้ปวด	yah gâa ḅòo·at
	สำหรับเด็ก	săm·ràp dèk
baby wipes	ผ้าเช็ดมือเปียก	pâh chét meu
		ḅèe·ak
disposable	ผ้าอ้อมแบบ	pâh ôrm bàap
nappies	ใช้แล้วทิ้ง	chái láa·ou tíng
tissues	กระดาษทิชชู่	grà·dàht tít·chôo

Do you hire ...?	มี ... ให้เช่าไหม	mee ... hâi chôw măi
prams	รถเข็น	rót kĕn
strollers	รถเข็นแบบพับได้	rót kĕn bàap páp dâi

Is there space for a pram?
มีที่สำหรับรถเข็นไหม
mee têe săm·ràp rót kĕn măi

Could I have some paper and pencils, please?
ขอกระดาษเขียนเล่นและ
kŏr grà·dàht kĕe·an lên láa
ดินสอหน่อย
din·sŏr nòy

Are there any good places to take children around here?
แถวนี้มีที่ดีๆ สำหรับเด็กไหม
tăa·ou née mee têe dee
dee săm·ràp dèk măi

Are children allowed?
เด็กเข้าได้ไหม
dèk kôw dâi măi

Where can I change a nappy?
เปลี่ยนผ้าอ้อมได้ที่ไหน
ḅlèe·an pâh ôrm dâi têe năi

Do you mind if I breast-feed here?
ที่นี่ให้นมลูกได้ไหม
têe née hâi nom lôok dâi măi

Is this suitable for ... -year-old children?
อันนี้เหมาะสมสำหรับเด็ก
an née mò sŏm săm·ràp
อายุ ... ขวบไหม
dèk ah·yú ... kòo·ap măi

For ages see **numbers & amounts**, page 35.

Do you know a doctor who's good with children?
รู้จักหมอที่เก่งเรื่องเด็กไหม
róo jàk mŏr têe gèng
rêu·ang dèk măi

For health issues, see **health**, page 191.

talking about children

When's the baby due?
กำหนดคลอดวันที่เท่าไร
gam-nòt klôrt wan têe
tôw rai

Have you thought of a name for the baby yet?
หาชื่อให้เด็กได้หรือยัง
hăh chêu hâi dèk dâi
rěu yang

Is this your first child?
เป็นลูกคนแรกไหม
ben lôok kon râak măi

How many children do you have?
มีลูกกี่คน
mee lôok gèe kon

What a beautiful child!
เด็กน่ารักจริงๆ
dèk nâh rák jing jing

Is it a boy or a girl?
เป็นผู้หญิงหรือผู้ชาย
ben pôo yĭng rěu pôo chai

How old is he/she?
อายุกี่ขวบ
ah-yú gèe kòo·ap

Does he/she go to school?
เข้าโรงเรียนหรือยัง
kôw rohng ree·an rěu yang

What's his/her name?
เขาชื่ออะไร
kŏw chêu à-rai

Is he/she well-behaved?
เป็นเด็กดีหรือเปล่า
ben dèk dee rěu blòw

He/She ...	เขา ...	kŏw ...
has your eyes	มีตาเหมือนคุณ	mee đah měu·an kun
looks like you	หน้าเหมือนคุณ	nâh měu·an kun

talking with children

When is your birthday?
วันไหนวันเกิดของหนู — wan năi wan gèut kŏrng nŏo

Do you go to school?
หนูไปโรงเรียนไหม — nŏo bai rohng ree·an măi

Do you go to kindergarten?
หนูไปอนุบาลไหม — nŏo bai à-nú-bahn măi

What grade are you in?
ที่โรงเรียนหนูอยู่ชั้นอะไร — têe rohng ree·an nŏo yòo chán à-rai

Do you like ...?	หนูชอบ ... ไหม	nŏo chôrp ... măi
school	โรงเรียน	rohng ree·an
sport	กีฬา	gee-lah
your teacher	อาจารย์ของหนู	ah-jahn kŏrng nŏo

Do you learn English?
เรียนภาษาอังกฤษไหม — ree·an pah-săh ang-grìt măi

I come from very far away.
ฉันมาจากที่ไกลมาก — chăn mah jàhk têe glai mâhk

---

rug rats

When speaking to children it's customary to use endearing forms of address that may change with the age and gender of the child. The informal second-person pronoun teu เธอ (you) may be used for children above thirteen years of age, but younger children are often addressed as nŏo หนู (lit: mouse). The best way to address a teenager is by their nickname. If in doubt, just ask:

What's your nickname?
ชื่อเล่นคืออะไร — chêu lên keu à-rai

SOCIAL > meeting people

basics

พื้นฐาน

Yes.	ใช่	châi
No.	ไม่	mâi
Please.	ขอ	kŏr
Thank you (very much).	ขอบคุณ (มาก ๆ)	kòrp kun (mâhk mâhk)
You're welcome.	ยินดี	yin dee
Excuse me. (to get attention)	ขอโทษ	kŏr tôht
Excuse me. (to get past)	ขออภัย	kŏr à-pai
Sorry.	ขอโทษ	kŏr tôht

greetings & goodbyes

การทักทายและการลา

In Thailand instead of asking 'What are you up to?', it's customary to ask 'Where are you going?', 'Where have you been?' and even 'Have you eaten?'. How you choose to answer is not so important – these greetings are really just a way of affirming a friendly connection.

Hello.	สวัสดี	sà-wàt-dee
Hi.	หวัสดี	wàt-dee
Where are you going?	ไปไหน	pai năi
Where have you been?	ไปไหนมา	pai năi mah
Have you eaten?	กินข้าวหรือยัง	gin kôw rĕu yang

Good day. (for morning, afternoon and evening)
สวัสดี　　　　　　　　　　　　sà-wàt-dee

Good night.
ราตรีสวัสดิ์　　　　　　　　　rah-dree sà-wàt

How are you?
สบายดีไหม　　　　　　　　　sà-bai dee măi

Fine. And you?
สบายดี ครับ/ค่ะ แล้วคุณล่ะ　　sà-bai dee kráp/kâ, láa·ou
　　　　　　　　　　　　　　　kun lâ m/f

What's your name?
คุณชื่ออะไร　　　　　　　　　kun chêu à-rai

My name is …
ผม/ดิฉัน ชื่อ …　　　　　　　pŏm/dì-chăn chêu … m/f

I'd like to introduce you to …
นี่คือ …　　　　　　　　　　　nêe keu …

This is my …	นี่คือ … ของ ผม/ดิฉัน	nêe keu … kŏrng pŏm/dì-chăn m/f
child	ลูก	lôok
colleague	เพื่อน งาน	pêu·an ngahn
friend	เพื่อน	pêu·an
husband	ผัว	pŏo·a
partner (intimate)	แฟน	faan
wife	เมีย	mee·a

For other family members, see **family**, page 107.

I'm pleased to meet you.
ยินดีที่ได้รู้จัก　　　　　　　yin-dee têe dâi róo jàk

See you later.
เดี๋ยวพบกันใหม่　　　　　　　dĕe·o póp gan mài

Goodbye.	ลาก่อน	lah gòrn
See you!	เจอกันนะ	jeu gan ná
Good night.	ราตรีสวัสดิ์	rah-đree sà-wàt
Bon voyage!	เดินทางด้วย	deun tahng dôo·ay
	สวัสดิภาพนะ	sà-wàt-dì-pâhp ná

addressing people

Thais will quickly establish your age when they first meet you which helps to establish the appropriate forms of address. An older person is addressed as pêe พี่ (elder) while a younger person will be addressed as nórng น้อง (younger) or more likely just by name. Kinship terms are used even for people who aren't related. So a woman may be called bâa ป้า or náa น้า (auntie), or even yai ยาย (grandma) and a man may be called lung ลุง (uncle) or bòo ปู่ (grandpa). The Thai language does have words that correspond to the English terms Mr/Ms/Mrs/Miss but these are only ever used in writing:

Mr	นาย	nai
Ms/Mrs	นาง	nahng
Miss	นางสาว	nahng sŏw

monkey business

When speaking of people of high social rank it's custom-ary to use the appropriate pronoun (usually tâhn ท่าน). This applies especially to monks and royalty. Monks and the royal family are treated with high reverence, so if you want to be sure of not offending anyone, tread lightly when discussing them.

making conversation

What a beautiful day!
อากาศดีนะ
ah-gàat dee ná

It's so hot today!
วันนี้ร้อนจัง
wan née rórn jang

It's very cold today!
วันนี้หนาวมาก
wan née nŏw mâhk

Do you live here?
คุณอยู่ที่นี่หรือเปล่า
kun yòo têe née rĕu ฿lòw

Where do you come from?
คุณมาจากไหน
kun mah jàhk năi

Where are you going?
จะไปไหน
jà ฿ai năi

What are you doing?
กำลังทำอะไรอยู่
gam-lang tam à-rai yòo

Do you like it here?
ชอบที่นี่ไหม
chôrp têe née măi

I love it here.
ชอบที่นี่มาก
chôrp têe née mâhk

---

wâi me?

Although Western codes of behaviour are becoming more familiar in Thailand, the country still has its own proud traditions. One of these is the wâi ไหว้, the prayer-like gesture of hands held together in front of the chin, which is used in everyday interactions. The wâi is generally used in situations where Westerners would shake hands. Thus you would wâi when meeting a person for the first time, and also when meeting a person after an absence, or for the first time for that day. A wâi is always called for when meeting a person older than you or with a respected social position. Usually the younger person is expected to wâi first.

What's this called?
อันนี้เรียกว่าอะไร

an née rêe·ak wâh à-rai

Can I take a photo (of you)?
ถ่ายรูป (คุณ) ได้ไหม

tài rôop (kun) dâi măi

That's (beautiful), isn't it!
นั่น (สวย) นะ

nân (sŏo·ay) ná

Just joking.
พูดเล่นเฉย ๆ

pôot lên chĕu·i chĕu·i

Are you here on holiday?
คุณมาที่นี่พักผ่อนหรือเปล่า

kun mah têe née pák pòrn
rĕu blòw

I'm here … ฉันมาที่นี้ มา…

chăn mah têe née
mah …

for a holiday	พักผ่อน	pák pòrn
on business	ทำธุระ	tam tú-rá
to study	ศึกษา	sèuk-săh

How long are you here for?
คุณจะมาพักที่นี่นานเท่าไร

kun jà mah pák têe née
nahn tôw-rai

I'm here for (four) days/weeks.
มาพักที่นี่ (สี่) วัน/อาทิตย์

mah pák têe née (sèe)
wan/ah-tít

nationalities

Where are you from?
คุณมาจากไหน

kun mah jàhk năi

I'm from … ผม/ดิฉัน มาจาก
ประเทศ …

pŏm/dì-chăn mah
jàhk brà-têt … m/f

Australia	ออสเตรเลีย	or-sà-drair-lee·a
Canada	แคนาดา	kaa-nah-dah
Singapore	สิงคโปร์	sĭng-ká-boh

age

How old …?	… อายุเท่าไร	… ah-yú tôw-rai
are you	คุณ	kun
is your daughter	ลูกสาวของคุณ	lôok sŏw kŏrng kun
is your son	ลูกชายของคุณ	lôok chai kŏrng kun

I'm … years old.
ฉันอายุ … ปี   chăn ah-yú … ƀee

He/She is … years old.
เขาอายุ … ปี   kŏw ah-yú … ƀee

Too old!
อายุมากเกินไป   ah-yú mâhk geun ƀai

I'm younger than I look.
ฉันอายุน้อยกว่าที่คิด   chăn ah-yú nóy gwàh têe kít

For your age, see **numbers & amounts**, page 35.

occupations & studies

What's your occupation?
คุณมีอาชีพอะไร   kun mee ah-chêep à-rai

I'm a …	ฉันเป็น …	chăn ƀen …
civil servant	ข้าราชการ	kâh râht-chá-gahn
farmer	ชาวไร่	chow râi
journalist	นักข่าว	nák kòw
teacher	ครู	kroo

I work in ...	ฉันทำงานทางด้าน ...	chăn tam ngahn tahng dâhn ...
administration	บริหาร	bor-rí-hărn
health	สุขภาพ	sùk-kà-pâhp
sales & marketing	การค้าและตลาด	gahn káh láa đà-làht

I'm ...	ฉัน ...	chăn ...
retired	ปลดเกษียณแล้ว	blòt gà-sĕe·an láa·ou
self-employed	ทำธุรกิจส่วนตัว	tam tú-rá-gìt sòo·an đoo·a
unemployed	ว่างงาน	wâhng ngahn

What are you studying?
คุณกำลังเรียนอะไร
kun gam-lang ree·an à-rai yòo

I'm studying ...	ผม/ดิฉัน กำลังเรียน ...	pŏm/dì-chăn gam-lang ree·an ... m/f
humanities	มนุษยศาสตร์	má-nút-sà-yá-sàht
science	วิทยาศาสตร์	wít-tá-yah-sàht
Thai	ภาษาไทย	pah-săh tai

family

ครอบครัว

When talking about families in Thailand you can't just say 'I have three brothers and two sisters' as it isn't the gender that counts, but the age. So a Thai would say 'I have three youngers and two elders'. You'd have to enquire further to find out how many of those were sisters and how many brothers.

Do you have a ...?	มี ... ไหม	mee ... măi
I (don't) have a ...	(ไม่) มี ...	(mâi) mee ...
brother (older)	พี่ชาย	pêe chai
brother (younger)	น้องชาย	nórng chai
daughter	ลูกสาว	lôok sŏw
family	ครอบครัว	krôrp kroo·a
father (pol)	บิดา	bì-dah
father (inf)	พ่อ	pôr
husband (pol)	สามี	săh-mee
husband (inf)	ผัว	pŏo·a
mother (pol)	มารดา	mahn-dah
mother (inf)	แม่	mâa
partner (intimate)	แฟน	faan
sister (older)	พี่สาว	pêe sŏw
sister (younger)	น้องสาว	nórng sŏw
son	ลูกชาย	lôok chai
wife (pol)	ภรรยา	pan-rá-yah
wife (inf)	เมีย	mee·a

I'm ...	ผม/ดิฉัน ...	pŏm/dì-chăn ... m/f
married	แต่งงานแล้ว	đàang ngahn láa·ou
not married	ยังไม่แต่งงาน	yang mâi đàang ngahn
separated	หย่ากันแล้ว	yàh gan láa·ou
single	เป็นโสดอยู่	ben sòht yòo

I live with someone.
อยู่ร่วมกับคนอื่น | yòo rôo·am gàp kon èun

Are you married?
คุณแต่งงานหรือยัง | kun đàang ngahn rĕu yang

Do you have any children?
มีลูกหรือยัง | mee lôok rĕu yang

Not yet.
ยัง | yang

Speaking about your or somebody else's extended family is complicated in Thai as you need to specify which side of the family you're referring to, and sometimes even how old the person is relative to the mother or father. Use the table below to find out how to talk about aunts, uncles and grandparents:

uncle	(mother's older brother)	ลุง	lung
	(mother's younger brother)	น้า	náh
	(father's older brother)	ลุง	lung
	(father's younger brother)	อา	ah
aunt	(mother's older sister)	ป้า	bâh
	(mother's younger sister)	อา	ah
	(father's older sister)	ป้า	bâh
	(father's younger sister)	อา	ah
grandmother	(mother's side)	ยาย	yai
	(father's side)	ย่า	yâh
grandfather	(mother's side)	ตา	đah
	(father's side)	ปู่	bòo

farewells

การลา

Tomorrow is my last day here.
พรุ่งนี้เป็นวันสุดท้ายที่นี่   prûng née ben wan sùt tái têe née

Here's my ...   นี่คือ ... ของผม/ดิฉัน   nêe keu ... kŏrng pŏm/dì-chăn m/f

What's your ...?   ... ของคุณคืออะไร   ... kŏrng kun keu à-rai
     address   ที่อยู่   têe yòo
     email address   ที่อยู่อีเมล   têe yòo ee-men
     phone number   เบอร์โทรศัพท์   beu toh-rá-sàp

If you come to (Scotland) you can stay with me.
ถ้ามา (ประเทศสกอตแลนด์)
มาพักกับฉันได้

tâh mah bra-têt (sà-kórt-laan) mah pák gàp chăn dâi

Keep in touch!
ติดต่อมานะ

dìt dòr mah ná

It's been great meeting you.
ดีใจมากที่ได้พบกับคุณ

dee jai mâhk têe dâi póp gàp kun

local talk

Hey!	เฮ้ย	héu·i
Great!	ยอด	yôrt
Sure.	แน่นอน	nâa norn
Maybe.	บางที	bahng tee
No way!	ไม่มีทาง	mâi mee tahng
Just a minute.	เดี๋ยวก่อน	dĕe·o gòrn
It's OK.	ไม่เป็นไร	mâi ben rai
No problem.	ไม่มีปัญหา	mâi mee ban-hăh
Oh, no!	ตายแล้ว	đai láa·ou
Oh my god!	คุณพระช่วย	kun prá chôo·ay

well wishing

การอวยพร

Bless you!	จงเจริญ	jong jà-reun
Bon voyage!	เดินทางโดย สวัสดิภาพนะ	deun tahng dôo·ay sà-wàt-dì-pâhp
Congratulations!	ขอแสดงความ ยินดีด้วย	kŏr sà-daang kwahm yin-dee dôo·ay
Good luck!	โชคดีนะ	chôhk dee ná
Happy birthday!	สุขสันต์วันเกิด	sùk-săn wan gèut
Merry Christmas!	สุขสันต์วันคริสต์มาส	sùk-săn wan krít-mâht
Happy New Year!	สวัสดีปีใหม่	sà-wàt-dee bee mài

common interests

แหล่งความสนใจทั่วไป

Do you like ...?	ชอบ ... ไหม	chôrp ... măi
I (don't) like ...	ผม/ดิฉัน (ไม่)	pŏm/dì-chăn (mâi)
	ชอบ ...	chôrp ... m/f
cooking	ทำอาหาร	tam ah-hăhn
dancing	เต้นรำ	đên ram
drawing	เขียนภาพ	kĕe·an pâhp
music	ดนตรี	don-đree
painting	ระบายสี	rá-bai sĕe
photography	ถ่ายภาพ	tài pâhp
socialising	การสังคม	gahn săng-kom
surfing the Internet	เล่นอินเตอร์เนต	lên in-đeu-nét
travelling	การท่องเที่ยว	gahn tôrng têe·o
watching TV	ดูโทรทัศน์	doo toh-rá-tát
Where can I enrol in ...?	จะเข้า ... ได้ที่ไหน	jà kôw ... dâi têe năi
Can you recommend a ...?	คุณแนะนำที่ ... ได้ไหม	kun náa nam têe ... dâi măi
Thai cookery course	เรียนทำอาหารไทย	ree·an tam ah-hăhn tai
Thai language course	เรียนภาษาไทย	ree·an pah-săh tai
massage course	เรียนนวดแผนโบราณ	ree·an nôo·at păan boh-rahn
meditation course	เรียนวิธีทำสมาธิ	ree·an wí-tee tam sà-mah-tí

What do you do in your spare time?

คุณทำอะไรเวลาว่าง   kun tam à-rai wair-lah wâhng

For sporting activities, see **sport**, page 137.

music

Do you ...?	คุณ ... ไหม	kun ... măi
dance	เต้นรำ	đên ram
go to concerts	ไปดูการแสดง	bai doo gahn sà-daang
listen to music	ฟังดนตรี	fang don-đree
play an instrument	เล่นเครื่องดนตรี	lên krêu·ang don-đree

What ... do you like?	คุณชอบ ... อะไรบ้าง	kun chôrp ... à-rai bâhng
bands	วงดนตรี	wong don-đree
music	ดนตรี	don-đree
singers	นักร้อง	nák rórng

classical music	เพลงคลาสิค	pleng klah-sìk
blues	เพลงบลูส์	pleng bloo
electronic music	เพลงเทคโน	pleng ték-noh
jazz	ดนตรีแจ๊ซ	don-đree jáat
pop	เพลงป๊อบ	pleng bórp
rock	เพลงร้อค	pleng rórk
world music	ดนตรีโลก	don-đree lôhk

Planning to go to a concert? See **tickets**, page 46 and **going out**, page 121.

cinema & theatre

หนังและละคร

What's showing at the cinema tonight?
มีอะไรฉายที่โรงหนังคืนนี้   mee à-rai chăi têe rohng năng keun née

What's showing at the theatre tonight?
มีอะไรแสดงที่โรงละคร คืนนี้   mee à-rai sà-daang têe rohng lá-korn keun née

Is it in English?
เป็นภาษาอังกฤษไหม

ฺben pah-săh ang-grìt măi

Does it have (English) subtitles?
มีบรรยาย (ภาษาอังกฤษ)
ด้วยไหม

mee ban-yai (pah-săh
ang-grìt) dôo·ay măi

Who's in it?
ใครแสดง

krai sà-daang

Have you seen …?
คุณเคยดู … ไหม

kun keu·i doo … măi

Is this seat taken?
ที่นั่งนี้มีใครเอาหรือยัง

têe nâng née mee krai
ow rĕu yang

I feel like going to a …	ผม/ดิฉัน รู้สึก อยากจะไปดู …	pŏm/dì-chăn róo-sèuk yàhk jà ฺbai doo… m/f
Did you like the …?	คุณชอบ … ไหม	kun chôrp … măi
film	หนัง	năng
folk opera	ลิเก	lí-gair
Ramayana play	โขน	kŏhn
Thai dancing	รำไทย	ram tai
maw lam	หมอลำ	mŏr lam
temple fair	งานวัด	ngahn wát
I (don't) like …	ผม/ดิฉัน (ไม่) ชอบ …	pŏm/dì-chăn (mâi) chôrp … m/f
action movies	หนังบู๊	năng ฺbóo
animated films	หนังการ์ตูน	năng gah-đoon
comedies	หนังตลก	năng đà-lòk
documentaries	สารคดี	săh-rá-ká-dee
erotic movies	หนังโป๊	năng ฺbóh
Thai cinema	หนังไทย	năng tai
horror movies	หนังผี	năng pĕe
sci-fi movies	หนังวิทยาศาสตร์	năng wít-tá- yah-sàht
short films	หนังเรื่องสั้น	năng rêu·ang sân

I thought it was …	ผม/ดิฉัน คิดว่ามัน …	pǒm/dì-chǎn kít
		wâh man … m/f
excellent	ยอด	yôrt
long	ยาว	yow
OK	ก็โอเค	gôr oh-kair

thai tunes

From Western-inspired house beats to flowing classical melodies, Thailand resounds with music. Listen out for some of these distinctively Thai styles:

traditional Thai music
เพลงไทยเดิม   pleng tai deum

Thai country music
เพลงลูกทุ่ง   pleng lôok tûng

country music of Lao and Northeastern Thailand (*maw lam*)
เพลงหมอลำ   pleng mŏr lam

Thai classical orchestra
คนตรีปี่พาทย์   don-đree bèe pâht

bamboo xylophone music
คนตรีระนาด   don-đree rá-nâat

Thai folk opera (*li-ke*)
เพลงลิเก   pleng lí-gair

feelings

Key words in expressing emotions in Thai are jai ใจ (heart or mind) and occasionally ah·rom อารมณ์ (similar to the English 'mood'). The phrase ah·rom dee อารมณ์ดี means 'a good mood', while ah·rom mâi dee อารมณ์ไม่ดี means 'bad mood' or 'not a good mood'. The expression ah·rom sĕe·a อารมณ์เสีย refers to 'a mood turning sour'.

Are you ...?	คุณ ... ไหม	kun ... mǎi
I'm (not) ...	ผม/ดิฉัน (ไม่) ...	pǒm/dì·chǎn (mâi) ... m/f
annoyed	รำคาญ	ram-kahn
cold	หนาว	nŏw
disappointed	ผิดหวัง	pìt wǎng
embarrassed	อับอาย	àp-ai
happy	ดีใจ	dee jai
hot	ร้อน	rórn
hungry	หิว	hěw
in a hurry	รีบร้อน	rêep rórn
sad	เศร้า	sôw
surprised	ประหลาดใจ	bràlàht jai
thirsty	หิวน้ำ	hěw nám
tired	เหนื่อย	nèu·ay
worried	กังวล	gang-won

If feeling unwell, see **health**, page 191.

opinions

Did you like it?
คุณชอบไหม   kun chôrp măi

What do you think of it?
คุณว่าอย่างไร   kun wâh yàhng rai

I thought it	ผม/ดิฉัน	pŏm/dì-chăn
was ...	คิดว่ามัน ...	kít wâh man ... m/f
It's ...	มัน ...	man ...
awful	สุดแย่	sùt yâa
beautiful	น่าประทับใจ	nâh bràr-táp jai
boring	น่าเบื่อ	nâh bèu-a
great	เยี่ยม	yêe·am
interesting	น่าสนใจ	nâh sŏn-jai
OK	ก็โอเค	gôr oh-kair
strange	แปลก	blàak
too expensive	แพงเกินไป	paang geun bai

mood swings

a little	นิดหน่อย	nít-nòy
I'm a little	ผม/ดิฉัน รู้สึกผิด	pŏm/dì-chăn róo-sèuk
disappointed.	หวังนิดหน่อย	pìt wăng nít-nòy m/f
extremely	อย่างยิ่ง	yàhng yîng
I'm extremely	ผม/ดิฉัน เสียใจ	pŏm/dì-chăn sĕe·a
sorry.	อย่างยิ่ง	jai yàhng yîng m/f
very	มาก	mâhk
I feel very lucky.	ผม/ดิฉัน รู้สึก	pŏm/dì-chăn róo-sèuk
	โชคดีมาก	chôhk dee mâhk m/f

politics & social issues

Who do you vote for?
คุณลงคะแนนเสียงให้ใคร

kun long ká-naan sĕe·ang
hâi krai

I support the ... party.
ผม/ดิฉัน สนับสนุนพรรค ...

pŏm/dì-chăn sà-nàp sà-nŭn
pák ... m/f

I'm a member of
the ... party.

I'm a member of the ... party.	ผม/ดิฉัน เป็นสมาชิก พรรค ...	pŏm/dì-chăn ben sà-mah-chik pák ... m/f
communist	คอมมิวนิสต์	korm-mew-nít
conservative	หัวเก่า	hŏo·a gòw
democratic	ประชาธิปไตย	brà-chah-tí-bà-đai
green	อนุรักษ์นิยม	à-nú-rák ní-yom
liberal (progressive)	เสรีนิยม	săir-ree ní-yom
social democratic	ประชาธิปไตย สังคมนิยม	brà-chah-tí-bà-đai săng-kom ní-yom
socialist	สังคมนิยม	săng-kom ní-yom

---

a matter of heart

The Thai word jai ใจ is used extensively in everyday
conversation. It can mean both 'heart' (centre of the
emotional self) or 'mind'. When it's attached to the end
of a word it describes an emotional state, whereas at the
beginning of a word it describes a personality trait.

น้อยใจ	nóy jai	**to be peeved**
ใจน้อย	jai nóy	**to be petty**
ร้อนใจ	rórn jai	**to be agitated**
ใจร้อน	jai rórn	**to be impetuous**
ดีใจ	dee jai	**to be happy**
ใจดี	jai dee	**to be kind**

the life of the party

Democrat Party	พรรคประชาธิปัตย์	pák bràchah-tí-bàt
New Aspiration Party	พรรคความหวังใหม่	pák kwahm wǎng mài
Social Action Party	พรรคกิจสังคม	pák gìt sǎng-kom
Thai Nation Party	พรรคชาติไทย	pák châht tai
Thai Progress Party	พรรคชาติพัฒนา	pák châht pá-tá-nah
Thai Rak Thai Party	พรรคไทยรักไทย	pák tai rák tai

Did you hear about …?
ได้ยินเรื่อง … ไหม
dâi yin rêu·ang … mǎi

Do you agree with it?
เห็นด้วยไหม
hěn dôo·ay mǎi

I (don't) agree with …
ผม/ดิฉัน (ไม่) เห็นด้วยกับ …
pǒm/dì-chǎn (mâi) hěn dôo·ay gàp … m/f

How do people feel about …?
คนรู้สึกอย่างไรเรื่อง …
kon róo-sèuk yàhng rai rêu·ang …

In my country we're concerned about …
ในประเทศของผม/ดิฉัน
เราสนใจเรื่อง …
nai brà-têt kǒrng pǒm/dì-chǎn
row sǒn-jai rêu·ang … m/f

How can we protest against …?
เราจะประท้วงเรื่อง …
ได้อย่างไร
row jà bràtóo·ang
rêu·ang … dâi yàhng rai

How can we support …?
เราจะสนับสนุนเรื่อง …
ได้อย่างไร
row jà sà-nàp sà-nǔn
rêu·ang … dâi yàhng rai

AIDS	โรคเอดส์	rôhk èt
animal rights	สิทธิของสัตว์	sìt-tí kŏrng sàt
	เดรัจฉาน	dair-rát-chăhn
corruption	ความทุจริต	kwahm tú-jà-rìt
crime	อัชญากรรม	àt-chá-yah-gam
discrimination	การกีดกัน	gahn gèet gan
drugs	ยาเสพติด	yah sèp đìt
the economy	เศรษฐกิจ	sèt-tà-gìt
education	การศึกษา	gahn sèuk-săh
the environment	สิ่งแวดล้อม	sìng wâat lórm
equal opportunity	การให้โอกาส	gahn hâi oh-gàht
	เท่าเทียมกัน	tôw tee·am gan
globalisation	โลกาภิวัติ	loh-gah-pí-wát
human rights	สิทธิมนุษยชน	sìt-tí má-nút-sà-yá- chon
immigration	การอพยพเข้าเมือง	gahn òp-pá-yóp kôw meu·ang
indigenous issues	เรื่องคนพื้นเมือง	rêu·ang kon péun meu·ang
indigenous rights	สิทธิของคนพื้นเมือง	sìt-tí kŏrng kon péun meu·ang
inequality	ความไม่เสมอภาค	kwahm mâi sà-mĕu pâhk
the monarchy	สถาบันมหากษัตริย์	sà-tăh-ban má-hăh gà-sàt
party politics	การเมืองระหว่าง พรรค	gahn meu·ang rá- wàhng pák
racism	การเหยียดผิว	gahn yèe·at pĕw
sex tourism	การเที่ยวทางเพศ	gahn têe·o tahng pêt
sexism	เพศนิยม	pêt ní-yom
social welfare	การประชา สงเคราะห์	gahn bprà-chah sŏng-kró
terrorism	การก่อการร้าย	gahn gòr gahn rái
unemployment	ความว่างงาน	kwahm wâhng ngahn
US foreign policy	นโยบายต่างประเทศ ของสหรัฐฐอเมริกา	ná-yoh-bai đàhng bprà-têt kŏrng sà-hà- rát à-mair-rí-gah
the war in ...	สงครามใน ...	sŏng-krahm nai ...

feelings & opinions

119

the environment

Is there a ... problem here?
ที่นี่มีปัญหาเรื่อง ... ไหม

têe née mee ban-hăh
rêu·ang ... măi

What should be done about ...?
ควรจะทำอย่างไรเรื่อง ...

koo·an jà tam yàhng rai
rêu·ang ...

conservation	การอนุรักษ์สิ่งแวดล้อม	gahn à-nú-rák sìng wâat lórm
deforestation	การทำลายป่า	gahn tam lai bàh
drought	ภาวะขาดแคลนน้ำ	pah-wá kàht klaan nám
ecosystem	ระบบนิเวศ	rá-bòp ní-wêt
endangered species	สัตว์ที่ใกล้จะสูญพันธุ์	sàt têe glâi jà sŏon pan
hydroelectricity	พลังไฟฟ้าจากน้ำ	pá-lang fai fáh jàhk nám
irrigation	การทดน้ำ	gahn tót nám
pesticides	ยาฆ่าแมลง	yah kâh má-laang
pollution	มลภาวะ	mon-pah-wá
toxic waste	ขยะมีพิษ	kà-yà mee pít
water supply	แหล่งน้ำใช้	làang nám chái

Is this a protected ...?	อันนี้เป็น ... สงวนไหม	an née ben ... sà-ngŏo·an măi
jungle	ป่า	bàh
park	อุทยาน	ù-tá-yahn
species	สัตว์	sàt

where to go

ที่ไป

What's there to do in the evenings?
มีอะไรบ้างให้ทำตอนเย็น

mee à-rai bâhng hâi tam đorn yen

Where shall we go?
จะไปไหนกันดี

jà bai năi gan dee

What's on …?	มีอะไรทำ …	mee à-rai tam …
locally	แถวๆ นี้	tăe·ou tăe·ou née
this weekend	เสาร์อาทิตย์นี้	sŏw ah-tít née
today	วันนี้	wan née
tonight	คืนนี้	keun née
Where can I find …?	จะหา … ได้ที่ไหน	jà hăh … dâi têe năi
clubs	ไนท์คลับ	nai kláp
gay venues	สถานบันเทิง สำหรับคนเกย์	sà-tăhn ban-teung săm-ràp kon gair
places to eat	ที่ทานอาหาร	têe tahn ah-hăhn
pubs	ผับ	pàp
Is there a local … guide?	มีคู่มือ … สำหรับ แถวนี้ไหม	mee kôo meu … săm- ràp tăe·ou née măi
entertainment	สถานบันเทิง	sà-tăhn ban-teung
film	ภาพยนตร์	pâhp-pá-yon
gay	เกย์	gair
music	ดนตรี	don-đree

I feel like going to a ...	ผม/ดิฉัน รู้สึก อยากจะไป ...	pŏm/dì-chăn róo-sèuk yàhk jà bai ... m/f
bar	บาร์	bah
café	ร้านกาแฟ	ráhn gah-faa
concert	ดูการแสดง	doo gahn sà-daang
film	ดูหนัง	doo năng
full moon party	งานปาร์ตี้พระจันทร์เต็มดวง	ngahn bah-đêe prá jan đem doo·ang
karaoke bar	คาราโอเกะ	kah-rah-oh-gé
nightclub	ไนท์คลับ	nai kláp
party	งานปาร์ตี้	ngahn bah-đêe
performance	ดูงานแสดง	doo ngahn sà-daang
pub	ผับ	pàp
restaurant	ร้านอาหาร	ráhn ah-hăhn

For more on bars and drinks, see **eating out**, page 153.

invitations

การเชิญชวน

What are you doing ...?	คุณทำอะไรอยู่ ...	kun tam à-rai yòo ...
now	เดี๋ยวนี้	dĕe·o née
this weekend	เสาร์อาทิตย์นี้	sŏw ah-tít née
tonight	คืนนี้	keun née

Would you like to go (for a) ...?	อยากจะไป ... ไหม	yàhk jà bai ... măi
I feel like going (for a) ...	ฉันรู้สึกอยากจะไป ...	chăn róo-sèuk yàhk jà bai ...
coffee	กินกาแฟ	gin gah-faa
dancing	เต้นรำ	đên ram
drink	ดื่ม	dèum
meal	ทานอาหาร	tahn ah-hăhn
out somewhere	เที่ยวข้างนอก	têe·o kâhng nôrk
walk	เดินเล่น	deun lên

My round.
ตาของฉันนะ   đah kŏrng chăn ná

Do you know a good restaurant?
รู้จักร้านอาหารดีๆไหม   róo jàk ráhn ah-hăhn dee
dee măi

Do you want to come to the concert with me?
คุณอยากจะไปงานแสดง   kun yàhk jà bai ngahn
กับฉันไหม   sà-daang gàp chăn măi

We're having a party.
เรากำลังจัดงานเลี้ยงอยู่   row gam-lang jàt ngahn
lée·ang yòo

You should come.
คุณน่าจะมานะ   kun nâh jà mah ná

responding to invitations

Sure!
ได้เลย   dâi leu·i

Yes, I'd love to.
ไป ครับ/ค่ะ ดีใจมากเลย   bai kráp/kâ, dee jai mâhk
leu·i m/f

That's very kind of you.
คุณใจดีนะ   kun jai dee ná

No, I'm afraid I can't.
ขอโทษนะไปไม่ได้   kŏr tôht ná, bai mâi dâi

Sorry, I can't sing.
ขอโทษ ร้องเพลงไม่เป็น   kŏr tôht, rórng pleng mâi ben

Sorry, I can't dance.
ขอโทษ เต้นรำไม่เป็น   kŏr tôht, đên ram mâi ben

What about tomorrow?
พรุ่งนี้ได้ไหม   prûng née dâi măi

arranging to meet

What time will we meet?
จะพบกันกี่โมง · jà póp gan gèe mohng

Where will we meet?
จะพบกันที่ไหน · jà póp gan têe năi

Let's meet at ...   พบกัน ... ดีไหม   póp gan ... dee măi
  (eight pm)   (สองทุ่ม)   (sŏrng tûm)
  the (entrance)   ที่ (ทางเข้า)   têe (tahng kôw)

I'll pick you up.
ฉันจะมารับคุณ · chăn jà mah ráp kun

Are you ready?
พร้อมหรือยัง · prórm rĕu yang

I'm ready.
พร้อมแล้ว · prórm láa·ou

'shitting' yourself

The word kêe ขี้ on its own means 'shit', but if you chat enough with the Thai people you'll hear this word used in a wealth of different ways. At its most colourful, kêe is used to describe the 'by-products' of someone's personality in negative character traits such as kêe gèe·at ขี้เกียจ (lazy), kêe gloo·a ขี้กลัว (timid), kêe klàht ขี้ขลาด (cowardly), kêe móh ขี้โม้ (boastful), and kêe moh-hŏh ขี้โมโห (hot-tempered). It's also used to describe all manner of real by-products such as kêe lêu·ay ขี้เลื่อย (saw dust), kêe lèk ขี้เหล็ก (iron filings), and kêe gleu·a ขี้เกลือ (salty residue).

At its most vulgar kêe denotes various secretions of the body – as in kêe đah ขี้ตา (eye excretion, ie 'sleep'), kêe hŏo ขี้หู (ear wax), kêe môok ขี้มูก (snot) and kêe klai ขี้ไคล (grime of the skin). The words you'll hear if you're giving too small a tip are kêe nĕe·o ขี้เหนียว (stingy), often creatively translated as 'sticky shit'.

I'll be coming later.
ฉันจะมาทีหลัง — chăn jà mah tee lăng

Where will you be?
คุณจะอยู่ที่ไหน — kun jà yòo têe năi

If I'm not there by (nine pm), don't wait for me.
ถ้าถึงเวลา (สามทุ่ม) ฉัน
ไม่มา ไม่ต้องรอนะ — tâh tĕung wair-lah (săhm túm) chăn mâi mah mâi đôrng ror ná

OK!
ตกลง — đòk long

I'll see you then.
เจอกันตอนนั้น — jeu gan đorn nán

See you later.
เดี๋ยวพบกันทีหลัง — dĕe·o póp gan têe lăng

See you tomorrow.
เดี๋ยวพบกันพรุ่งนี้ — dĕe·o póp gan prûng née

I'm looking forward to it.
ตื่นเต้นจัง — đèun đên jang

Sorry I'm late.
ขอโทษที่มาช้า — kŏr tôht têe mah cháh

Never mind.
ไม่เป็นไร — mâi ɓen rai

drugs

ยาเสพติด

I don't take drugs.
ฉันไม่เสพยา — chăn mâi sèp yah

I take ... occasionally.
ฉัน เอา ... เป็นบางครั้ง — chăn ow ... ɓen bahng kráng

Do you want to have a smoke?
จะสูบไหม — jà sòop măi

Do you have a light?
มีไฟไหม mee fai măi

Where can I find clean syringes?
จะหาเข็มฉีดที่สะอาดได้ที่ไหน jà hăh kĕm chèet têe sà-àht
dâi têe năi

I'm high.
เมาแล้ว mow láa·ou

what's your poison?

amphetamines	ยาบ้า	yah bâh
cocaine	โคเคน	koh-ken
ecstasy	ยาอี	yah ee
heroin	เฮโรอีน	hair-roh-een
LSD	แอลเอสดี	aan-et-dee
opium	ฝิ่น	fin
psilocybin mushrooms	เห็ดขี้ควาย	hèt kêe kwai

asking someone out

การขอไปเที่ยวกัน

Would you like to do something (tomorrow)?
คุณอยากจะไปทำอะไรสัก
อย่าง (พรุ่งนี้) ไหม

kun yàhk jà ɓai tam à-rai sàk
yàhng (prûng née) măi

Where would you like to go (tonight)?
คุณอยากจะไปไหน (คืนนี้)

kun yàhk jà ɓai năi (keun
née)

Yes, I'd love to.
ไปครับ/ค่ะ ดีใจมาก

ɓai kráp/kâ, dee jai mâhk m/f

I'm busy.
ฉันติดธุระ

chăn đìt tú-rá

What a babe!
น่ารักจัง

nâh rák jang

He/She gets around.
เขา/เธอเที่ยวเก่งนะ

kŏw/teu têe·o gèng ná

local talk		
He/She is (a) …	เขา/เธอ …	kŏw/teu …
babe	น่ารักจัง	nâh rák jang
bastard	เลว	le·ou
bitch	สำส่อน	săm sòrn
hot	เร้าร้อน	rôw rórn

pick-up lines

Would you like a drink?
จะดื่มอะไรไหม   jà dèum à-rai mǎi

You look like someone I know.
คุณนี้หน้าคุ้นๆ   kun née nâh kún kún

You're a fantastic dancer.
คุณเต้นรำเก่งมากเลย   kun đên ram gèng mâhk leu·i

Can I …?   … ได้ไหม   … dâi mǎi
  dance with you   เต้นกับคุณ   đên gàp kun
  sit here   นั่งที่นี้   nâng têe née
  take you home   พาคุณกลับบ้าน   pah kun glàp bâhn

rejections

I'm here with my boyfriend/girlfriend.
ฉันอยู่กับแฟน   chǎn yòo gàp faan

Excuse me, I have to go now.
ขอโทษนะ ต้องไปแล้ว   kǒr tôht ná, đôrng bai láa·ou

I'd rather not.
คิดว่าไม่นะ   kít wâh mâi ná

No, thank you.
ไม่นะ ครับ/ค่ะ ขอบคุณ   mâi ná kráp/kâ, kòrp kun m/f

the hard word

Leave me alone!   อย่ายุ่งกับฉัน   yàh yûng gàp chǎn
Piss off!   ไปให้พ้น   bai hâi pón

getting closer

I like you very much.
ฉันชอบคุณมากๆ   chăn chôrp kun mâhk mâhk

Can I kiss you?
จูบคุณได้ไหม   jòop kun dâi măi

Do you want to come inside for a while?
จะเข้ามาข้างในหน่อยไหม   jà kôw mah kâhng nai nòy măi

Do you want a massage?
อยากให้นวดไหม   yàhk hâi nôo·at măi

safe sex

ร่วมเพศแบบปลอดภัย

Do you have a condom?
มีถุงยางไหม   mee tŭng yahng măi

Let's use a condom.
ใช้ถุงยางกันเถิด   chái tŭng yahng gan tèut

I won't do it without protection.
ฉันจะไม่ทำถ้าไม่มี   chăn jà mâi tam tâh mâi mee
อะไรป้องกัน   à-rai bôrng gan

sex

การร่วมเพศ

I want to make love to you.
ฉันอยากจะร่วมรักกับเธอ   chăn yàhk jà rôo·am rák gàp teu

Kiss me.	จูบฉันเถิด	jòop chăn tèut
I want you.	ต้องการเธอแล้ว	đôrng gahn teu láa·ou
Let's go to bed.	ไปที่นอนนะ	bai têe norn ná
Touch me here.	แตะฉันตรงนี้	đàa chăn đrong née

Do you like this?	แบบนี้ชอบไหม	bàap née chôrp mǎi
I (don't) like that.	(ไม่) ชอบ	(mâi) chôrp
I think we should stop now.	คิดว่าหยุดดีกว่า	kít wâh yùt dee gwàh
Oh yeah!	ใช่เลย	châi leu·i
Oh my god!	คุณพระช่วย	kun prá chôo·ay
That's great.	ยอดเลย	yôrt leu·i
Easy tiger!	ใจเย็นๆนะ	jai yen yen ná
faster	เร็วขึ้น	re·ou kêun
harder	แรงขึ้น	raang kêun
slower	ช้าลง	cháh long
softer	เบาลง	bow long

It's my first time.
นี่เป็นครั้งแรก   nêe ben kráng râak

It helps to have a sense of humour.
ต้องมีอารมณ์ขันหน่อย   đôrng mee ah-rom kǎn nòy

Don't worry, I'll do it myself.
ไม่ต้องกังวล ฉันจะทำเอง   mâi đôrng gang-won, chǎn jà tam eng

afterwards

ช่วงหลัง

That was …	นั่นก็ …	nân gôr …
amazing	น่าอัศจรรย์	nâh àt-sà-jan
weird	แปลก	blàak
wild	รุนแรง	run raang
Can I …?	… ได้ไหม	… dâi mǎi
call you	โทรคุณ	toh kun
meet you tomorrow	พบกับคุณพรุ่งนี้	póp gàp kun prûng née
stay over	ค้างที่นี่	káhng têe née

love

I love you.
ฉันรักเธอ | chăn rák teu

You're great.
คุณนี่ยอดเลย | kun nêe yôrt leu·i

I think we're good together.
ฉันคิดว่าเราสองคนเข้ากันได้ดี | chăn kít wâh row sŏrng
kon kôw gan dâi dee

Will you ...? | เธอจะ ... ไหม | teu jà ... măi
  go out with me | ไปเที่ยวกับฉัน | bai têe·o gàp chăn
  live with me | มาอยู่กับฉัน | mah yòo gàp chăn
  marry me | แต่งงานกับฉัน | đàang ngahn gàp
chăn

sweet nothings		
Darling	สุดที่รัก	sùt têe rák
Honey	ยอดรัก	yôrt rák
My love	ที่รัก	têe rák
Sweetheart	หวานใจ	wăhn jai

problems

Are you seeing someone else?
เธอกำลังพบกับคนอื่นไหม | teu gam-lang póp gàp kon
èun măi

He/She is just a friend.
เขาแค่เพื่อนเฉยๆ | kŏw kâa pêu·an chĕu·i chĕu·i

You're just using me for sex.
เธอใช้ฉันแค่ประโลม
ทางเพศเฉยๆ | teu chái chăn kâa brà-lohm
tahng pêt chĕu·i chĕu·i

I never want to see you again.
ฉันไม่อยากจะเห็นหน้าเธอ
อีกแล้ว

chăn mâi yàhk jà hĕn nâh
teu èek láa·ou

I don't think it's working out.
ฉันรู้สึกว่ามันกำลังเป็น
ไปไม่ได้

chăn róo-sèuk wâh man
gam-lang ben bai mâi dâi

We'll work it out.
เราจะหาทางแก้ไข

row jà hăh tahng gâa kăi

leaving

I have to leave tomorrow.
ฉันต้องไปพรุ่งนี้

chăn đôrng bai prûng née

I'll ...   ฉันจะ ...   chăn jà ...
  come and   มาเยี่ยมคุณ   mah yêe·am kun
    visit you
  keep in touch   ติดต่อนะ   đit đòr ná
  miss you   คิดถึงคุณ   kít tĕung kun

beliefs & cultural differences
ความเชื่อถือและความแตกต่างทางวัฒนธรรม

religion

ศาสนา

What's your religion?
คุณนับถือศาสนาอะไร
kun náp-tĕu sàht-sà-năh à-rai

I'm not religious.
ฉันไม่สนใจเรื่องศาสนา
chăn mâi sŏn-jai rêu·ang
sàht-sà-năh

Buddhist	ชาวพุทธ	chow pút
Catholic	คริสตัง	krít-sà-đang
Christian	คริสเตียน	krít-sà-đee·an
Hindu	ชาวฮินดู	chow hin-doo
Jewish	ชาวยิว	chow yew
Muslim	ชาวอิสลาม	chow ìt-sà-lahm

I (don't) believe	ผม/ดิฉัน (ไม่)	pŏm/dì-chăn (mâi)
in ...	เชื่อเรื่อง ...	chêu·a rêu·ang ... m/f
astrology	โหราศาสตร์	hŏh-rah-sàht
fate	ชะตากรรม	chá-đah gam
God	พระเจ้า	prá jôw

Can I ... here?	... ที่นี่ได้ไหม	... têe née dâi măi
Where can I ...?	จะ ... ได้ที่ไหน	jà ... dâi têe năi
attend a service	ร่วมพิธี	rôo·am pí-tee
practise meditation	ฝึกสมาธิ	fèuk sà-mah-tí
pray	สวดมนต์	sòo·at mon

Is there a meditation teacher here?
ที่นี่มีอาจารย์สอนสมาธิไหม
têe née mee ah-jahn sŏrn
sà-mah-tí măi

chanting	การสวดมนต์	gahn sòo·at mon
meditation	การทำสมาธิ	gahn tam sà·mah·tí
monastery	วัด	wát
novice monk	เณร	nen
nun	แม่ชี	mâa chee
ordained monk	พระ	prá
shrine	แท่นพระ	tâan prá
stupa	พระสถูป	prá sà·tòop
temple	วัด	wát

cultural differences

ความแตกต่างทางวัฒนธรรม

Is this a local or national custom?
นี่เป็นประเภณีประจำ
ชาติหรือเฉพาะท้องถิ่น
nêe ben brà-pair-nee brà-jam
châht rĕu chá-pó tórng tìn

I don't want to offend you.
ผม/ดิฉัน ไม่อยากจะทำ
ผิดประเพณีของคุณ
pŏm/dì-chăn mâi yàhk jà
tam pìt brà-pair-nee kŏrng
kun m/f

I'm not used to this.
ผม/ดิฉัน ไม่คุ้นเคยกับ
การทำอย่างนี้
pŏm/dì-chăn mâi kún keu·i
gàp gahn tam yàhng née m/f

I'd rather not join in.
ผม/ดิฉัน คิดว่าไม่ร่วมดีกว่า
pŏm/dì-chăn kít wâh mâi
rôo·am dee gwàh m/f

I didn't mean to do anything wrong.
ผม/ดิฉันไม่ได้เจตนาทำ
อะไรผิด
pŏm/dì-chăn mâi dâi
jèt-đà-nah tam à-rai pìt m/f

I'm sorry, it's against my …	ขอโทษนะ มันขัด กับ … ของ ผม/ดิฉัน	kŏr tôht ná man kàt gàp … kŏrng pŏm/ dì-chăn m/f
beliefs	ความเชื่อถือ	kwahm chêu·a tĕu
religion	ศาสนา	sàht-sà-năh

When's the gallery open?
หอแสดงเปิดกี่โมง
hŏr sà-daang bèut gèe mohng

When's the museum open?
พิพิธพันธ์ เปิดกี่โมง
pí-pít-tá-pan bèut gèe mohng

What kind of art are you interested in?
คุณสนใจศิลปะแบบไหน
kun sŏn-jai sĭn-lá-bà bàap năi

What's in the collection?
มีอะไรบ้างในชุดนี้
mee à-rai bâhng nai chút née

What do you think of ...?
คุณคิดอย่างไรเรื่อง ...
kun kít yàhng rai rêu·ang ...

I'm interested in ...
ผม/ดิฉัน สนใจ ...
pŏm/dì-chăn sŏn-jai ... m/f

I like the works of ...
ผม/ดิฉัน ชอบงานของ ...
pŏm/dì-chăn chôrp ngahn kŏrng ... m/f

It reminds me of ...
ทำให้นึกถึง ...
tam hâi néuk tĕung ...

... art	ศิลปะ ...	sĭn-lá-bà ...
graphic	การเขียน	gahn kĕe·an
modern	สมัยใหม่	sà-măi mài
performance	การแสดง	gahn sà-daang

past glories

Sukhothai period (13th–15th centuries AD)
ยุคสุโขทัย
yúk sù-kŏh-tai

Ayuthaya period (14th–18th centuries AD)
ยุคอยุธยา
yuk à-yút-tá-yah

Srivijaya period (7th–13th centuries AD)
ยุคศรีวิชัย
yúk sĕe-wí-chai

artwork	งานศิลปะ	ngahn sĭn-lá-bà
curator	ผู้ดูแล	pôo doo laa
design	การออกแบบ	gahn òrk bàap
etching	ภาพแกะพิมพ์	pâhp gàa pim
exhibit	งานแสดง	ngahn sà-daang
exhibition hall	หอนิทรรศการ	hŏr ní-tát-sà-gahn
installation	งานติดตั้ง	ngahn dìt đâng
opening	งานเปิด	ngahn bèut
painter	ช่างเขียน	châhng kĕe·an
painting	ภาพระบาย	pâhp rá-bai
period	ยุค	yúk
print	ภาพพิมพ์	pâhp pim
sculptor	ช่างปั้น	châhng bân
sculpture (cut)	รูปสลัก	rôop sà-làk
sculpture (moulded)	รูปปั้น	rôop bân
statue	รูปหล่อ	rôop lòr
studio	ห้องทำงาน	hôrng tam ngahn
style	แบบ	bàap
technique	เทคนิค	ték-ník

sporting interests

ความสนใจเกี่ยวกับกีฬา

What sport do you ...?	คุณ ... กีฬาอะไร	kun ... gee-lah à-rai
play	เล่น	lên
follow	ติดตาม	đìt đahm

I play (do) ...	ผม/ดิฉัน เล่น ...	pŏm/dì-chăn lên ... m/f
I follow ...	ผม/ดิฉัน ติดตาม ...	pŏm/dì-chăn đìt đahm ... m/f
athletics	กรีฑา	gree-tah
badminton	แบดมินตัน	bàat-min-đan
basketball	บาสเกตบอล	bah-sà-gèt born
boxing	มวยสากล	moo-ay săh-gon
football (soccer)	ฟุตบอล	fút-born
karate	คาราเต้	kah-rah-tê
muay Thai	มวยไทย	moo-ay tai
table tennis	ปิงปอง	bing-borng
takraw	เซปักตะกร้อ	sair bàk đà-grôr
tennis	เทนนิส	ten-nít
scuba diving	การดำน้ำใช้ถังออกซิเยน	gahn dam nám chái tăng òok-sí-yen
volleyball	วอลเลย์บอล	worn-lair-born

I ...	ผม/ดิฉัน ...	pŏm/dì-chăn ... m/f
cycle	ขี่จักรยาน	kèe jàk-gà-yahn
run	วิ่ง	wîng
walk	เดิน	deun

Do you like (soccer)?
คุณชอบ (ฟุตบอล) ไหม   kun chôrp (fút-born) măi

Yes, very much.
ชอบมาก   chôrp mâhk

Not really.
ไม่เท่าไร   mâi tôw-rai

I like watching it.
ชอบดู   chôrp doo

Who's your	ใครเป็น ...	krai ben ... têe
favourite ...?	ที่คุณชอบที่สุด	kun chôrp têe-sùt
sportsperson	นักกีฬา	nák gee-lah
team	ทีมกีฬา	teem gee-lah

going to a game

การไปดูเกม

Would you like to go to a game?
คุณอยากจะไปดูเกมไหม   kun yàhk jà bai doo gem măi

Who are you supporting?
คุณเชียร์ใคร   kun chee·a krai

Who's ...?	ใครกำลัง ... อยู่	krai gam-lang ... yòo
playing	เล่น	lên
winning	ชนะ	chá-ná

sports talk		
What a ...!	... ยอดเลย	... yôrt leu·i
goal	ประตู	brà-doo
hit	ต่อย	dòy
kick	เตะ	dè
pass	ส่งลูก	sòng lôok
performance	เล่น	lên

Thai boxing, or *muay Thai* is a national sport of international popularity. Keep ahead of the action with these boxing terms:

boxing ring	เวทีมวย	wair-tee moo·ay
elbow	ศอก	sòrk
kick	เตะ	dè
knee	เข่า	kòw
knockout	ชนะน็อค	chá·na nórk
points decision	ชนะคะแนน	chá·ná ká·naan
punch	ชก	chók
referee	กรรมการ	gam·má·gahn
round	ยก	yók

That was a ... game!	นั่นเป็นเกม ...	nân ben gem ...
bad	ห่วย	hoo·ay
boring	น่าเบื่อ	nâh bèu·a
great	เยี่ยม	yêe·am

playing sport

การเล่นกีฬา

Do you want to play?
คุณอยากจะเล่นไหม
kun yàhk jà lên măi

Can I join in?
ฉันร่วมด้วยได้ไหม
chăn rôo·am dôo·ay dâi măi

That would be great.
นั่นก็เยี่ยม
nân gôr yêe·am

I can't.
ไม่ได้
mâi dâi

I have an injury.
ฉันบาดเจ็บ
chăn bàht jèp

đâam körng kun/chăn		
แต้มของ คุณ/ฉัน		**Your/My point.**
đè mah hâi chăn		
เตะมาให้ฉัน		**Kick it to me!**
kòrp kun săm-ràp gahn lên		
ขอบคุณสำหรับการเล่น		**Thanks for the game.**
kun lên gèng ná		
คุณเล่นเก่งนะ		**You're a good player.**
sòng lôok mah hâi chăn		
ส่งลูกมาให้ฉัน		**Pass it to me!**

Where's a good place to ...?	ที่ไหนมีที่ที่ ... ดี	têe năi mee têe têe ... dee
fish	หาปลา	hăh blah
go horse riding	ขี่ม้า	kèe máh
run	วิ่ง	wîng
snorkel	ดำน้ำใช้ท่อ	dam nám chái
	หายใจ	tôr hăi jai
surf	เล่นโต้คลื่น	lên đôh klêun

Where's the nearest ...?	ที่ไหน ...	têe năi ... têe glâi
	ที่ใกล้เคียง	kee·ang
golf course	สนามกอล์ฟ	sà-năhm gòrp
gym	ห้องออกกำลังกาย	hôrng òrk
		gam-lang gai
swimming pool	สระว่ายน้ำ	sà wâi nám
tennis court	สนามเทนนิส	sà-năhm ten-nít

Do I have to be a member to attend?

ต้องเป็นสมาชิกจึงจะไปได้ไหม đôrng ben sà-mah-chík
jeung jà bai dâi măi

Is there a women-only session?
มีเวลาสำหรับเฉพาะผู้หญิงไหม   mee wair-lah săm-ràp
                                   chà-pó pôo yĭng măi

Where are the changing rooms?
ห้องเปลี่ยนผ้าอยู่ที่ไหน   hôrng blèe·an pâh yòo
                                 têe năi

What's the	คิดค่า ... ละเท่าไร	kít kâh ... lá tôw-rai
charge per ...?		
day	วัน	wan
game	เกม	gem
hour	ชั่วโมง	chôo·a mohng
visit	ครั้ง	kráng

Can I hire a ...?	เช่า ... ได้ไหม	chôw ... dâi măi
ball	ลูกบอล	lôok born
bicycle	จักรยาน	jàk-gà-yahn
court	สนาม	sà-năhm
racquet	ไม้ตี	mái đee

diving

การดำน้ำ

Where's a good diving site?
ที่ไหนมีที่ดำน้ำที่ดี   têe năi mee têe dam nám
                              têe dee

Is the visibility good?
การมองเห็นชัดไหม   gahn morng hěn chát măi

How deep is the dive?
ดำได้ลึกเท่าไร   dam dâi léuk tôw-rai

I need an air fill.
ต้องเติมออกซิเยน   dôrng đeum òok-sí-yen

Are there ...?	มี ... ไหม	mee ... măi
currents	กระแสน้ำแรง	grà-săa nám raang
sharks	ปลาฉลาม	blah chà-lăhm
whales	ปลาวาฬ	blah-wahn

I want to hire (a) ...	อยากจะเช่า ...	yàhk jà chôw ...
buoyancy vest	เสื้อชูชีพ	sêu·a choo chêep
diving equipment	อุปกรณ์ดำน้ำ	ùp·bà·gorn dam nám
flippers	ตีนกบ	đeen gòp
mask	หน้ากากดำน้ำ	nâh gàhk dam nám
regulator	เครื่องปรับลม	krêu·ang bràp lom
snorkel	ท่อหายใจ	tôr hǎi jai
tank	ถังออกซิเยน	tǎng òrk·sí·yen
weight belt	เข็มขัดถ่วงน้ำหนัก	kěm·kàt tòo·ang nám·nàk
wetsuit	ชุดหนัง	chút nǎng

I'd like to ...	ฉันอยากจะ ...	chǎn yàhk jà ...
explore caves	ไปสำรวจถ้ำ	bai sǎm·ròo·at tâm
explore wrecks	ไปสำรวจซาก เรือเก่า	bai sǎm·ròo·at sâhk reu·a gòw
go night diving	ไปดำน้ำกลางคืน	bai dam nám glahng keun
go scuba diving	ไปดำน้ำใช้ถัง ออกซิเยน	bai dam nám chái tǎng òrk·sí·yen
go snorkelling	ไปดำน้ำใช้ท่อ หายใจ	bai dam nám chái tôr hǎi jai
join a diving tour	ไปเข้าคณะดำน้ำ	bai kôw ká·ná dam nám
learn to dive	เรียนวิธีดำน้ำ	ree·an wí·tee dam nám

buddy	เพื่อน	pêu·an
cave	ถ้ำ	tâm
diving boat	เรือสำหรับการ ไปดำน้ำ	reu·a sǎm·ràp gahn bai dam nám
diving course	หลักสูตรดำน้ำ	làk sòot dam nám
night dive	ดำน้ำกลางคืน	dam nám glahng keun
wreck	ซากเรือเก่า	sâhk reu·a gòw

soccer

Who plays for (Thai Farmers Bank)?
ใครเล่นให้ทีม (ธนาคาร
กสิกรไทย)
krai lên hâi teem (tá-nah-kahn gà-sì-gorn tai)

He's a great player.
เขาเป็นนักเล่นที่เก่ง
kŏw ɓen nák lên têe gèng

He played brilliantly in the match against (Cambodia).
เขาเล่นเก่งมากตอนที่เล่น
แข่งกับ (เขมร)
kŏw lên gèng mâhk đorn têe lên kàang gàp (kà-mĕn)

Which team is at the top of the league?
ทีมไหนอยู่ที่หนึ่งในการแข่งขัน
teem năi yòo têe nèung nai gahn kàang kăn

What a great/terrible team!
ทีมนี้ยอด/ฮวยเลย
teem née yôrt/hoo·ay leu·i

ball	ลูกบอล	lôok born
coach	โค้ช	kóht
corner	เตะมุม	đè mum
expulsion	ไล่ออก	lâi òrk
fan	แฟนบอล	faan born
foul	ฟาวส์	fow
free kick	เตะกินเปล่า	đè gin ɓlòw
goal	ประตู	ɓrà-đoo
goalkeeper	ผู้รักษาประตู	pôo rák-sah ɓrà-đoo
manager	ผู้จัดการทีม	pôo-jàt-gahn teem
offside	ล้ำหน้า	lám nâh
penalty	เตะลูกโทษ	đè lôok tôht
player	นักเล่น	nák lên
red card	ใบแดง	bai daang
referee	กรรมการผู้ตัดสิน	gam-má-gahn pôo đàt sĭn
striker	ตัวยิง	đoo·a ying
throw in	ทุ่มเข้า	tûm kôw
yellow card	ใบเหลือง	bai lĕu·ang

tennis

I'd like to play tennis.
อยากจะเล่นเทนนิส   yàhk jà lên ten-nít

Can we play at night?
เล่นกลางคืนได้ไหม   lên glahng keun dâi măi

I need my racquet restrung.
ต้องตึงเอ็นไม้เทนนิสใหม่   đôrng đeung en mái
ten-nít mài

ace	เสิร์ฟลูกม่า	sèup lôok kâh
advantage	ได้เปรียบ	dâi ʉ̀rèe·ap
fault	ฟอลท์	forn
game, set, match	จบการแข่งขัน	jòp gahn kàang kăn
grass	หญ้า	yâh
hard court	สนามแข็ง	sà-năhm kăang
net	เนต	nét
play doubles	เล่นคู่	lên kôo
racquet	ไม้ตี	mái đee
serve	เสิร์ฟ	sèup
set	เซท	sét
tennis ball	ลูกบอล	lôok born

scoring

What's the score?	ได้คะแนนเท่าไร	dâi ká-naan tôw-rai
draw/even	เสมอกัน	sà-mĕr gan
love (zero)	ศูนย์	sŏon
match-point	แต้มชนะการแข่งขัน	đâam chá-ná gahn kàang kăn
nil (zero)	สูญ	sŏon

water sports

Can I book a lesson?
จอง บทเรียนได้ไหม · jorng bòt ree·an dâi măi

Can I hire (a) ...	เช่า ... ได้ไหม	chôw ... dâi măi
boat	เรือ	reu·a
canoe	เรือคนู	reu·a ká-noo
kayak	เรือไคยัก	reu·a kai-yák
life jacket	เสื้อชูชีพ	sêu·a choo chêep
snorkelling gear	อุปกรณ์ดำน้ำใช้ท่อหายใจ	ùp-bà-gorn dam nám chái tôr hăi jai
water-skis	สกีน้ำ	sà-gee nám
wetsuit	ชุดหนัง	chút năng

Are there any ...?	มี ... ไหม	mee ... măi
reefs	หินโสโครก	hĭn sŏh-krôhk
rips	กระแสใต้น้ำ	grà-săa đâi nám
water hazards	อันตรายในน้ำ	an-đà-rai nai nám

guide	ไกด์	gai
motorboat	เรือติดเครื่อง	reu·a đìt krêu·ang
oars	ไม้พาย	mái pai
sailing boat	เรือใบ	reu·a bai
surfboard	กระดานโต้คลื่น	grà-dahn đôh klêun
surfing	การเล่นกระดานโต้คลื่น	gahn lên grà-dahn đôh klêun
wave	คลื่น	klêun
windsurfing	การเล่นกระดานโต้ลม	gahn lên grà-dahn đôh lom

golf

How much ...?	... เท่าไร	... tôw-rai
for a round	เล่นรอบหนี้	lên rôrp nèung
to play 9/18	เล่นเก้า/สิบแปด	lên gôw/sìp-bàat
holes	หลุม	lŭm

Can I hire golf clubs?
เช่าไม้ตีได้ไหม   chôw mái đee dâi măi

What's the dress code?
ต้องแต่งตัวอย่างไร   đôrng đàang đoo-a yàhng rai

Do I need golf shoes?
ต้องใช้รองเท้ากอล์ฟหรือเปล่า   đôrng chái rorng tów gòrp
          rĕu ḃlòw

Soft or hard spikes?
ปุ่มแข็งหรือปุ่มนุ่ม   ḃùm kăng rĕu ḃùm nûm

---

put a smile on your dial

Thailand has been called the Land of Smiles, and not without reason. It's cool to smile, and Thai people seem to smile and laugh at the oddest times (such as if you trip over something or make a mistake). It's important to realise that they're not laughing at you, but with you: it's a way of releasing the tension of embarrassment and saying it's OK.

Thais feel negative emotions just as much as anyone else, but the culture does not encourage the outward expression of them. It's considered bad form to blow up in anger in public, and trying to intimidate someone into doing what you want with a loud voice and red face will only make you look bad.

hiking

การเดินป่า

Where can I ...?	จะ ... ได้ที่ไหน	jà ... dâi têe năi
buy supplies	ซื้อเสบียง	séu sà-bee·ang
find someone	หาคนที่รู้จักพื้น	hăh kon têe róo jàk
who knows	ที่แถวๆ นี้	péun têe tăa·ou
this area		tăa·ou née
get a map	หาแผนที่	hăh păan têe
hire hiking	เช่าอุปกรณ์เดินป่า	chôw ùp-bà-gorn
gear		deun bàh

How ...?	... เท่าไร	... tôw-rai
high is the climb	การปีนสูง	gahn been sŏong
long is the trail	ทางไกล	tahng glai

Do we need a guide?
ต้องมีไกด์ไหม   đôrng mee gai măi

Are there guided treks?
มีการนำทางเดินป่าไหม   mee gahn nam tahng deun
bàh măi

Can you recommend a trekking company?
คุณแนะนำบริษัทนำ   kun náa-nam bor-rí-sàt nam
เที่ยวตามป่าได้ไหม   têe·o đahm bàh dâi măi

How many people will be on the trek?
จะเดินป่ากี่คน   jà deun bàh gèe kon

Do you provide transport?
บริการรถถึงที่ด้วยไหม   bor-rí-gahn rót tĕung têe
dôo·ay măi

Exactly when does the trek begin and end?
การเดินเริ่มต้นและจบลง   gahn deun rêum đôn láa
ที่ไหนกันแน่   jòp long têe năi gan nâa

Will there be other tourists in the area at the same time?

จะมีนักท่องเที่ยวคนอื่นอยู่แถว
นั้นในเวลาเดียวกันไหม

jà mee nák tôrng têe·o kon èun yòo tǎa·ou nán nai wair·lah dee·o gan mǎi

Can the guide speak the local languages?

ไกด์พูดภาษาท้องถิ่นได้ไหม

gai pôot pah-sǎh tórng tìn dâi mǎi

Is it safe?

ปลอดภัยไหม

blòrt pai mǎi

Are there land mines in the area?

มีทุ่นระเบิดฝังอยู่แถวนี้ไหม

mee tûn rá-bèut fǎng yòo tǎa·ou née mǎi

Is it safe to leave the trail?

ถ้าออกจากทางจะปลอดภัยไหม

tâh òrk jàhk tahng jà blòrt pai mǎi

When does it get dark?

ตกค่ำกี่โมง

dòk kâm gèe mohng

Do we need to take ...?	จะต้องเอา ... ไป ด้วยไหม	jà dôrng ow ... bai dôo·ay mǎi
bedding	เครื่องนอน	krêu·ang norn
food	อาหาร	ah-hǎhn
water	น้ำ	nám
Is the track ...?	ทาง ... ไหม	tahng ... mǎi
(well-)marked	หมายไว้ (ชัด)	mǎi wái (chát)
open	เปิด	bèut
scenic	มีทิวทัศน์สวย	mee tew-tát sǒo·ay
Which is the ... route?	ทางไหน .... ที่สุด	tahng nǎi ... têe sùt
easiest	ง่าย	ngâi
most interesting	น่าสนใจ	nâh sǒn-jai
shortest	ใกล้	glâi

Where can I find the …?	จะหา ... ได้ที่ไหน	jà hăh ... dâi têe năi
camping ground	ค่ายพัก	kâi pák
nearest village	หมู่บ้านใกล้ที่สุด	mòo bâhn glâi têe sùt
showers	ห้องน้ำฝักบัว	hôrng nám fàk boo·a
toilets	ห้องส้วม	hôrng sôo·am

Where have you come from?
คุณเดินทางมาจากไหน   kun deun tahng mah jàhk năi

How long did it take?
ใช้เวลานานเท่าไร   chái wair-lah nahn tôw-rai

Does this path go to …?
ทางนี้ไป ... ไหม   tahng née bai ... măi

Can I go through here?
ไปทางนี้ได้ไหม   bai tahng née dâi măi

Is the water OK to drink?
น้ำกินได้ไหม   nám gin dâi măi

I'm lost.
ฉันหลงทาง   chăn lŏng tahng

Where can I buy …?	จะซื้อ ... ได้ที่ไหน	jà séu ... dâi têe năi
bottled water	น้ำดื่มขวด	nám dèum kòo·at
iodine	ไอโอดีน	ai-oh-deen
mosquito repellent	ยากันยุง	yah gan yung
water purification tablets	ยาเม็ดทำให้น้ำบริสุทธิ์	yah mét tam hâi nám bor-rí-sùt

beach

ชายหาด

Where's the … beach?	ชายหาด ... อยู่ที่ไหน	chai hàht ... yòo têe năi
best	ที่ดีที่สุด	têe dee têe sùt
nearest	ที่ใกล้ที่สุด	têe glâi têe sùt
public	สาธารณะ	săh-tah-rá-ná

ห้ามกระโดดน้ำ
hâhm grà-dòht nám   **No Diving.**

ห้ามว่ายน้ำ
hâhm wâi nám   **No Swimming.**

Is it safe to dive here?
ที่นี่กระโดดน้ำปลอดภัยไหม   têe née grà-dòht nám Ъlòrt
           pai măi

Is it safe to swim here?
ที่นี่ว่ายน้ำปลอดภัยไหม   têe née wâi nám Ъlòrt
           pai măi

What time is high/low tide?
น้ำ ขึ้น/ลง กี่โมง   nám kêun/long gèe mohng

Do we have to pay?
จะต้องเสียเงินไหม   jà đôrng sĕe·a ngeun măi

Where can I hire a …?	จะเช่า … ได้ที่ไหน	jà chôw … dâi têe năi
sea canoe	เรือคนูทะเล	reu·a ká-noo tá-lair
windsurfer	กระดานโต้ลม	grà-dahn đôh lom
How much for a/an …?	… เท่าไร	… tôw-rai
chair	เก้าอี้	gôw-êe
umbrella	ร่ม	rôm

rá-wang grà-săa đâi nám
ระวังกระแสใต้น้ำ   **Be careful of the undertow!**

an-đà-rai
อันตราย   **It's dangerous!**

weather

What's the weather like?
อากาศเป็นอย่างไร   ah-gàht ɓen yàhng rai

What will the weather be like tomorrow?
พรุ่งนี้อากาศจะเป็นอย่างไร   prûng-née ah-gàht jà ɓen
                                 yàhng rai

It's ...	มัน ...	man ...
cloudy	ฟ้าคลุ้ม	fáh klúm
cold	หนาว	nŏw
fine	แจ่มใส	jàam săi
flooding	กำลังน้ำท่วม	gam-lang nám tôo·am
hot	ร้อน	rórn
raining	มีฝน	mee fŏn
sunny	แดดจ้า	dàat jâh
warm	อุ่น	ùn
windy	มีลม	mee lom

Where can I buy ...?	จะซื้อ ... ได้ที่ไหน	jà séu .... dâi têe năi
a rain jacket	เสื้อกันฝน	sêu·a gan fŏn
an umbrella	ร่ม	rôm

For words and phrases related to seasons, see **time & dates**,
page 37.

flora & fauna

What ... is that?	นั่น ... อะไร	nân ... à-rai
animal	สัตว์	sàt
flower	ดอกไม้	dòrk mái
plant	ต้น	đôn
tree	ต้นไม้	đôn mái

What's it used for?
ใช้ประโยชน์อะไร
chái brà-yòht à-rai

Can you eat the fruit?
ผลมันกินได้ไหม
pŏn man gin dâi măi

Is it ...?	มัน ... ไหม	man ... măi
common	หาง่าย	hăh ngâi
dangerous	อันตราย	an-đà-rai
endangered	ใกล้จะสูญพันธุ์	glâi jà sŏon pan
protected	เป็นของสงวน	ben kŏrng
		sà-ngŏo·an
rare	หายาก	hăh yâhk

the call of the wild

bamboo	ไม้ไผ่	mái pài
cobra	งูเห่า	ngoo hòw
elephant	ช้าง	cháhng
king cobra	งูจงอาง	ngoo jong-ahng
monkey	ลิง	ling
orchid	กล้วยไม้	glôo·ay mái
tiger	เสือโคร่ง	sĕu·a krôhng

The cultural importance of food in Thailand can hardly be underestimated. In fact, a common Thai pleasantary is gin kôw rěu yang กินข้าวหรือยัง which means 'Have you eaten yet?'. If your answer is yang ยัง (lit: not yet) this chapter will help you put food on your plate.

key language

ศัพท์สำคัญ

breakfast	อาหารเช้า	ah-hǎhn chów
lunch	อาหารกลางวัน	ah-hǎhn glahng wan
dinner	อาหารเย็น	ah-hǎhn yen
snack	อาหารว่าง	ah-hǎhn wâhng

I'd like ...	ผม/ดิฉัน ต้องการ ...	pǒm/dì-chǎn đôrng gahn ... m/f

Please.	ขอ	kǒr
Thank you.	ขอบคุณ	kòrp kun
I'm starving!	หิวจะตาย	hěw jà đai

finding a place to eat

การหาที่จะทานอาหาร

Where would you go for ...?	ถ้าคุณจะ ... คุณจะ ไปไหน	tâh kun jà ... kun jà Đai nǎi
a cheap meal	ไปหาอาหา รราคาถูกๆ	Đai hǎh ah-hǎhn rah-kah tòok tòok
local specialities	ไปหาอาหารรส เด็ดๆของแถวนี้	Đai hǎh ah-hǎhn rót dèt dèt kǒrng tǎe·ou née

Can you recommend a ...	แนะนำ ... ได้ไหม	náa-nam ... dâi măi
bar	บาร์	bah
café	ร้านกาแฟ	ráhn gah-faa
Hainan chicken shop	ร้านข้าวมันไก่	ráhn kôw man gài
noodle shop	ร้านก๋วยเตี๋ยว	ráhn gŏo·ay đĕe·o
rice and curry shop	ร้านข้าวราดแกง	ráhn kôw râht gaang
rice and red pork shop	ร้านข้าวหมูแดง	ráhn kôw mŏo daang
rice gruel shop	ร้านโจ๊ก	ráhn jóhk
rice soup shop	ร้านข้าวต้ม	ráhn kôw đôm
restaurant	ร้านอาหาร	ráhn ah-hăhn

I'd like to reserve a table for ...	ผม/ดิฉัน อยากจะ จองโต๊ะสำหรับ ...	pŏm/dì-chăn yàhk jà jorng đó săm-ràp ... m/f
(two) people	(สอง) คน	(sŏrng) kon
(eight pm)	เวลา (สองทุ่ม)	wair-lah (sŏrng tûm)

I'd like ..., please.	ขอ ... หน่อย	kŏr ... nòy
a menu	รายการอาหาร	rai gahn ah-hăhn
in English	เป็นภาษาอังกฤษ	฿en pah-săh ang-grìt
a table	โต๊ะสำหรับ	đó săm-ràp
for (five)	(ห้า) คน	(hâh) kon
nonsmoking	ที่เขตห้ามสูบบุหรี่	têe kèt hâhm sòop bù-rèe
smoking	ที่เขตสูบบุหรี่ได้	têe kèt sòop bù-rèe dâi
the drink list	รายการเครื่องดื่ม	rai gahn krêu·ang dèum
the menu	รายการอาหาร	rai gahn ah-hăhn

Are you still serving food?
ยังบริการอาหารไหม   yang bor-rí-gahn ah-hăhn măi

How long is the wait?
ต้องรอนานเท่าไร   đôrng ror nahn tôw-rai

at the restaurant

What would you recommend?
คุณแนะนำอะไรบ้าง

kun náe-nam à-rai bâhng

What's in that dish?
จานนั้นมีอะไร

jahn nán mee à-rai

I'll have that.
เอาอันนั้นนะ

ow an nán ná

Is service included in the bill?
ค่าบริการรวมในบิลล์ด้วยไหม

kâh bor-rí-gahn roo·am nai bin dôo·ay măi

Are these complimentary?
ของเหล่านี้แถมไหม

kŏrng lòw née tăam măi

I'd like ...   อยากจะทาน ...   yàhk jà tahn ...
  the chicken   ไก่   gài
  a local   อาหารพิเศษของ   ah-hăhn pí-sèt
  speciality   ถิ่นนี้สักอย่างหนึ่ง   kŏrng tìn née sàk yàhng nèung
  a meal fit   อาหารอย่างดี   ah-hăhn yàhng
  for a king   dee

eating out

155

I'd like it with ...	ต้องการแบบมี ...	đôrng gahn bàap mee ...
I'd like it without ...	ต้องการแบบไม่มี ...	đôrng gahn bàap mâi mee ...
chilli	พริก	prík
garlic	กระเทียม	grà-tee·am
nuts	ถั่ว	tòo·a
oil	น้ำมัน	nám man

For other specific meal requests, see **vegetarian & special meals**, page 169.

---

listen for ...

kun chôrp ... mǎi
คุณชอบ ... ไหม **Do you like ...?**

jà hâi jàt tam yàhng rai
จะให้จัดทำอย่างไร **How would you like that cooked?**

pǒm/dì-chǎn kǒr náa-nam ... m/f
ผม/ดิฉัน ขอแนะนำ ... **I suggest the ...**

For more words you might see on a menu, see the **culinary reader**, page 171.

at the table

ที่โต๊ะอาหาร

Please bring ...	ขอ ... หน่อย	kǒr ... nòy
the bill	บิลล์	bin
a cloth	ผ้า	pâh
a serviette	ผ้าเช็ดปาก	pâh chét bàhk
a (wine)glass	แก้ว(ไวน์)	gâa·ou (wai)

อาหารเรียกน้ำย่อย	ah-hăhn rêe·ak nám yôy	**Appetisers**
น้ำซุป	nám súp	**Soups**
อาหารว่าง	ah-hăhn wâhng	**Entrées**
ผักสด	pàk sòt	**Salads**
อาหารจานหลัก	ah-hăhn jahn làk	**Main Courses**
ของหวาน	kŏrng wăhn	**Desserts**
เหล้าให้เจริญอาหาร	lôw hâi jà-reun ah-hăhn	**Aperitifs**
น้ำอัดลม	nám àt lom	**Soft Drinks**
สุรา	sù-rah	**Spirits**
เบียร์	bee·a	**Beer**
ไวน์ขาว	wai kŏw	**White Wine**
ไวน์แดง	wai daang	**Red Wine**

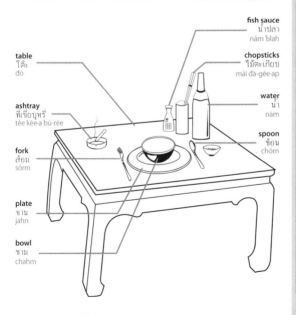

fish sauce
น้ำปลา
nám blah

table
โต๊ะ
dó

chopsticks
ไม้ตะเกียบ
mái đà·gèe·ap

ashtray
ที่เขี่ยบุหรี่
têe kèe·a bù·rèe

water
น้ำ
nám

fork
ส้อม
sôrm

spoon
ช้อน
chórn

plate
จาน
jahn

bowl
ชาม
chahm

talking food

I love this dish.
อาหารนี้ชอบจัง　　　　　　　ah-hǎhn née chôrp jang

I love the local cuisine.
ชอบอาหารท้องถิ่นมาก　　　　chôrp ah-hàhn tórng
　　　　　　　　　　　　　tìn mâhk

That was delicious!
อร่อยมาก　　　　　　　　　à-ròy mâhk

My compliments to the chef.
ขอฝากคำชมให้พ่อครัวด้วย　　kŏr fàhk kam chom hâi pôr
　　　　　　　　　　　　　kroo·a dôo·ay

I'm full.
อิ่มแล้ว　　　　　　　　　　ìm láa·ou

This is ...　　　　อันนี้ ...　　　　an née ...
　　(too) cold　　เย็น (เกินไป)　　yen (geun bai)
　　spicy　　　　เผ็ด　　　　　　pèt
　　superb　　　อร่อยมาก　　　à-ròy mâhk

breakfast

What's a typical breakfast?
ปกติอาหารเช้าทานอะไร　　　bò-gà-đì ah-hǎhn chów
　　　　　　　　　　　　　tahn à-rai

bacon　　　หมูเบค่อน　　　mǒo bair-kôrn
bread　　　ขนมปัง　　　　kà-nǒm bang
butter　　　เนย　　　　　　neu·i
cereal　　　ซีเรียล　　　　see-ree·an

... egg(s)	ไข่ ...	kài ...
boiled	ต้ม	đôm
fried	ดาว	dow
hard-boiled	ต้มแข็ง	dôm kăang
poached	ทอดน้ำ	tôrt nám
scrambled	กวน	goo·an

omelette	ไข่เจียว	kài jee·o
milk	นม	nom
muesli	มิวส์ลี่	mew-lêe
rice gruel	โจ๊ก	jóhk
rice gruel with egg	โจ๊กใส่ไข่	jóhk sài kài
rice soup	ข้าวต้ม	kôw đôm
toast	ขนมปังปิ้ง	kà-nŏm ƃang ƃîng

For other breakfast items, see **self-catering**, page 165, and the **culinary reader**, page 171.

street food

อาหารว่าง

What's that called?
อันนั้นเรียกว่าอะไร — an nán rêe·ak wâh à-rai

coconut roasties	ขนมครก	kà-nŏm krók
deep-fried dough	ปาท่องโก๋	ƃah-tôrng-gŏh
steamed buns	ซาลาเปา	sah-lah-ƃow
mixed nuts	ไก่สามอย่าง	gài săhm yàhng
rice noodles	ก๋วยเตี๋ยว	gŏo·ay đĕe·o
roast chicken and sticky rice	ข้าวเหนียวไก่ย่าง	kôw nĕe·o gài yâhng
roast fish/meat balls	ลูกชิ้นปลา/เนื้อปิ้ง	lôok chín ƃlah/néu·a ƃîng
sweet sticky rice in bamboo	ข้าวหลาม	kôw lăhm
baked custard sweet	ขนมหม้อแกง	kà-nŏm môr gaang

condiments

Do you have ...?	มี ... ไหม	mee ... măi
chilli sauce	น้ำพริก	nám prík
dipping sauces	น้ำจิ้ม	nám jîm
fish sauce	น้ำปลา	nám Ъlah
ground peanuts	ถั่วลิสงป่น	tòo·a lí·sŏng Ъòn
ground red pepper	พริกป่น	prík Ъòn
ketchup/tomato sauce	ซอสมะเขือเทศ	sórt má·kĕu·a têt
pepper	พริกไทย	prík tai
salt	เกลือ	gleu·a
sliced hot chillies in fish sauce	พริกน้ำปลา	prík nám Ъlah
sliced chillies in vinegar	พริกน้ำส้ม	prík nám sôm

For additional items, see the **culinary reader**, page 171.

methods of preparation

วิธีจัดอาหาร

I'd like it ...	ต้องการ ...	đôrng gahn ...
I don't want it ...	ไม่ต้องการ ...	mâi đôrng gahn ...
spicy	เผ็ด	pèt
boiled	ต้ม	đôm
deep-fried	ทอด	tôrt
fried	ผัด	pàt
grilled	ย่าง	yâhng
medium	ปานกลาง	Ъahn glahng
rare	ไม่สุกมาก	mâi sùk mâhk
re-heated	อุ่นใหม่	ùn mài
steamed	นึ่ง	nêung
well-done	สุกมากหน่อย	sùk mâhk nòy
without ...	ไม่มี ...	mâi mee ...

160

in the bar

Excuse me!
ขออภัย — kŏr à-pai

I'm next.
ฉันต่อไป — chăn đòr bai

I'll have …
จะเอา … — jà ow …

Same again, please.
ขออีกครั้งหนึ่ง — kŏr èek kráng nèung

No ice, thanks.
ไม่ใส่น้ำแข็ง ขอบคุณ — mâi sài nám kăang kòrp kun

I'll buy you a drink.
ฉันจะซื้อของดื่มให้คุณ — chăn jà séu kŏrng dèum hâi kun

What would you like?
จะรับอะไร — jà ráp à-rai

It's my round.
ตาของฉันนะ — đah kŏrng chăn ná

How much is that?
เท่าไร — tôw-rai

Do you serve meals here?
ที่นี่บริการอาหารด้วยไหม — têe née bor-rí-gahn ah-hăhn dôo·ay măi

---

listen for …

kít wâh kun dèum mâhk por láa·ou ná
คิดว่าคุณดื่มมากพอแล้วนะ — **I think you've had enough.**

kun jà ráp à-rai
คุณจะรับอะไร — **What are you having?**

sàng kráng sùt tái ná kráp/kâ **m/f**
สั่งครั้งสุดท้ายนะ ครับ/ค่ะ — **Last orders.**

nonalcoholic drinks

เครื่องดื่มที่ไม่มีแอลกอฮอล์

... mineral water	น้ำแร่ ...	nám râa ...
sparkling	อัดลม	àt lom
still	ธรรมดา	tam-má-dah
... water	น้ำ ...	nám ...
boiled	ต้ม	đôm
purified	บริสุทธิ์	bor-rí-sùt
Chinese tea	น้ำชาจีน	nám chah jeen
iced coffee	กาแฟเย็น	gah-faa yen
iced lime juice with sugar	น้ำมะนาวใส่น้ำตาล	nám má-now sài nám-đahn
iced tea	น้ำชาเย็น	nám chah yen
orange juice	น้ำส้มคั้น	nám sôm kán
soft drink	น้ำอัดลม	nám àt lom
(hot) water	น้ำ (ร้อน)	nám (rórn)
(cup of) coffee	กาแฟ (ถ้วยหนึ่ง)	gah-faa (tôo-ay nèung)
(cup of) tea	ชา (ถ้วยหนึ่ง)	chah (tôo-ay nèung)
... with milk	... ใส่นม	... sài nom
... without sugar	... ไม่ใส่น้ำตาล	... mâi sài nám-đahn
tea leaves	ใบชา	bai chah

coffee

black coffee	กาแฟดำ	gah-faa dam
decaffeinated coffee	กาแฟไม่มีกาเฟอีน	gah-faa mâi mee ga-fair-een
iced coffee	กาแฟเย็น	gah-faa yen
strong coffee	กาแฟแก่	gah-faa gàe
Thai filtered coffee	กาแฟถุง	gah-faa tǔng
weak coffee	กาแฟอ่อน	gah-faa òrn
white coffee	ใส่นม	sài nom

alcoholic drinks

a shot of …	… ช็อตหนึ่ง	… chórt nèung
distilled spirits	เหล้า	lôw
gin	จิน	jin
herbal liquor	เหล้ายาดอง	lôw yah dorng
jungle liquor	เหล้าเถื่อน	lôw tèu·an
Mekong whisky	วิสกีแม่โขง	wít·sà·gee mâa kŏhng
rum	เหล้ารัม	lôw ram
vodka	เหล้าวอดก้า	lôw vôrt·gâh
whisky	วิสกี้	wít·sà·gêe
white liquor	เหล้าขาว	lôw kŏw
a bottle/glass of … wine	ไวน์ … แก้วหนึ่ง/ ขวดหนึ่ง	wai … gâa·ou nèung/ kòo·at nèung
red	แดง	daang
white	ขาว	kŏw
a … of beer	เบียร์ … หนึ่ง	bee·a … nèung
glass	แก้ว	gâa·ou
jug	เหยือก	yèu·ak
large bottle	ขวดใหญ่ขวด	kòo·at yài kòo·at
pint	ไพนต์	pai
small bottle	ขวดเล็กขวด	kòo·at lék kòo·at

garçon!

When calling for the attention of a waiter or waitress, make sure you use the correct form of address. A waiter is called bŏy บ๋อย which is easy enough to remember – just think of the English word 'boy' and raise the tone as if you are asking a question.

A waitress is referred to as nórng น้อง (lit: younger) but this may also be used for both sexes.

drinking up

Cheers!
ไชโย — chai-yoh

This is hitting the spot.
เข้าท่า — kôw tâh

I feel fantastic!
รู้สึกดีมาก — róo-sèuk dee mâhk

I think I've had one too many.
สงสัยฉันดื่มมากไปสัก — sŏng-săi chăn dèum mâhk bai
แก้วหนึ่งกระมัง — sàk gâa·ou nèung grà-mang

I'm feeling drunk.
เมาแล้ว — mow láa·ou

I feel ill.
รู้สึกไม่สบาย — róo-sèuk mâi sà-bai

I think I'm going to throw up.
สงสัยจะอ้วก — sŏng-săi jà ôo·ak

Where's the toilet?
ห้องส้วมอยู่ไหน — hôrng sôo·am yòo năi

I'm tired, I'd better go home.
เหนื่อยแล้ว กลับบ้านดีกว่า — nèu·ay láa·ou, glàp bâhn dee
gwàh

Can you call a taxi for me?
เรียกแท็กซี่ให้หน่อยได้ไหม — rêe·ak táak-sêe hâi nòy dâi măi

I don't think you should drive.
คิดว่าคุณไม่ขับรถดีกว่า — kít wâh kun mâi kàp rót dee
gwàh

buying food

การซื้ออาหาร

What's the local speciality?
อาหารรสเด็ดๆ ของแถว
นี้คืออะไร
ah-hǎhn rót dèt dèt kǒrng
tǎa·ou née keu à-rai

What's that?
นั่นคืออะไร
nân keu à-rai

Can I taste it?
ชิ้มได้ไหม
chím dâi mǎi

Can I have a bag, please?
ขอถุงใบหนึ่ง
kǒr tǔng bai nèung

How much is (a kilo of mangoes)?
(มะม่วงกิโลหนึ่ง) เท่าไร
(má-môo·ang gì-loh nèung)
tôw-rai

How much?
เท่าไร
tôw-rai

Less.	น้อยลง	nóy long
A bit more.	มากขึ้นหน่อย	mâhk kêun nòy
Enough!	พอแล้ว	por láa·ou

listen for ...

mee à-rai jà hâi chôo·ay mǎi
มีอะไรจะให้ช่วยไหม   **Can I help you?**

jà ow à-rai kráp/ká **m/f**
จะเอาอะไรครับ/คะ   **What would you like?**

jà ow à-rai èek mǎi
จะเอาอะไรอีกไหม   **Would you like anything else?**

(háh) bàht
(ห้า) บาท   **That's (five) baht.**

I'd like ...	ต้องการ ...	đôrng gahn ...
(200) grams	(สองร้อย) กรัม	(sŏrng róy) gram
half a dozen	ครึ่งโหล	krêung lŏh
a dozen	โหลหนึ่ง	lŏh nèung
half a kilo	ครึ่งกิโล	krêung gì-loh
a kilo	กิโลหนึ่ง	gì-loh nèung
(two) kilos	(สอง) กิโล	(sŏrng) gì-loh
a bottle	ขวดหนึ่ง	kòo·at nèung
a jar	กระปุกหนึ่ง	grà-ɓùk nèung
a packet	ห่อหนึ่ง	hòr nèung
a piece	ชิ้นหนึ่ง	chín nèung
(three) pieces	(สาม) ชิ้น	(săhm) chín
a slice	ชิ้นหนึ่ง	chín nèung
(six) slices	(หก) ชิ้น	(hòk) chín
a tin	กระป๋องหนึ่ง	grà-ɓŏrng nèung
(just) a little	(แต่) นิดหน่อย	(đàa) nít-nòy
more	อีก	èek
that one	อันนั้น	an nán
this one	อันนี้	an née

Do you have ...?	มี ... ไหม	mee ... măi
anything cheaper	ถูกกว่า	tòok gwàh
other kinds	ชนิดอื่น	chá-nít èun

cooked	สุก	sùk
cured	บ่ม	bòm
dried	ตากแห้ง	đàhk hâang
fresh	สด	sòt
frozen	แช่แข็ง	châa kăang
smoked	อบควัน	òp kwan
raw	ดิบ	dìp
pickled	ดอง	dorng

Where can I find the ... section?	จะหาแผนก ... ได้ที่ไหน	jà hǎh pà-nàak ... dâi têe nǎi
dairy	อาหารจำพวกนม	ah-hǎhn jam-pôo·ak nom
fish	ปลา	Ьlah
frozen goods	อาหารแช่แข็ง	ah-hǎhn châa kǎang
fruit and vegetable	ผักผลไม้	pàk pǒn-lá-mái
meat	เนื้อ	néu·a
poultry	เนื้อไก่	néu·a gài

---

fruity farangs

One of the first words that many people learn in Thailand is fà-ràng ฝรั่ง which means a foreigner of Western descent. There are several theories as to the origin of the word. One of the most popular is that fà-ràng is an abbreviation of fà-ràng seht (French person).

More accurately, the word relates to the Germanic Franks who participated in the crusades. The name gave rise to the arabic word *faranji* meaning European Christian (hence 'foreigner' in the Middle East) and reached Thailand via Persian trade routes.

Neighbouring countries have very similar words for foreigner. In Cambodia, Westerners are called *barang*, and in Vietnam they are called *pha-rang* or *pha-lang-xa*. In Thailand fà-ràng also means 'guava' (possibly because guavas are not native to Thailand), so Westerners seen eating guavas may find themselves the butt of silly puns.

cooking utensils

Could I please borrow a/an ...?	ขอยืม ... หน่อย	kŏr yeum ... nòy
I need a/an ...	ต้องการ ...	đôrng gahn ...
bottle opener	เครื่องเปิดขวด	krêu·ang bèut kòo·at
bowl	ชาม	chahm
can opener	เครื่องเปิดกระป๋อง	krêu·ang bèut grà-bŏrng
chopping board	เขียง	kĕe·ang
chopsticks	ตะเกียบ	đà-gèe·ap
corkscrew	เหล็กไขจุกขวด	lèk kăi jùk kòo·at
cup	ถ้วย	tôo·ay
fork	ส้อม	sôrm
fridge	ตู้เย็น	đôo yen
frying pan	กระทะ	grà-tá
glass	แก้ว	gâa·ou
knife	มีด	mêet
meat cleaver	มีดสับ	mêet sàp
microwave	ตู้ไมโครเวฟ	đôo mai-kroh-wêp
oven	เตาอบ	đow òp
plate	จาน	jahn
rice cooker	หม้อหุงข้าว	môr hŭng kôw
saucepan	หม้อ	môr
spoon	ช้อน	chórn
wok	กระทะ	grà-tá

vegetarian & special meals

ordering food

การสั่งอาหาร

I eat only vegetarian food.

ผม/ดิฉัน ทานแต่อาหารเจ · pŏm/dì-chăn tahn đàa ah-hăhn jair **m/f**

Is there a … restaurant near here?

มีร้านอาหาร … อยู่แถวๆ นี้ไหม · mee ráhn ah-hăhn … yòo tăa·ou tăa·ou née măi

Do you have … food?	มีอาหาร … ไหม	mee ah-hăhn … măi
halal	อาหารที่จัดทำตาม หลักศาสนาอิสลาม	ah-hăhn têe jàt tam đahm làk sàht-sà-năh ìt-sà-lahm
kosher	อาหารที่จัดทำตาม หลักศาสนายิว	ah-hăhn têe jàt tam đahm làk sàht-sà-năh yew
vegetarian	เจ	jair

I don't eat … · ผม/ดิฉัน ไม่ทาน … · pŏm/dì-chăn mâi tahn … **m/f**

Is it cooked in/ with …? · อันนี้ทำกับ … ไหม · an née tam gàp … măi

Could you prepare a meal without …?	ทำอาหารไม่ ใส่ … ได้ไหม	tam ah-hăhn mâi sài … dâi măi
butter	เนย	neu·i
eggs	ไข่	kài
fish	ปลา	Ƅlah
meat stock	ซุปก้อนเนื้อ	súp gôrn néu·a
MSG	ชูรส	choo-rót
pork	เนื้อหมู	néu·a mŏo
poultry	เนื้อไก่	néu·a gài
red meat	เนื้อแดง	néu·a daang

169

special diets & allergies

I'm (a) ...	ผม/ดิฉัน ...	pŏm/dì-chăn ... m/f
vegan	ไม่ทานอาหารที่	mâi tahn ah-hăhn
	มาจากสัตว์	têe mah jàhk sàt
vegetarian	ทานอาหารเจ	tahn ah-hăhn jair

I'm on a special diet.

ผม/ดิฉัน ทานอาหารพิเศษ	pŏm/dì-chăn tahn ah-hăhn pí-sèt m/f

I'm allergic to ...	ผม/ดิฉัน แพ้ ...	pŏm/dì-chăn páa ...
chilli	พริก	prík
dairy produce	อาหารจำพวกนม	ah-hăhn jam-pôo·ak nom
eggs	ไข่	kài
gelatine	วุ้น	wún
gluten	แป้ง	bâang
honey	น้ำผึ้ง	nám pêung
MSG	ชูรส	choo-rót
nuts	ถั่ว	tòo·a
seafood	อาหารทะเล	ah-hăhn tá-lair
shellfish	หอย	hŏy

---

go nuts

Note that in Thai the generic word for nuts (tòo·a ถั่ว) also includes beans. So you need to specify precisely which variety of nuts you are allergic to. Refer to the dictionary for individual nut varieties.

These Thai dishes and ingredients are listed alphabetically, by pronunciation, so you can easily understand what's on offer and ask for what takes your fancy. A more detailed food glossary can be found in Lonely Planet's *World Food Thailand*.

Can you recommend a local speciality?

แนะนำ อาหารรสเด็ดๆของ
แถวนี้ได้ไหม

náa-nam ah-hǎhn rót dèt
dèt kŏrng tǎa·ou née dâi mǎi

Do you serve …?

มี … ไหม

mee … mǎi

B

bai đeu·i ใบเตย *pandanus leaves – used primarily to add a vanilla-like flavour to Thai sweets*

bai đorng ใบตอง *banana leaves*

bai gà-prow ใบกะเพรา *'holy basil' – so-called due to its sacred status in India*

bai hŏh-rá-pah ใบโหระพา *'sweet basil' – a hardy, large-leafed plant used in certain* gaang *(curries), seafood dishes & especially* pàt pèt *(hot stir-fries)*

bai maang-lák ใบแมงลัก *known variously as Thai basil, lemon basil or mint basil – popular in soups & as a condiment for* kà-nŏm jeen nám yah *&* láhp

bai má-gròot ใบมะกรูด *kaffir lime leaves*

bai sà-rá-nàa ใบสะระแหน่ *native spearmint leaves used in* yam *&* láhp *& eaten raw in North-Eastern Thailand*

bà-mèe บะหมี่ *yellowish noodles made from wheat flour & sometimes egg*

bà-mèe gée·o boo บะหมี่เกี๊ยวปู *soup containing* bà-mèe*, won ton & crab meat*

bà-mèe hâang บะหมี่แห้ง *bà-mèe served in a bowl with a little garlic oil, meat, seafood or vegetables*

bà-mèe nám บะหมี่น้ำ *bà-mèe with broth, meat, seafood or vegetables*

boo·a loy บัวลอย *'floating lotus' – boiled sticky rice dumplings in a white syrup of sweetened & lightly salted coconut milk*

bòo·ap บวบ *gourd*

bòo·ap lèe·am บวบเหลี่ยม *sponge gourd*

bòo·ap ngoo บวบงู *snake gourd*

฿

ฺbah-tôrng-gŏh ปาท่องโก๋ *fried wheat pastry similar to an unsweetened doughnut*

ฺbèt เป็ด *duck*

ฺbèt đǔn เป็ดตุ๋น *steamed duck soup generally featuring a broth darkened by soy sauce & spices such as cinnamon, star anise or Chinese five-spice*

ฺbèt yâhng เป็ดย่าง *roast duck*

ฺblah ปลา *fish*

ฺblah bèuk ปลาบึก *giant Mekong catfish*

blah chôrn ปลาช่อน *serpent-headed fish –
a freshwater variety*

blah dàak ปลาแดก *see* blah-ráh

blah dàat dee-o ปลาแดดเดียว *'half-day
dried fish' – fried & served with a spicy
mango salad*

blah dùk ปลาดุก *catfish*

blah gà-dàk ปลากะตัก *type of anchovy
used in* nám blah *(fish sauce)*

blah gà-pong ปลากะพง *seabass • ocean
perch*

blah gōw ปลาเก๋า *grouper • reef cod*

blah grà-bòrk ปลากระบอก *mullet*

blah kem ปลาเค็ม *preserved salted fish*

blah klúk kà-mín ปลาคลุกขมิ้น *fresh fish
rubbed with a paste of turmeric, garlic &
salt before grilling or frying*

blah lǎi ปลาไหล *freshwater eel*

blah lòt ปลาหลด *saltwater eel*

blah mèuk glôo-ay ปลาหมึกกล้วย
squid • calamari

blah mèuk grà-dorng ปลาหมึกกระดอง
cuttlefish

blah mèuk pàt pǒng gà-rèe
ปลาหมึกผัดผงกะหรี่ *squid stir-fried in
curry powder*

blah mèuk bîng ปลาหมึกปิ้ง *dried, roasted
squid flattened into a sheet via a hand-
cranked press then toasted over hot coals –
a favourite night-time street snack*

blah nèung ปลานึ่ง *freshwater fish
steamed with Thai lemon basil,
lemongrass & any other vegetables
(North-East Thailand)*

blah nin ปลานิล *tilapia (variety of fish)*

blah pǒw ปลาเผา *fish wrapped in banana
leaves or foil & roasted over (or covered
in) hot coals*

blah sah-deen ปลาซาร์ดีน *sardine*

blah sǎm-lee ปลาสำลี *cottonfish*

blah sǎm-lee dàat dee-o ปลาสำลีแดดเดียว
'half-day-dried cottonfish' – whole

cottonfish sliced lengthways & left to
dry in the sun for half a day, then fried
quickly in a wok

blah sǎm-lee pǒw ปลาสำลีเผา *'fire-roasted
cottonfish' – cottonfish roasted over
coals*

blah too ปลาทู *mackerel*

blah tôrt ปลาทอด *fried fish*

blah-ráh ปลาร้า *'rotten fish' –
unpasteurised version of* nám blah *sold
in earthenware jars (North-East Thailand)*

bó đàak โป๊ะแตก *'broken fish trap soup' –*
đôm yam *with the addition of either
sweet or holy basil & a melange of
seafood, usually including squid, crab,
fish, mussels & shrimp*

boo ปู *crab*

boo nah ปูนา *field crabs*

boo òp wún-sên ปูอบวุ้นเส้น *bean thread
noodles baked in a lidded, clay pot with
crab & seasonings*

boo pàt pǒng gà-rèe ปูผัดผงกะหรี่ *crab in
the shell stir-fried in curry powder & eggs*

boo tá-lair ปูทะเล *sea crab*

bor-bée-a ปอเปี๊ยะ *egg rolls*

bor-bée-a sòt ปอเปี๊ยะสด *fresh spring rolls*

bor-bée-a tôrt ปอเปี๊ยะทอด *fried spring rolls*

C

chá-om ชะอม *bitter acacia leaf*

chom-pôo ชมพู่ *rose apple*

D

đaang moh แตงโม *watermelon*

đà-gôh ตะโก้ *popular steamed sweet made
from tapioca flour & coconut milk over a
layer of sweetened seaweed gelatine*

đà-krai ตะไคร้ *lemongrass – used in curry
pastes,* tôm yam, *yam & certain kinds
of* lâhp

đam màhk hùng คำหมากหุ่ง *see* sôm đam

đam sôm คำส้ม *see* sôm đam

đam-ráp gàp kòw คำรับกับข้าว *basic handed-down recipes*

đôm ต้ม *Isaan soup similar to* đôm yam *made with lemongrass, galangal, spring onions, kaffir lime leaves & fresh whole* prík kêe nôo, *seasoned before serving with lime juice & fish sauce (also known as* đôm sáap)

đôm ɓrèe-o ต้มเปรี้ยว *'boiled sour' –* đôm yam *soup with added tamarind*

đôm fák ต้มฟัก *Isaan* đôm *made with green squash, often eaten with duck salad*

đôm gài sài bai má-kǎhm òrn ต้มไก่ใส่ใบมะขามอ่อน *Isaan* đôm *made with chicken & tamarind leaves*

đôm kàh gài ต้มข่าไก่ *'boiled galangal chicken' – includes lime, chilli & coconut milk (Central Thailand)*

đôm sáap ต้มแซบ *see* đôm

đôm woo-a ต้มวัว *Isaan* đôm *made with beef tripe & liver*

đôm yam ต้มยำ *popular soup made with chilli, lemongrass, lime & usually seafood*

đôm yam gûng ต้มยำกุ้ง *shrimp yam*

đôm yam hâang ต้มยำแห้ง *a dry version of* đôm yam gûng

đôm yam ɓó đaak ต้มยำโป๊ะแตก đôm yam *with mixed seafood*

đôn glòo-ay ต้นกล้วย *cross-section of the heart of the banana stalk*

đôn hǒrm ต้นหอม *'fragrant plant' – spring onion or scallions*

đôw hôo เต้าหู้ *tofu (soybean curd)*

đôw jêe-o เต้าเจี้ยว *paste of salted, fermented soybeans, either yellow or black*

đôw jêe-o dam เต้าเจี้ยวดำ *black-bean sauce*

F

fák ฟัก *gourd • squash*

fák kěe-o ฟักเขียว *wax gourd*

fák ngoo ฟักงู *snake or winter melon*

fák torng ฟักทอง *golden squash or Thai pumpkin*

fà-ràng ฝรั่ง *guava (the word also refers to a Westerner of European descent)*

fěu เฝอ *another name for* gǒo-ay-đěe-o *(rice noodles)*

fǒy torng ฝอยทอง *'golden threads' – small bundle of sweetened egg-yolk threads in Thai desserts*

G

gaang แกง *classic chilli-based curries for which Thai cuisine is famous, as well as any dish with a lot of liquid (thus it can refer to soups)*

gaang ɓàh แกงป่า *'forest curry' – spicy curry which uses no coconut milk*

gaang đai ɓlah แกงไตปลา *curry made with fish stomach, green beans, pickled bamboo shoots & potatoes (South Thailand)*

gaang gah-yôo แกงกาหยู *curry made with fresh cashews – popular in Phuket & Ranong*

gaang gà-rèe gài แกงกะหรี่ไก่ *curry similar to an Indian curry, containing potatoes & chicken*

gaang hang-lair แกงฮังเล *rich Burmese-style curry with no coconut milk*

gaang hó แกงโฮะ *spicy soup featuring pickled bamboo shoots (North Thailand)*

gaang jèut แกงจืด *'bland soup' – plain Cantonese-influenced soup in which cubes of soft tofu, green squash, Chinese radish, bitter gourd, ground pork & mung bean noodles are common ingredients* gaang jèut wún sên แกงจืดวุ้นเส้น *mung bean noodle soup*, gaang jèut with wún-sên

gaang kaa แกงแค *soup made with 'sawtooth coriander' & bitter eggplant (North Thailand)*

gaang kà-nǔn แกงขนุน *jackfruit curry – favoured in Northern Thailand but found elsewhere as well*

gaang kěe-o wǎhn แกงเขียวหวาน *green curry*

gaang kôw-a sôm sàp-bà-rót แกงคั่วส้มสัปปะรด *pan-roasted pineapple curry with sea crab*

gaang lee-ang แกงเลียง *spicy soup of green or black peppercorns, sponge gourd, baby corn, cauliflower & various greens, substantiated with pieces of chicken, shrimp or ground pork – probably one of the oldest recipes in Thailand*

gaang lěu-ang แกงเหลือง *'yellow curry' – spicy dish of fish cooked with green squash, pineapple, green beans & green papaya (South Thailand)*

gaang mát-sà-màn แกงมัสมั่น *Indian-influenced Muslim curry featuring a cumin, cinnamon & cardamom spice mix*

gaang mét má-môo-ang hǐm-má-pahn แกงเม็ดมะม่วงหิมพานต์ *curry made with fresh cashews*

gaang morn แกงมอญ *Mon curry*

gaang pàk hóo-an แกงผักฮ้วน *soup containing tamarind juice (North Thailand)*

gaang pàk wǎhn แกงผักหวาน *soup with 'sweet greens' (North Thailand)*

gaang pá-naang แกงพะแนง *similar to a regular red curry but thicker, milder & without vegetables*

gaang pèt แกงเผ็ด *red curry*

gaang pèt bèt yâhng แกงเผ็ดเป็ดย่าง *duck roasted Chinese-style in five-spice seasoning & mixed into Thai red curry*

gaang râht kôw แกงราดข้าว *curry over rice*

gaang sôm แกงส้ม *soupy, sweet, salty & sour curry made with dried chillies, shallots, garlic & Chinese key (grà-chai) pestled with salt, gà-bì & fish sauce*

gaang yòo-ak แกงหยวก *curry featuring banana palm heart & jackfruit (North Thailand)*

gah-làh กาหลา *'torch ginger' – thinly-sliced flower buds from a wild ginger plant, sometimes used in the Southern Thai rice salad kôw yam*

gài ไก่ *chicken*

gài bair-dong ไก่เบตง *Betong dish of steamed chicken, chopped & seasoned with locally made soy sauce then stir-fried with vegetables*

gài bing ไก่ปิ้ง *chicken grilled in the North-Eastern (Isaan) style (see gài yâhng)*

gài dǔn ไก่ตุ๋น *steamed chicken soup generally featuring a broth darkened by soy sauce & spices such as cinnamon, star anise or Chinese five-spice mixture*

gài hòr bai đeu-i ไก่ห่อใบเตย *chicken marinated in soy sauce & wrapped in pandanus leaves along with sesame oil, garlic & coriander root, then fried or grilled & served with a dipping sauce similar to the marinade*

gài pàt kǐng ไก่ผัดขิง *chicken stir-fried with ginger, garlic & chillies, seasoned with fish sauce*

gài pàt mét má-môo-ang hǐm-má-pahn ไก่ผัดเม็ดมะม่วงหิมพานต์ *sliced chicken stir-fried in dried chillies & cashews*

gài sǎhm yâhng ไก่สามอย่าง *'three kinds of chicken' – chicken, chopped ginger, peanuts, chilli peppers & lime pieces to be mixed together & eaten by hand*

gài tôrt ไก่ทอด *fried chicken*

gài yâhng ไก่ย่าง *Isaan-style grilled chicken* (bîng gài *or* gài bîng *in Isaan dialect) marinated in garlic, coriander root, black pepper & salt or fish sauce & cooked slowly over hot coals*

gà-bì กะปิ *shrimp paste*

gàp glâam กับแกล้ม *'drinking food' – dishes specifically meant to be eaten while drinking alcoholic beverages*

gà-rèe กะหรี่ *Thai equivalent of the Anglo-Indian term 'curry'*

gà-tí กะทิ *coconut milk*

gée-o เกี๊ยว *won ton – triangle of dough wrapped around ground pork or fish*

glàh กล้า *rice sprouts*

glôo-ay กล้วย *banana*

glôo-ay bòo-at chee กล้วยบวชชี *'bananas ordaining as nuns' – banana chunks floating in a white syrup of sweetened & lightly salted coconut milk*

glôo-ay hŏrm กล้วยหอม *fragrant banana*

glôo-ay kài กล้วยไข่ *'egg banana' – native to Kamphaeng Phet*

glôo-ay lép meu nahng กล้วยเล็บมือนาง *'princess fingernail banana'– native to Chumphon Province in Southern Thailand*

glôo-ay nám wáh กล้วยน้ำว้า *thick-bodied, medium-length banana*

glôo-ay tôrt กล้วยทอด *batter-fried banana*

goh-bÊe โกปี๊ *Hokkien dialect for coffee, used especially in Trang province*

goh-bÊe dam โกปี๊ดำ *sweetened black coffee (Trang province)*

goh-bÊe dam mâi sài nám-dahn โกปี๊ดำไม่ใส่น้ำตาล *unsweetened black coffee (Trang province)*

gŏo-ay đĕe-o ก๋วยเตี๋ยว *rice noodles made from pure rice flour mixed with water to form a paste which is then steamed to form wide, flat sheets*

gŏo-ay đĕe-o hâhng ก๋วยเตี๋ยวแห้ง *dry rice noodles*

gŏo-ay đĕe-o hâhng sù-kŏh-tai ก๋วยเตี๋ยวแห้งสุโขทัย *'Sukothai dry rice noodles' – thin rice noodles served in a bowl with peanuts, barbecued pork, ground dried chilli, green beans & bean sprouts*

gŏo-ay đĕe-o jan-tá-bù-ree ก๋วยเตี๋ยวจันทบูรณ์ *dried rice noodles (Chantaburi)*

gŏo-ay đĕe-o lôok chín blah ก๋วยเตี๋ยวลูกชิ้นปลา *rice noodles with fish balls*

gŏo-ay đĕe-o nám ก๋วยเตี๋ยวน้ำ *rice noodles served in a bowl of plain chicken or beef stock with bits of meat, pickled cabbage & a coriander-leaf garnish*

gŏo-ay đĕe-o pàt ก๋วยเตี๋ยวผัด *fried rice noodles with sliced meat, Chinese kale, soy sauce & various seasonings – a favourite crowd-pleaser at temple festivals all over the country*

gŏo-ay đĕe-o pàt kêe mow ก๋วยเตี๋ยวผัดขี้เมา *'drunkard's fried noodles' – wide rice noodles, fresh basil leaves, chicken or pork, seasonings & fresh sliced chillies*

gŏo-ay đĕe-o pàt tai ก๋วยเตี๋ยวผัดไทย *a plate of thin rice noodles stir-fried with dried or fresh shrimp, beansprouts, fried tofu, egg & seasonings (pàt tai for short)*

gŏo-ay đĕe-o râht nâh ก๋วยเตี๋ยวราดหน้า *noodles braised in a light gravy made with cornstarch-thickened stock, then combined with either pork or chicken, Chinese broccoli or Chinese kale & oyster sauce*

gŏo-ay đĕe-o râht nâh tá-lair ก๋วยเตี๋ยวราดหน้าทะเล râht nâh *with seafood* gŏo·ay đĕe·o reu·a ก๋วยเตี๋ยวเรือ 'boat noodles' – concoction of dark beef broth & rice noodles originally sold only on boats that frequented the canals of Rangsit

gŏo·ay jáp ก๋วยจั๊บ thick broth of sliced Chinese mushrooms & bits of chicken or pork

gòp กบ frog – used as food in Northern & North-Eastern Thailand

gôy ก้อย raw spicy minced-meat salad

gôy woo·a ก้อยวัว raw spicy minced-meat salad of beef

grà-chai กระชาย Chinese key – root in the ginger family used as a traditional remedy for a number of gastrointestinal ailments

grà-yah sãh-rot กระยาสารท rice & peanut sweet, popular at certain Buddhist festivals

gûng กุ้ง refers to a variety of different shrimps, prawns & lobsters

gûng gù-lah dam กุ้งกุลาดำ tiger prawn

gûng mang-gorn กุ้งมังกร 'dragon prawn' – refers to lobster

gûng pàt kĭng กุ้งผัดขิง prawns stir-fried in ginger

gûng pàt sà-đor กุ้งผัดสะเดา beans stir-fried with chillies, shrimp & shrimp paste (South Thailand)

gûng súp ƀâang tôrt กุ้งชุบแป้งทอด batter-fried shrimp

H

hăhng gà-tí หางกะทิ coconut milk

hèt hŏrm เห็ดหอม shiitake mushrooms

hŏm daang หอมแดง shallots • scallions

hŏo·a ƀlee หัวปลี banana flower – a purplish, oval-shaped bud that has a tart & astringent mouth feel when eaten raw as an accompaniment to lâhp in the North-East

hŏo·a chai tów หัวไชเท้า Chinese radish

hŏo·a gà-tí หัวกะทิ coconut cream

hŏo·a pàk gàht หัวผักกาด giant white radish

hòr mòk ห่อหมก soufflé-like dish made by steaming a mixture of red curry paste, beaten eggs, coconut milk & fish in a banana-leaf cup (Central Thailand)

hòr mòk hŏy má-laang pŏo ห่อหมกหอยแมลงภู่ hòr mòk cooked inside green mussel shells

hòr mòk tá-lair ห่อหมกทะเล hòr mòk made by steaming a mixture of red curry paste, beaten eggs, coconut milk & mixed seafood in a banana-leaf cup (Central Thailand)

hŏy หอย clams & oysters (generic)

hŏy kraang หอยแครง cockle

hŏy má-laang pŏo หอยแมลงภู่ green mussel

hŏy nahng rom หอยนางรม oyster

hŏy pàt หอยผัด scallop

hŏy tôrt หอยทอด fresh oysters quickly fried with beaten eggs, mung bean sprouts & sliced spring onions (Central Thailand)

J

jàa·ou แจ่ว see nám jàa·ou

jàa·ou hórn แจ่วฮ้อน North-Eastern version of Central Thailand's popular Thai sukiyaki (sù-gêe-yah-gêe) but includes mung bean noodles, thin-sliced beef, beef entrails, egg, water spinach, cabbage & cherry tomatoes

jóhk โจ๊ก thick rice soup or congee

jóhk gài โจ๊กไก่ thick rice soup with chicken

jóhk mŏo โจ๊กหมู thick rice soup with pork meatballs

K

kàh ข่า galangal (also known as Thai ginger)

kài ไข่ egg

kài bîng ไข่ปิ้ง eggs in their shells skewered on a sharp piece of bamboo & grilled over hot coals kài ʙlah mòk ไข่ปลาหมก *egg, fish & red curry paste steamed in a banana-leaf cup & topped with strips of kaffir lime leaves* (South Thailand)

kài jee-o ไข่เจียว *Thai omelette – offered as a side dish or filler for a multidish meal*

kài lôok kěu-i ไข่ลูกเขย *'son-in-law eggs' – eggs that are boiled then fried and served with a sweet sauce*

kài mót daang ไข่มดแดง *red ant larvae used in soups* (North-East Thailand)

kài pǎm ไข่ผำ *small green plant that grows on the surface of ponds, bogs & other still waters* (North-East Thailand)

kài pàt hèt hǒo nǒo ไข่ผัดเห็ดหูหนู *eggs stir-fried with mouse-ear mushrooms*

kài yát sâi ไข่ยัดไส้ *omelette wrapped around a filling of fried ground pork, tomatoes, onions & chillies*

kà-min ขมิ้น *turmeric – popular in Southern Thai cooking*

kà-nǒm ขนม *Thai sweets*

kà-nǒm bêu-ang ขนมเบื้อง *Vietnamese vegetable crepe prepared in a wok*

kà-nǒm ʙow-láng ขนมเปาลั้ง *mix of black sticky rice, shrimp, coconut, black pepper & chilli steamed in a banana-leaf packet – favoured by Thai Muslims in Ao Phang-Nga*

kà-nǒm jeen ขนมจีน *'Chinese Pastry' – rice noodles produced by pushing rice-flour paste through a sieve into boiling water – served on a plate & mixed with various curries*

kà-nǒm jeen chow nám ขนมจีนซาวน้ำ *noodle dish featuring a mixture of pineapple, coconut, dried shrimp, ginger & garlic served with* kà-nǒm jeen

kà-nǒm jeen nám ngée-o ขนมจีนน้ำเงี้ยว *sweet & spicy Yunnanese noodle dish with pork rib meat, tomatoes & black-bean sauce fried with a curry paste of chillies,* coriander root, lemongrass, galangal, turmeric, shallots, garlic & shrimp paste

kà-nǒm jeen nám yah ขนมจีนน้ำยา *thin Chinese rice noodles doused in a Malay-style ground fish curry sauce served with fresh cucumbers, steamed long green beans, parboiled mung bean sprouts, grated papaya, pickled cabbage & fresh pineapple chunks* (South Thailand)

kà-nǒm jeen tôrt man ขนมจีนทอดมัน *thin rice noodles with fried fish cake from Phetchaburi*

kà-nǒm jèep ขนมจีบ *Chinese dumplings filled with shrimp or pork*

kà-nǒm krók ขนมครก *lightly salted & sweetened mixture of coconut milk & rice flour poured into half-round moulds in a large, round iron grill*

kà-nǒm môr gaang ขนมหม้อแกง *double-layered baked custard from Phetchaburi, made with pureed mung beans, eggs, coconut milk & sugar*

kà-nǒm tee-an ขนมเทียน *'candle pastry' – mixture of rice or corn flour, sweetened coconut milk & sesame seeds, steamed in a tall slender banana-leaf packet*

kà-nǒm tôo-ay ขนมถ้วย *sweet made from tapioca flour & coconut milk steamed in tiny porcelain cups*

kà-nǔn ขนุน *jackfruit (also known as* màhk mêe *in Isaan dialect)*

kéun-chài ขึ้นฉ่าย *Chinese celery*

king ขิง *ginger*

kǒrng cham ของชำ *refers to sundries like vegetable oil, fish sauce, sugar, soy sauce, salt, coffee, dried noodles, canned food, rice, curry paste, eggs, liquor & cigarettes*

kǒrng wǎhn ของหวาน *sweets*

kòw ข้าว *rice*

kòw ʙlòw ข้าวเปล่า *plain rice*

kòw bow ข้าวเบา *'light rice' – early season rice*

kôw ỳrà-dàp din ข้าวประดับดิน *'earth-adorning rice'* – small lumps of rice left as offerings at the base of temple stupas or beneath banyan trees during Buddhist festivals

kôw ỳbûn ข้าวปุ้น *Lao/Isaan term for* ka-nŏm jeen

kôw châa ข้าวแช่ *soupy rice eaten with small bowls of assorted foods*

kôw châa pét-bù-ree ข้าวแช่เพชรบุรี *moist chilled rice served with sweetmeats – a hot season Mon speciality*

kôw ỳdôm ข้าวต้ม *boiled rice soup, a popular late-night meal*

kôw ỳdôm gà-tí ข้าวต้มกะทิ *Thai sweets made of sticky rice, coconut milk & grated coconut wrapped in a banana leaf*

kôw ỳdôm mát ข้าวต้มมัด *Thai sweets made of sticky rice & coconut milk, black-beans or banana pieces wrapped in a banana leaf*

kôw ỳdôn reu-doo ข้าวต้นฤดู *'early season' rice*

kôw gaang ข้าวแกง *curry over rice*

kôw glahng ข้าวกลาง *'middle rice' – rice that matures mid-season*

kôw glàm ข้าวก่ำ *type of sticky rice with a deep purple, almost black hue, for use in desserts and, in Northern Thailand, to produce a mild home-made rice wine of the same name*

kôw glòrng ข้าวกล้อง *brown rice*

kôw grèe-ap gûng ข้าวเกรียบกุ้ง *shrimp chips*

kôw hŏrm má-lí ข้าวหอมมะลิ *jasmine rice*

kôw jŏw ข้าวเจ้า *white rice*

kôw kôo-a ỳbòn ข้าวคั่วป่น *uncooked rice dry-roasted in a pan till it begins to brown, then pulverised with a mortar & pestle – one of the most important ingredients in lâhp*

kôw lähm ข้าวหลาม *sticky rice & coconut steamed in a bamboo joint, a Nakhon Pathom speciality*

kôw man gài ข้าวมันไก่ *Hainanese dish of sliced steamed chicken over rice cooked in chicken broth & garlic*

kôw mòk gài ข้าวหมกไก่ *Southern version of chicken biryani – rice & chicken cooked together with cloves, cinnamon & turmeric, traditionally served with a bowl of plain chicken broth, a roasted chilli sauce & sliced cucumbers, sugar & red chillies*

kôw mŏo daang ข้าวหมูแดง *red pork over rice*

kôw nah ỳbee ข้าวนาปี *'one-field-per-year' rice*

kôw nah ỳbrang ข้าวนาปรัง *'off-season' rice*

kôw nàk ข้าวหนัก *'heavy rice' – late season rice*

kôw nĕe-o ข้าวเหนียว *sticky rice that is popular in Northern & North-Eastern Thailand*

kôw nĕe-o má-môo-ang ข้าวเหนียวมะม่วง *sliced fresh ripe mangoes served with sticky rice and sweetened with coconut milk*

kôw pàt ข้าวผัด *fried rice*

kôw pàt bai gà-prow ข้าวผัดใบกะเพรา *chicken or pork stir-fry served over rice with basil*

kôw pàt mŏo kài dow ข้าวผัดหมูไข่ดาว *fried rice with pork and a fried egg*

kôw pàt nãam ข้าวผัดแหนม *fried rice with nãam*

kôw pôht ข้าวโพด *corn*

kôw pôht òrn ข้าวโพดอ่อน *baby corn*

kôw ráht gaang ข้าวราดแกง *curry over rice*

kôw râi ข้าวไร่ *plantation rice or mountain rice*

kôw săhn ข้าวสาร *unmilled rice*

kôw sŏo-ay ข้าวสวย *cooked rice*

kôw soy ข้าวซอย *a Shan or Yunnanese egg-noodle dish with chicken or beef curry, served with shallot wedges, sweet-spicy pickled cabbage, lime & a thick red chilli sauce*

kôw yam ข้าวยำ *traditional breakfast of cooked dry rice, grated toasted coconut, bean sprouts, kaffir lime leaves, lemongrass & dried shrimp, with powdered chilli & lime (South Thailand)*

krêu·ang gaang เครื่องแกง *curry paste created by mashing, pounding & grinding an array of ingredients with a stone mortar & pestle to form an aromatic, thick & very pungent-tasting paste (also known as* nám prík gaang*)*

krêu·ang gaang pèt เครื่องแกงเผ็ด *red krêu·ang gaang made with dried red chillies*

L

lahng sàht ลางสาด *oval-shaped fruit with white fragrant flesh, grown in Utaradit Province*

làhp ลาบ *spicy minced meat salad made by tossing minced meat, poultry or freshwater fish with lime juice, fish sauce, chillies, fresh mint leaves, chopped spring onion & pulverised rice (North-Eastern Thailand)*

làhp bèt ลาบเป็ด *duck* làhp*, an Ubon Ratchathani speciality*

làhp bèt daang ลาบเป็ดแดง *red duck* làhp *which uses duck blood as part of the sauce*

làhp bèt kŏw ลาบเป็ดขาว *white duck* làhp

làhp sùk ลาบสุก *cooked* làhp

lam yai ลำไย *longan fruit (also known as 'dragon's eyes')*

lá-mút ละมุด *sapodilla fruit*

lôok chín ปลาh ลูกชิ้นปลา *fish balls*

lôok grà-wahn ลูกกระวาน *cardamom*

lôok súp ลูกชุบ *'dipped fruit' – sweets made of soybean paste, sugar & coconut milk that are boiled, coloured & fashioned to look exactly like miniature fruits & vegetables*

M

maang dah nah แมงดานา *a water beetle found in rice fields & used in certain kinds of* nám prík *(chilli & shrimp paste)*

má-dà-bà มะตะบะ *roti (unleavened bread) stuffed with chopped chicken or beef with onions & spices*

má-fai มะไฟ *rambeh fruit*

má-gòrk มะกอก *astringent-flavoured fruit resembling a small mango (also known in English as ambarella, Thai olive or Otaheite apple)*

má-gròot มะกรูด *kaffir lime – small citrus fruit with a bumpy & wrinkled skin*

má-kǎhm มะขาม *tamarind*

má-kǎhm ɓèe-ak มะขามเปียก *the flesh & seeds of the husked tamarind fruit pressed into red-brown clumps*

má-kěu·a มะเขือ *eggplant • aubergine*

má-kěu·a ɓró มะเขือเปราะ *'Thai eggplant' – popular curry ingredient*

má-kěu·a poo·ang มะเขือพวง *'pea eggplant' – popular curry ingredient, especially for* gaang kêe-o-wǎhn

má-kěu·a têt มะเขือเทศ *tomatoes*

má-kěu·a yow มะเขือยาว *'long eggplant' – also called Japanese eggplant or Oriental eggplant in English*

má-lá-gor มะละกอ *paw paw • papaya*

má-môo·ang มะม่วง *mango*

man fà-ràng มันฝรั่ง *potato*

man fà-ràng tôrt มันฝรั่งทอด *fried potatoes*

man gâa·ou มันแกว *yam root • jicama*

má-now มะนาว *lime*

má-práw มะพร้าว *coconut*

má-prow òrn มะพร้าวอ่อน *young green coconut*

mèe pan หมี่พัน *spicy mix of thin rice noodles, bean sprouts & coriander leaf rolled in rice paper – a speciality of Laplae district in Utaradit Province*

mèe·ang kam เมี่ยงคำ *do-it-yourself appetiser in which chunks of ginger, shallot, peanuts, coconut flakes, lime & dried shrimp are wrapped in wild tea leaves or lettuce*

mét má-môo·ang hím-má-pahn tôrt เม็ดมะม่วงหิมพานต์ทอด *fried cashew nuts*

môo หมู *pork*

môo bîng หมูปิ้ง *toasted pork*

môo daang หมูแดง *strips of bright red barbecued pork*

môo sǎhm chán หมูสามชั้น *'three level pork' – cuts that include meat, fat & skin*

môo sàp หมูสับ *ground pork*

môo yâhng หมูย่าง *grilled strips of pork eaten with spicy dipping sauces*

môo yor หมูยอ *sausage resembling a large German frankfurter*

N

nǎam แหนม *pickled pork*

nǎam môr แหนมหม้อ *'pot sausage' – sausage made of ground pork, pork rind & cooked sticky rice & fermented in a clay pot with salt, garlic & chilli (North Thailand)*

nòr mái หน่อไม้ *bamboo shoots*

nòr mái ฺbrèe·o หน่อไม้เปรี้ยว *pickled bamboo shoots*

nám ฺblah น้ำปลา *fish sauce – thin, clear, amber sauce made from fermented anchovies & used to season Thai dishes*

nám ฺboo น้ำปู *condiment made by pounding small field crabs into a paste*

& then cooking the paste in water until it becomes a slightly sticky black liquid (North Thailand)

nám đôw น้ำเต้า *bottle gourd*

nám jàa·ou น้ำแจ่ว *Isaan dipping sauce for chicken, made by pounding dried red chilli flakes with shallots, shrimp paste & a little tamarind juice to make a thick jam-like sauce (also known as* jàa·ou)

nám jim น้ำจิ้ม *dipping sauces*

nám jim ah-hǎhn tá-lair น้ำจิ้มอาหารทะเล *seafood dipping sauce, with* prík nám ฺblah *with the addition of minced garlic, lime juice & sugar*

nám jim gài น้ำจิ้มไก่ *chicken dipping sauce – a mixture of dried red chilli flakes, honey (or sugar) & rice vinegar*

nám kǎang gót น้ำแข็งกด *frozen sweets made with ice, sugar, & a little fruit juice*

nám kǎang sài น้ำแข็งใส *desserts with ice*

nám keu·i น้ำเคย *sauce consisting of palm sugar, raw cane sugar, shrimp paste, fish sauce, salt, black pepper, shallots, galangal, kaffir lime leaves & lemongrass (South Thailand)*

nám mêe·ang น้ำเมี่ยง *ginger, shallot, shrimp paste, fish sauce & honey dip eaten with* mèe·ang kam

nám ngée·o น้ำเงี้ยว *sweet & spicy topping for* kà-nǒm jeen *(North Thailand)*

nám ôy น้ำอ้อย *raw, lumpy cane sugar • sugar cane juice*

nám prík น้ำพริก *thick chilli- & shrimp-paste dip usually eaten with fresh raw or steamed vegetables • a spicy-sweet peanut sauce used as a topping for* kà-nǒm jeen *(rice noodles)*

nám prík chée fáh น้ำพริกชี้ฟ้า *dipping sauce featuring dried chilli, garlic oil, salt & sugar –often cooked briefly to blend all the flavours & darken the chilli (North-East Thailand)* nám prík đah daang น้ำพริกตาแดง *'red eye chilli dip'* – very dry & hot dip

nám prík gaang น้ำพริกแกง *see* krêu·ang gaang

nám prík gà·bi น้ำพริกกะปิ nám prík *made with shrimp paste & fresh* prík kêe nöo *('mouse-dropping' chilli), usually eaten with mackerel that has been steamed & fried, or with fried serpent-headed fish (Central Thailand)*

nám prík kàh น้ำพริกข่า *chilli dip made with galangal – often served with steamed or roasted fresh mushrooms (North Thailand)*

nám prík maang dah น้ำพริกแมงดา *water beetle chilli paste*

nám prík nám boo น้ำพริกน้ำปู *chilli paste made with* nám boo, *shallots, garlic & dried chillies (North Thailand)*

nám prík nùm น้ำพริกหนุ่ม *young chilli-paste dip made of fresh green chillies & roasted eggplant (North Thailand)*

nám prík órng น้ำพริกอ่อง *chilli paste made by pounding dried red chillies, ground pork, tomatoes, lemongrass & various herbs, then cooking them till the pork is done (North Thailand)*

nám prík pǒw น้ำพริกเผา *thick paste made with dried chillies roasted together with* gà·bi *& then mortar-blended with fish sauce & a little sugar or honey (often eaten with* gài yâhng)

nám prík sée·rah-chah น้ำพริกศรีราชา *thick, orange, salty-sweet-sour-spicy bottled chilli sauce from Si Racha (south-east of Bangkok on the Gulf of Thailand)*

nám see-éw น้ำซีอิ๊ว *soy sauce*

nám sôm prík น้ำส้มพริก *sliced green chillies in vinegar*

nám yah น้ำยา *standard curry topping for* kà-nŏm jeen, *made of Chinese key* (grà-chai) *& ground or pounded fish*

nám-đahn béep น้ำตาลปีบ *soft, light palm sugar paste – the most raw form of palm sugar*

néu·a เนื้อ *beef*

néu·a đǔn เนื้อตุ๋น *steamed beef soup generally featuring a broth darkened by soy sauce & spices such as cinnamon, star anise or Chinese five-spice*

néu·a nám đòk เนื้อน้ำตก *'waterfall beef' – sliced barbecued beef in a savoury dressing of lime juice, ground chilli & other seasonings*

néu·a pàt nám-man hǒy เนื้อผัดน้ำมันหอย *beef stir-fried in oyster sauce*

nóy-nàh น้อยหน่า *custard apple*

P

pàt tai ผัดไทย *abbreviation of* gǒo·ay đěe·o pàt tai

prík bòn พริกป่น *dried red chilli (usually* nám prík chée fáh), *flaked or ground to a near powder*

prík chée·fáh พริกชี้ฟ้า *'sky-pointing chilli' – also known as spur chilli, Thai Chilli and Japanese chilli*

prík kêe nǒo พริกขี้หนู *'mouse-dropping chilli' – the hottest chilli in Thailand (also known as bird's-eye chilli)*

prík nám blah พริกน้ำปลา *standard condiment of sliced fresh red & green* prík kêe nǒo *(chilli) floating in fish sauce*

prík nám sôm พริกน้ำส้ม *young* prík yòo·ak *pickled in vinegar – a condiment popular with noodle dishes & Chinese food*

prík tai พริกไทย *black pepper (also known in English as Thai pepper)*

prík wǎhn พริกหวาน *'sweet pepper' – green bell pepper*

prík yòo·ak พริกหยวก *banana-stalk chilli – a large chilli usually cooked or pickled*

R

ráht nâh ราดหน้า *shortened name for any gŏo-ay-đĕe-o ráht nâh dish, frequently used when ordering*

ráht prík ราดพริก *prík smothered in garlic, chillies & onions – usually accompanies freshwater fish*

roh-đee โรตี *fried, round & flat wheat bread descended from the Indian paratha*

roh-đee gaang โรตีแกง *roti dipped in the sauce from a chicken, beef or crab curry*

roh-đee glŏo-ay โรตีกล้วย *roti stuffed with fresh banana chunks or banana paste & sprinkled with sugar & condensed milk*

roh-đee kài โรตีไข่ *roti cooked with egg*

S

sah-lah-bow ซาลาเปา *steamed buns filled with stewed pork or sweet bean paste*

see-éw dam ซีอิ๊วดำ *'black soy' – heavy, dark soy sauce*

see-éw kŏw ซีอิ๊วขาว *'white soy' – light soy sauce*

sow nám ขาวน้ำ *sauce of pineapple, dried shrimp, coconut, ginger & garlic used as a topping for kà-nŏm jeen*

súp kà-nŭn ซุปขนุน *jackfruit soup with kôw kôo-a bòn, lime juice & chilli (North-East Thailand)*

súp má-kĕu-a ซุปมะเขือ *eggplant soup with kôw kôo-a bòn, lime juice & chilli (North-East Thailand)*

súp nòr mái ซุปหน่อไม้ *'bamboo shoot soup' – boiled or pickled bamboo shoots with kôw kôo-a bòn, lime juice & chilli (North-East Thailand)*

sà-đé สะเต๊ะ *satay – short skewers of barbecued beef, pork or chicken that are served with a spicy peanut sauce*

sà-đé mŏo สะเต๊ะหมู *satay pork*

sà-đé néu-a สะเต๊ะเนื้อ *satay beef*

sà-đor สะดอ *a large, flat bean with a bitter taste (South Thailand)*

sâi ŏo-a ไส้อั่ว *sausage made from a curry paste of dried chillies, garlic, shallots, lemongrass & kaffir lime peel, blended with ground pork, stuffed into pork intestines & then fried to produce a spicy red sausage (North Thailand)*

săng-kà-yăh สังขยา *custard*

săng-kà-yăh fák torng สังขยาฟักทอง *custard-filled pumpkin*

sàp-bà-rót สับปะรด *pineapple*

sà-rá-nàa สะระแหน่ *mint*

sên lék เส้นเล็ก *thick rice noodles*

sên mèe เส้นหมี่ *thin rice noodles*

sên yài เส้นใหญ่ *medium-thick rice noodles*

sôm đam ส้มตำ *tart & spicy salad usually made with green paw paw (also known as đam-sôm or đam màhk hùng)*

sôm kĕe-o wăhn ส้มเขียวหวาน *mandarin orange*

sôm oh ส้มโอ *pomelo – popular in Northern Thailand*

sù-gêe สุกี้ *common abbreviation of sù-gêe-yah-gêe (see below)*

sù-gêe-yah-gêe สุกี้ยากี้ *'hotpot' – peculiar Thai-Japanese hybrid involving a large stationary pot sitting on a gas burner to which diners add raw ingredients such as mung bean noodles, egg, water spinach & cabbage (Central Thailand)*

T

tòo-a bòn ถั่วป่น *ground peanuts*

tòo-a fák yow ถั่วฝักยาว *long bean, yard bean, green bean, or cow pea*

tòo-a lan-đow ถั่วลันเตา *snow peas*

tòo-a lĕu-ang ถั่วเหลือง *soya bean*

tòo-a ngôrk ถั่วงอก *mung bean sprouts*

tòo-a poo ถั่วพู *angle bean – long green, bean-like vegetable which when cut into cross sections produces a four-pointed star*

tòo-a tòrt ถั่วทอด *fried peanuts*

táp-tim gròrp ทับทิมกรอบ *'crisp rubies' – red-dyed chunks of fresh water chestnut in a white syrup of sweetened & slightly salted coconut milk*

tôrt man ฺblah ทอดมันปลา *fried fish cake*

tôrt man gûng ทอดมันกุ้ง *fried shrimp cake*

W

wún-sên วุ้นเส้น *noodles made from mung bean & water to produce an almost clear noodle (sometimes called 'cellophane noodles', 'glass noodles' or 'bean thread noodles' in English)*

Y

yam ยำ *hot & tangy salad containing a blast of lime, chilli, fresh herbs & a choice of seafood, roast vegetables, noodles or meats*

yam ฺblah dùk foo ยำปลาดุกฟู *hot & tangy salad with fried shredded catfish, chillies, peanuts & a mango dressing*

yam ฺblah mèuk ยำปลาหมึก *hot & tangy salad with squid*

yam gài ยำไก่ *hot & tangy salad with chicken & mint*

yam hèt hŏrm ยำเห็ดหอม *hot & tangy salad made with fresh shiitake mushrooms*

yam kài dow ยำไข่ดาว *hot & tangy salad with fried eggs*

yam má-kĕu-a yow ยำมะเขือยาว *hot & tangy salad created by tossing a fresh-roasted or grilled long eggplant with shrimp, lime juice, ground pork, coriander leaf, chillies, garlic & fish sauce*

yam má-môo-ang ยำมะม่วง *hot & tangy salad with mango*

yam mét má-môo-ang hĭm-má-pahn ยำเม็ดมะม่วงหิมพานต์ *spicy cashew nut salad*

yam néu-a ยำเนื้อ *hot & tangy salad with grilled beef*

yam prík chée fáh ยำพริกชี้ฟ้า *hot & tangy salad featuring* nám prík chée fáh

yam săhm gròrp ยำสามกรอบ *fried squid, fish bladder & cashew nuts mixed with* nám ฺblah, *sugar, lime juice & chilli*

yam sôm oh ยำส้มโอ *hot & tangy salad made with pomelo (Chiang Mai)*

yam tòo-a poo ยำถั่วพู *hot & tangy salad with angle beans*

yam wún-sên ยำวุ้นเส้น *spicy salad made with warm mung bean noodles tossed with lime juice, fresh sliced* prík kêe nŏo, *mushrooms, dried or fresh shrimp, ground pork, coriander leaf, lime juice & fresh sliced chillies*

yêe-ràh ยี่หร่า *cumin*

> *Mátsàman kaeng kâew taa*
> *hǎwm yîiràa rót ráwn raeng*
> *chaai dai dâi kleun kaeng*
> *raeng yàak hâi fài fǎn hǎa*

'Mátsàman, curried by the jewel of my eye,
fragrant with cumin, hot strong taste
Any man who has tasted her curry,
cannot help but dream of her.'

King Rama II composed this verse during his 1809-24 reign and virtually every Thai child memorises it in school. The poem reinforces a traditional Thai claim that a woman who prepares a good curry is *sanèh plaai ja-wàk* (the charm at the end of the ladle). The fact that a Buddhist king wrote an ode associated with a dish that translates as 'Muslim curry' shows how Indian style curries have long been accepted into the cosmopolitan culture of Thai cuisine. Here's how you can make it yourself:

Khrêuang kaeng mátsàman (Muslim curry paste)

- 5   peeled shallots
- 4   green peppercorns
- 2   whole heads of garlic, peeled
- 2   cloves
- 1   teaspoon minced fresh galangal
- 1   teaspoon salt
- 1   tablespoon coriander seeds
- 1   teaspoon cumin seeds
- 1   teaspoon shrimp paste
- 1   tablespoon sliced fresh lemongrass
- 4   dried red prík chée-fáh (sky-pointing chillies)

Slice open the dried chillies, shake out and discard the seeds and soak the chillies in warm water until they are soft and flexible.

Roast all other ingredients, one at a time, in a dry skillet or wok until aromatic and only slightly browned. Grind and mash all ingredients together in a mortar until a thick red-brown paste is formed. Adds lyrical relish to chicken, beef or vegetable dishes.

Help!	ช่วยด้วย	chôo·ay dôo·ay
Stop!	หยุด	yùt
Go away!	ไปให้พ้น	ɓai hâi pón
Thief!	ขโมย	kà-moy
Fire!	ไฟไหม้	fai mâi
Watch out!	ระวัง	rá-wang

It's an emergency.
เป็นเหตุฉุกเฉิน
ɓen hèt chùk-chĕun

Call a doctor!
ตามหมอหน่อย
ɗahm mŏr nòy

Call an ambulance!
ตามรถพยาบาล
ɗahm rót pá-yah-bahn

I'm ill.
ผม/ดิฉัน ป่วย
pŏm/dì-chăn ɓòo·ay m/f

My friend is ill.
เพื่อนของ ผม/ดิฉัน ป่วย
pêu·an kŏrng pŏm/dì-chăn
ɓòo·ay m/f

My child is ill.
ลูกของ ผม/ดิฉัน ป่วย
lôok kŏrng pŏm/dì-chăn
ɓòo·ay m/f

My friend has had an overdose.
เพื่อนของฉันเสพยาเกินขนาด
pêu·an kŏrng chăn sèp yah
geun kà-nàht

He/She is having a/an …	เขากำลัง …	kŏw gam-lang …
allergic reaction	เกิดอาการแพ้	gèut ah-gahn páa
asthma attack	เป็นโรคหืด	ɓen rôhk hèut
baby	คลอดลูก	klôrt lôok
epileptic fit	เป็นลมบ้าหมู	ɓen lom bâh mŏo
heart attack	หัวใจวาย	hŏo·a jai wai

signs

แผนกฉุกเฉิน pà-nàak chùk-chĕun	**Emergency Department**
โรงพยาบาล rohng pá-yah-bahn	**Hospital**
ตำรวจ đam-ròo·at	**Police**
สถานีตำรวจ sà-tăh-nee đam-ròo·at	**Police Station**

Could you please help?
ช่วยได้ไหม

chôo·ay dâi măi

Can I use your phone?
ใช้โทรศัพท์ของคุณได้ไหม

chái toh-rá-sàp kŏrng kun
dâi măi

I'm lost.
ผม/ดิฉัน หลงทาง

pŏm/dì-chăn lŏng tahng m/f

Where are the toilets?
ห้องน้ำอยู่ที่ไหน

hôrng nám yòo têe năi

police

ตำรวจ

Where's the police station?
สถานีตำรวจอยู่ที่ไหน

sà-tăh-nee đam-ròo·at yòo
têe năi

Please telephone the Tourist Police.
ขอโทรตามตำรวจ
นักท่องเที่ยว

kŏr toh đahm đam-ròo·at
nák tôrng têe·o

I want to report an offence.
ผม/ดิฉัน อยากจะแจ้งความ   pŏm/dì-chăn yàhk jà jâang
kwahm m/f

I've been ...   ผม/ดิฉัน โดน ...   pŏm/dì-chăn
dohn ... m/f

He/She has been ...   เขาโดน ...   kŏw dohn ...
    assaulted   ทำร้ายร่างกาย   tam rái râhng gai
    drugged   วางยา   wahng yah
    raped   ข่มขืน   kòm kĕun
    robbed   ขโมย   kà-moy

It was him/her.
เป็นคนนั้น   ben kon nán

My ... was stolen.   ... ของ ผม/ดิฉัน   ... kŏrng pŏm dì-chăn
ถูกขโมย   tòok kà-moy m/f
    backpack   เป้   bâir
    handbag   กระเป๋าหิ้ว   grà-bŏw hêw
    jewellery   เพชรพลอย   pét ploy
    money   เงิน   ngeun
    wallet   กระเป๋าเงิน   grà-bŏw ngeun

I've lost my ...   ผม/ดิฉัน ทำ ...   pŏm/dì-chăn tam ...
หายแล้ว   hăi láa·ou m/f
    bags   กระเป๋า   grà-bŏw
    credit card   บัตรเครดิต   bàt krair-dìt
    papers   เอกสาร   èk-gà-săhn
    passport   หนังสือเดินทาง   năng-sĕu deun
tahng
    travellers cheques   เช็คเดินทาง   chék deun tahng

I have insurance.
ผม/ดิฉัน มีประกันอยู่   pŏm/dì-chăn mee brà-gan
yòo m/f

You're charged with ...	คุณโดนจับ ข้อหา ...	kun dohn jàp kôr hăh ...
He/She is charged with ...	เขาโดนจับ ข้อหา ...	kŏw dohn jàp kôr hăh ...
assault	ทำร้ายร่างกาย	tam rái râhng gai
disturbing the peace	ก่อกวนความสงบ	gòr goo·an kwahm sà-ngòp
drug trafficking	การค้ายาเสพติด	gahn káh yah sèp đit
littering	การทิ้งขยะ ไม่เป็นที่	gahn tíng kà-yà mâi ben têe
not having a visa	การไม่มีวีซ่า	gahn mâi mee wee-sâh
overstaying your visa	การอยู่เกินกำหนด ของวีซ่า	gahn yòo geun gam-nòt kŏrng wee-sâh
possession (of illegal substances)	การมีของผิด กฎหมายในความ ครอบครอง	gahn mee kŏrng pìt gòt-măi nai kwahm krôrp krorng
rape	การข่มขืน	gahn kòm kĕun
shoplifting	การขโมยของ ในร้าน	gahn kà-moy kŏrng nai ráhn
theft	การขโมย	gahn kà-moy
It's a ... fine.	เป็นการหมาย ปรับโทษ ...	ben gahn măi ràp tôht ...
littering	การทิ้งขยะ ไม่เป็นที่	gahn tíng kà-yà mâi ben têe
parking	การจอดรถผิด กฎหมาย	gahn jòrt rót pìt gòt-măi
speeding	การขับรถเร็ว เกินกำหนด	gahn kàp rót re·ou geun gam-nòt

What am I accused of?
ผม/ดิฉัน ถูกปรับข้อหาอะไร
pŏm/dì-chăn tòok bràp kôr hăh à-rai m/f

I'm sorry.
ขอโทษ
kŏr tôht

I (don't) understand.
(ไม่) เข้าใจ
(mâi) kôw jai

I didn't realise I was doing anything wrong.
ผม/ดิฉัน ไม่รู้เลยว่าทำ อะไรผิด
pŏm/dì-chăn mâi róo leu·i wâh tam à-rai pìt m/f

I didn't do it.
ผม/ดิฉัน ไม่ได้ทำ
pŏm/dì-chăn mâi dâi tam m/f

Can I pay an on-the-spot fine?
เสียค่าปรับที่นี่ได้ไหม
sĕe·a kâh bràp tée née dâi măi

I want to contact my embassy.
ผม/ดิฉัน อยากจะติดต่อสถานทูต
pŏm/dì-chăn yàhk jà đìt đòr sà-tăhn tôot m/f

I want to contact my consulate.
ผม/ดิฉัน อยากจะติดต่อกงศุล
pŏm/dì-chăn yàhk jà đìt đòr gong-sŭn m/f

Can I make a phone call?
โทรได้ไหม
toh dâi măi

Can I have a lawyer who speaks English?
ขอทนายความที่พูดภาษา อังกฤษได้ไหม
kŏr tá-nai kwahm tée pôot pah-săh ang-grìt dâi măi

I didn't know that was in there.
ผม/ดิฉัน ไม่รู้ก่อนเลยว่ามีสิ่ง นั้นอยู่ข้างในนั้น
pŏm/dì-chăn mâi róo gòrn leu·i wâh mee sìng nán yòo kâhng nai nán m/f

That's not mine.
นั่นไม่ใช่ของ ผม/ดิฉัน
nân mâi châi kŏrng pŏm/dì-chăn m/f

This drug is for personal use.
ยานี้สำหรับการใช้ส่วนตัว
yah née săm-ràp gahn chái sòo·an đoo·a

I have a prescription for this drug.

ผม/ดิฉัน มีใบสั่งจาก	pŏm/dì-chăn mee bai sàng
แพทย์สำหรับยานี้	jàhk pâat săm-ràp yah née m/f

What's the	กำหนดโทษเท่าไร	gam-nòt tôht tôw-
penalty for	สำหรับการมี ... ในค	rai săm-ràp gahn
possession of ...?	วามครอบครอง	mee ... nai kwahm
		krôrp krorng
amphetamines	ยาบ้า	yah bâh
heroin	เฮโรอีน	hair-roh-een
marijuana	กัญชา	gan-chah
opium	ยาฝิ่น	yah fin
psilocybin	เห็ดขี้ควาย	hèt kêe kwai
mushrooms		

Where's the nearest ...?	... ที่ใกล้เคียง อยู่ที่ไหน	... têe glâi kee·ang yòo têe năi
(night) chemist	ร้านขายยา (กลางคืน)	ráhn kăi yah (glahng keun)
dentist	หมอฟัน	mŏr fan
doctor	หมอ	mŏr
emergency department	แผนกฉุกเฉิน	pà·nàak chùk-chĕun
health centre (in rural areas)	สถานือนามัย	sà-tăh-nee à-nah-mai
hospital	โรงพยาบาล	rohng pá-yah-bahn
medical centre	คลินิก	klí-ník
optometrist	หมอตรวจสายตา	mŏr đròo·at săi đah

I need a doctor (who speaks English).
ผม/ดิฉัน ต้องการหมอ
(ที่พูดภาษาอังกฤษได้)
pŏm/dì-chăn đôrng gahn
mŏr (têe pôot pah-săh ang-
grìt dâi) m/f

Could I see a female doctor?
พบกับคุณหมอผู้หญิงได้ไหม
póp gàp kun mŏr pôo yĭng
dâi măi

Could the doctor come here?
หมอมาที่นี่ได้ไหม
mŏr mah têe née dâi măi

Is there an after-hours emergency number?
มีเบอร์โทรสำหรับเหตุฉุก
เฉินนอกเวลาทำงานไหม
mee beu toh săm-ràp hèt
chùk-chĕun nôrk wair-lah
tam ngahn măi

I've run out of my medication.
ยาของ ผม/ดิฉัน หมดแล้ว
yah kŏrng pŏm/dì-chăn
mòt láa·ou m/f

What's the problem?
เป็นอะไร ครับ/ค่ะ · ben à-rai kráp/kâ **m/f**

Where does it hurt?
เจ็บตรง ไหน · jèp đrong nǎi

Do you have a temperature?
มีไข้ไหม · mee kâi mǎi

How long have you been like this?
เป็นอย่าง นี้มานานเท่าไร · ben yàhng née mah nahn tôw-rai

Have you had this before?
เคยเป็นไหม · keu·i ben mǎi

Have you had unprotected sex?
ได้มีเพศสัมพันธ์โดยขาด · dâi mee pêt sǎm-pan doy kàht
การป้อง กันหรือเปล่า · gahn bôrng gan rěu blòw

Are you using contraception?
คุณใช้การคุมกำเนิด · kun chái gahn kum gam-
ไหม · nèut mǎi

Have you drunk unpurified water?
ได้ดื่มน้ำที่ไม่สะอาดไหม · dâi dèum nám têe mâi sà-àht mǎi

Are you allergic to anything?
คุณแพ้อะไร ไหม · kun páa à-rai mǎi

Are you on medication?
คุณกำลังใช้ยาอยู่ไหม · kun gam-lang chái yah yòo mǎi

How long are you travelling for?
คุณจะเดินทางนานเท่าไร · kun jà deun tahng nahn tôw-rai

You need to be admitted to hospital.
คุณจะต้อง เข้าโรง ง · kun jà đôrng kôw rohng
พยาบาล · pá-yah-bahn

You should have it checked when you go home.
เมื่อกลับถึงบ้านควรจะ · mêu·a glàp těung bâhn koo·an
ไปตรวจ · jà bai đròo·at

You should return home for treatment.
คุณควรจะกลับบ้าน · kun koo·an jà glàp bâhn
เพื่อรักษา · pêu·a rák-sǎh

You're a hypochondriac.
คุณอุปาทาน · kun ùp-bah-tahn

This is my usual medicine.
นี้คืออยาที่ ใช้ประจำ   née keu yah têe chái bràa-jam

I don't want a blood transfusion.
ไม่ต้อง การถ่ายโลหิต   mâi đôrng gahn tài loh-hìt

Please use a new syringe.
ขอใช้เข็มใหม่   kŏr chái kĕm mài

I have my own syringe.
ฉันมีเข็มของตัวเอง   chăn mee kĕm kŏrng đoo·a eng

Can I have a receipt for my insurance?
ขอใบเสร็จด้วยสำหรับ   kŏr bai sèt dôo·ay săm-ràp
บริษัทประกัน   bor-rí-sàt bràa-gan

I've been vaccinated against …	ผม/ดิฉันได้ฉีดป้อง กันโรค … แล้ว	pŏm/dì-chăn dâi chèet bôrng gan rôhk … láa·ou m/f
He/She has been vaccinated against …	เขาฉีดป้อง กันโรค … แล้ว	kŏw chèet bôrng gan rôhk … láa·ou
Japanese B encephalitis	ไข้สมอง งอักเสบ	kâi sà-mŏrng àk-sèp
rabies	พิษสุนัขบ้า	pít sù-nák bâh
tetanus	บาดทะยัก	bàht tá-yák
typhoid	ไข้รากสาดน้อย	kâi râhk sàht nóy
hepatitis A/B/C	ตับอักเสบ เอ/บี/ซี	đàp àk-sèp air/ bee/see

symptoms & conditions

อาการป่วย

I'm sick.
ผม/ดิฉัน ป่วย   pŏm/dì-chăn bòo·ay m/f

My friend/child is sick.
เพื่อน/ลูกของ ผม/   pêu·an/lôok kŏrng pŏm/
ดิฉัน ป่วย   dì-chăn bòo·ay m/f

It hurts here.
เจ็บตรง นี้   jèp đrong née

I've been ...	ผม/ดิฉัน ...	pŏm/dì-chăn ... **m/f**
He/She has been ...	เขา ...	kŏw ...
injured	บาดเจ็บ	bàht jèp
vomiting	อาเจียน	ah-jee·an

I feel ...	ผม/ดิฉันรู้สึก ...	pŏm/dì-chăn róo-sèuk ... **m/f**
anxious	กังวลใจ	gang-won jai
better	ดีขึ้น	dee kêun
depressed	กลุ้มใจ	glûm jai
dizzy	เวียนหัว	wee·an hŏo·a
hot and cold	หนาว ๆ ร้อน ๆ	nŏw nŏw rórn rórn
nauseous	คลื่นใส้	klêun sâi
shivery	ตัวสั่น	đoo·a sàn
strange	แปลกๆ	blàak blàak
weak	อ่อนเพลีย	òrn plee·a
worse	ทรุดลง	sút long

I have (a/an) ...	ผม/ดิฉัน ...	pŏm/dì-chăn ... **m/f**
He/She has (a/an) ...	เขา ...	kŏw ...
asthma	เป็นโรคหืด	ben rôhk hèut
constipation	เป็นท้องผูก	ben tórng pòok
cough	เป็นไอ	ben ai
dengue fever	เป็นไข้เลือดออก	ben kâi lêu·at òrk
depression	เป็นโรคกลุ้มใจ	ben rôhk glûm jai
diarrhoea	เป็นท้องร่วง	ben tórng rôo·ang
fever	เป็นไข้	ben kâi
fungal infection	ติดเชื้อรา	đìt chéu·a rah
heat exhaustion	แพ้แดด	páa dàat
heatstroke	แพ้แดด	páa dàat
intestinal worms	เป็นพยาธิ	ben pá-yâht
liver fluke	เป็นพยาธิใบไม้	ben pá-yâht bai mái
malaria	เป็นไข้มาเลเรีย	ben kâi mah-lair-ree·a
nausea	คลื่นใส้	klêun sâi
pain	ปวด	bòo·at
prickly heat	เป็นผด	ben pòt
sore throat	เจ็บคอ	jèp kor

I'm dehydrated.
ผม/ดิฉัน ขาดน้ำ · · · · · · · · · · · · pŏm/dì-chăn kàht nám **m/f**

I can't sleep.
นอนไม่หลับ · · · · · · · · · · · · · · · norn mâi làp

I think it's the medication I'm on.
คิดว่าเป็นเพราะยาที่ · · · · · · · · kít wâh Ђen pró yah têe
กำลังใช้อยู่ · · · · · · · · · · · · · · gam-lang chái yòo

women's health

สุขภาพผู้หญิง

(I think) I'm pregnant.
(ดิฉันคิดว่า) ตั้งท้องแล้ว · · · · (dì-chăn kít wâh) đâng
tórng láa·ou

I'm on the Pill.
ดิฉันกินยาคุมกำเนิดอยู่ · · · · · dì-chăn gin yah kum gam-
nèut yòo

---

the doctor may say ...

Are you using contraception?
คุณใช้การคุมกำเนิดไหม · · · · kun chái gahn kum gam-
nèut măi

Are you menstruating?
คุณเป็นระดูไหม · · · · · · · · · · · kun Ђen rá-doo măi

Are you pregnant?
คุณตั้งครรภ์หรือเปล่า · · · · · · · kun đâng kan rĕu Ђlòw

When did you last have your period?
คุณมีระดูครั้งที่แล้วเมื่อไร · · kun mee rá-doo kráng tee
láa·ou mêu·a rai

You're pregnant.
คุณตั้งครรภ์แล้ว · · · · · · · · · · kun đâng kan láa·ou

I haven't had my period for (six) weeks.

ดิฉันไม่ได้เป็นระดูมา
(หก) อาทิตย์แล้ว

dì-chǎn mâi dâi ben rá-doo
mah (hòk) ah-tít láa·ou

I've noticed a lump here.

สังเกตว่ามีก้อนเนื้ออยู่ตรงนี้

sǎng-gèt wâh mee gôrn
néu·a yòo drong née

I need ...	ดิฉันต้องการ ...	dì-chǎn đôrng gahn ...
a pregnancy test	ตรวจการตั้งท้อง	đròo·at gahn đâng tórng
contraception	การคุณกำเนิด	gahn kum gam-nèut
the morning-after pill	ยาคุมกำเนิดชนิดใช้วันหลัง	yah kum gam-nèut chá-nít chái wan lǎng

allergies

โรคภูมิแพ้

I'm allergic to ...	ผม/ดิฉัน แพ้ ...	pǒm/dì-chǎn páa ... m/f
He/She is allergic to ...	เขาแพ้ ...	kǒw páa ...
antibiotics	ยาปฏิชีวนะ	yah bà-đi-chee-wá-ná
anti-inflammatories	ยาแก้อักเสบ	yah gâa àk-sèp
aspirin	ยาแอสไพริน	yah àat-sà-pai-rin
bees	ตัวผึ้ง	đoo·a pêung
penicillin	ยาเพนนิซิลลิน	yah pen-ní-sin-lin
pollen	เกสรดอกไม้	gair-sǒrn dòrk mái
sulphur-based drugs	ยาที่ประกอบด้วยซัลเฟอร์	yah têe bràu-gòrp dôo·ay san-feu

For food-related allergies, see **vegetarian & special meals**, page 169.

parts of the body

My ... hurts.	... ของ ผม/ดิฉัน เจ็บ	... kŏrng pŏm/ dì-chăn jèp m/f
I can't move my ...	ขยับ ... ไม่ได้	kà-yàp ... mâi dâi
I have a cramp in my ...	เป็นตะคริวที่ ...	ɓen đà-krew têe ...
My ... is swollen.	... ของ ผม/ดิฉัน บวม	... kŏrng pŏm/ dì-chăn boo-am m/f

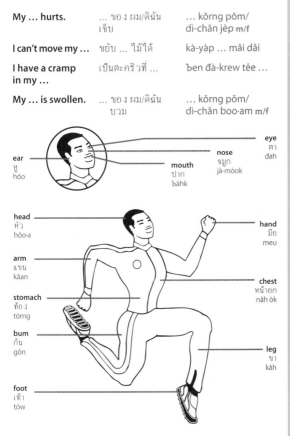

ear
หู
hŏo

eye
ตา
đah

nose
จมูก
jà-mòok

mouth
ปาก
ɓàhk

head
หัว
hŏo·a

hand
มือ
meu

arm
แขน
kăen

chest
หน้าอก
nâh òk

stomach
ท้อง
tórng

bum
ก้น
gôn

leg
ขา
kăh

foot
เท้า
tów

alternative treatments

I don't use (Western medicine).
ผม/ดิฉันไม่ใช้ (ยาตะวันตก)   pŏm/dì-chăn mâi chái (yah đà-wan đòk) **m/f**

I prefer ...
ผม/ดิฉันนิยม ...   pŏm/dì-chăn ní-yom ... **m/f**

Can I see someone
who practices ...?
พบกับหมอที่ชำนาญ
ทาง ... ได้ไหม   póp gàp mŏr têe cham-nahn tahng ... dâi măi

acupuncture	ฝังเข็ม	făng kĕm
herbal medicine	ยาสมุนไพร	yah sà-mŭn-prai
inner healing	การรักษาแบบใช้ พลังภายใน	gahn rák-săh bàap chái pá-lang pai nai
Thai massage	การนวดแผน โบราณ	gahn nôo·at păan boh-rahn
traditional Thai **medicine**	ยาพื้นเมืองของ ประเทศไทย	yah péun meu·ang kŏng bràdêt tai
naturopathy	การรักษาแบบบิ ธรรมชาต	gahn rák-săh bàap tam-má-châht
reflexology	การนวดเส้น	gahn nôo·at sên

chemist

I need something for ...
ต้องการยาสำหรับ ...   đôrng gahn yah săm-ràp ...

Do I need a prescription for ...?
ต้องมีใบสั่งยาสำหรับ ... ไหม   đôrng mee bai sàng yah săm-ràp ... măi

How many times a day?
วันละกี่ครั้ง   wan lá gèe kráng

Will it make me drowsy?
จะทำให้ ง่วงนอนไหม   jà tam hâi ngôo·ang norn măi

Twice a day ...	วันละสองครั้ง ...	wan lá sŏrng kráng ...
after meals	หลังอาหาร	lăng ah-hăhn
before meals	ก่อนอาหาร	gòrn ah-hăhn
with food	พร้อมอาหาร	prórm ah-hăhn

Have you taken this before?
เคยใช้ยาแบบนี้มาก่อนไหม
keu·i chái yah bàap née
mah gòrn măi

You must complete the course.
ต้องใช้ยาจนหมด
đôrng chái yah jon mòt

antifungal cream	ยาฆ่าเชื้อรา	yah kâh chéu·a rah
antimalarial medication	ยาป้องกันมาเลเรีย	yah bòrng gan mah-lair-ree·a
antiseptic	ยาฆ่าเชื้อ	yah kâh chéu·a
contraceptives	ยาคุมกำเนิด	yah kum gam-nèut
delousing preparation	ยาฆ่าเหา	yah kâh hŏw
diahorrea medicine	ยาระงับอาการท้องร่วง	yah rá-ngáp ah-gahn tórng rôo·ang
painkillers	ยาแก้ปวด	yah gâa bòo·at
thermometer	ปรอท	bà-ròrt
rehydration salts	เกลือแร่	gleu·a râa
water filter	กรองน้ำ	grorng nám

dentist

I have a ...	ผม/ดิฉัน ...	pŏm/dì-chăn ... m/f
broken tooth	ฟันหัก	fan hàk
cavity	ฟันผุ	fan pù
toothache	ปวดฟัน	bòo·at fan

I need (a/an) ...	ต้องการ ...	đôrng gahn ...
anaesthetic	ยาชา	yah chah
filling	อุดฟัน	ùt fan

I've lost a filling.
ที่อุดฟันหลุดไป   têe ùt fan lùt bai

My gums hurt.
เจ็บที่เหงือก   jèp têe ngèu·ak

I don't want it extracted.
ไม่อยากจะถอน   mâi yàak jà tŏrn

Ouch!
เอ๊ะ   ôw

the dentist may say ...

Open wide.
อ้าปากให้กว้าง   âh bàhk hâi gwâhng

This won't hurt a bit.
ไม่เจ็บหรอก   mâi jèp ròrk

Bite down on this.
กัดอันนี้ไว้   gàt an née wái

Don't move.
อย่าขยับ   yàh kà-yàp

Rinse!
บ้วนปาก   bôo·an bàhk

Come back, I haven't finished.
กลับมานะ ยังไม่เสร็จ   glàp mah ná, yang mâi sèt

The symbols ⓝ, ⓐ and ⓥ (indicating noun, adjective and verb) have been added for clarity where an English term could be either. Basic food terms have been included – for a more extensive list of ingredients and dishes, see the **culinary reader**.

A

abortion การทำแท้ง gahn tam táang

about เรื่อง rêu·ang

above ข้างบน kâhng bon

abroad ต่างประเทศ đàhng ʼbrà-têt

accident อุบัติเหตุ ù-bàt-đi-hèt

accommodation ที่พัก têe pák

account บัญชี ban-chee

across ข้ามจาก kâhm jàhk

activist นักประท้วง nák ʼbrà-tóo·ang

actor นักแสดง nák sà-daang

acupuncture การฝังเข็ม gahn fãng kĕm

adaptor หม้อแปลง môr ʼblaang

addiction การติด gahn đìt

address ที่อยู่ têe yòo

administration การบริหาร gahn bor-rí-hăhn

admission (price) ค่าเข้า kâh kôw

admit (let in) ให้เข้า hâi kôw

adult ผู้ใหญ่ pôo yài

advertisement การโฆษณา gahn koh-sà-nah

advice คำแนะนำ kam náa-nam

aerobics การเต้นแอโรบิก gahn đên aa-roh-bìk

aeroplane เครื่องบิน krêu·ang bin

Africa ทวีปแอฟริกา tá-wêep aa-frí-gah

after หลัง lăng

afternoon ตอนบ่าย đorn bài

(this) afternoon บ่าย (นี้) bài (née)

aftershave ครีมทาหลังโกนหนวด kreem tah lăng gohn nòo·at

again อีก èek

age อายุ ah-yú

(three days) ago (สามวัน) ที่แล้ว (săhm wan) tee láa·ou

agree (with an opinion) เห็นด้วย hĕn dôo·ay

agree (to do something) ตกลง đòk long

agriculture เกษตรกรรม gà-sèt-đà-gam

ahead ข้างหน้า kâhng nâh

AIDS โรคเอดส์ rôhk èd

air อากาศ ah-gàht

air-conditioned ปรับอากาศ ʼbràp ah-gàht

air-conditioned vehicle รถปรับอากาศ rót ʼbràp ah-gàht

air-conditioning แอร์ aa

airline สายการบิน săi gahn bin

airmail ไปรษณีย์อากาศ prai-sà-nee ah-gàht

airplane เครื่องบิน krêu·ang bin

airport สนามบิน sà-năhm bin

airport tax ภาษีสนามบิน pah-sĕe sà-năhm bin

aisle (on plane) ทางเดิน tahng deun

alarm clock นาฬิกาปลุก nah-lí-gah ʼblùk

alcohol เหล้า lôw

all ทั้งหมด táng mòt

allergy การแพ้ gahn páa

alley ซอย soy

almond เมล็ดอามันด์ má-lét ah-man

almost เกือบ gèu·ap
alone เดียว dèe·o
already แล้ว láa·ou
also ด้วย dôo·ay
altar แท่นพระ tâan prá
altitude ระดับสูง rá·dáp sŏong
always ตลอดไป đà·lòrt pai
ambassador ทูต tôot
ambulance รถพยาบาล rót pá·yah·bahn
American football ฟุตบอลอเมริกัน fút·born à·mair·rí·gan
anaemia โรคโลหิตจาง rôhk loh·hìt jahng
ancient โบราณ boh·rahn
and และ láa
angry โกรธ gròht
animal สัตว์ sàt
ankle ข้อเท้า kôr tów
another อีก (อัน) หนึ่ง èek (an) nèung
answer ⓝ คำตอบ kam đòrp
ant มด mót
antibiotics ยาปฏิชีวนะ yah pà·đi·chee·wá·ná
antinuclear ต่อต้านพลังงานนิวเคลียร์ đòr đâhn pá·lang ngahn new·klee·a
antique วัตถุโบราณ wát·tù boh·rahn
antiseptic ยาฆ่าเชื้อ yah kâh chéu·a
any ใด ๆ dai dai
apartment ห้องคอนโด hôrng korn·doh
appendix (body) ไส้ติ่ง sâi đìng
apple แอปเปิ้ล àap·bêun
appointment การนัด gahn nát
April เดือนเมษายน deu·an mair·săh·yon
archaeological ทางโบราณคดี tahng boh·rahn·ná·ká·dee
architect สถาปนิก sà·tăh·bà·ník
architecture สถาปัตยกรรม sà·tăh·bàt·đà·yá·gam
argue ทะเลาะ tá·ló
arm แขน kăan
aromatherapy การบำบัดโรคด้วยกลิ่นหอม gahn bam·bàt rôhk dôo·ay glìn hŏrm
arrest ⓥ จับกุม jàp gum
arrivals ขาเข้า kăh kôw

arrive มาถึง mah tĕung
art ศิลปะ sĭn·lá·bà
art gallery ห้องแสดงภาพ hôrng sà·daang pâhp
artist ศิลปิน sĭn·lá·bin
ashtray ที่เขี่ยบุหรี่ têe kèe·a bù·rèe
Asia ทวีปเอเชีย tá·wêep air·see·a
ask (a question) ถาม tăhm
ask (for something) ขอ kŏr
asparagus หน่อไม้ฝรั่ง nòr mái fà·ràng
aspirin ยาแอสไพริน yah àat·sà·pai·rin
asthma โรคหืด rôhk hèut
at ที่ têe
athletics การกรีฑา gahn gree·tah
atmosphere บรรยากาศ ban·yah·gàht
aubergine มะเขือ má·kĕu·a
August เดือนสิงหาคม deu·an sĭng·hăh·kom
aunt (father's younger sister) อา ah
aunt (older sister of either parent) ป้า bâh
Australia ประเทศออสเตรเลีย brà·têt or·sà·đrair·lee·a
Australian Rules Football ฟุตบอลออสเตรเลีย fút·born or·sà·đrair·lee·a
automated teller machine (ATM) ตู้เอทีเอ็ม đôo air tee em
autumn หน้าใบไม้ร่วง nâh bai mái rôo·ang
avenue ถนน tà·nŏn
awful แย่ yâa

B

B&W (film) (ฟิล์ม) ขาวดำ (fim) kŏw dam
baby ทารก tah·rók
baby food อาหารทารก ah·hăhn tah·rók
baby powder แป้งทารก bâang tah·rók
babysitter พี่เลี้ยงเด็ก pêe lée·ang dèk
back (body) หลัง lăng
back (position) หลัง lăng
back street ซอย soy

backpack เป้ báir

bacon หมูเบคอน mŏo bair-korn

bad เลว le-ou

bag ถุง tŭng

baggage กระเป๋า grà-bŏw

baggage allowance พิกัดน้ำหนักกระเป๋า
pí-gàt nám nàk grà-bŏw

baggage claim ที่รับกระเป๋า têe ráp
grà-bŏw

bakery ที่ขายขนมปัง têe kǎi kà-nŏm bang

balance (account) รายยอด ขนบัญชี rai yôrt
(ban-chee)

balcony ระเบียง rá-bee-ang

ball ลูกบอล lôok born

ballet การเต้นบัลเล่ต์ gahn đên ban-lâir

bamboo ไม้ไผ่ mái pài

bamboo shoot(s) หน่อไม้ nòr mái

banana กล้วย glôo-ay

band (music) วงดนตรี wong don-đree

bandage ผ้าพันแผล pâh pan plǎa

Band-Aid ปลาสเตอร์ blah-sà-đeu

bandit โจร john

Bangkok กรุงเทพ grung têp

bank ธนาคาร tá-nah-kahn

bank account บัญชีธนาคาร ban-chee
tá-nah-kahn

banknote ธนบัตร tá-ná-bàt

bar บาร์ bah

bar work งานในบาร์ ngahn nai bah

barber ช่างตัดผม chàhng đàt pŏm

baseball เบสบอล bèt-born

basket ตะกร้า đà-grâh

basketball บาสเกตบอล bah-sà-gèt-born

bath อาบน้ำ àhng nám

bathing suit ชุดว่ายน้ำ chút wâi nám

bathroom ห้องน้ำ hôrng nám

batik ปาเต๊ะ bah-dé

battery (flashlight) ถ่านไฟฉาย tàhn
fai chǎi

battery (car) หม้อแบตเตอรี่ môr bàat-
đeu-rêe

bay อ่าว òw

be เป็น ben

beach ชายหาด chai hàht

beach volleyball วอลเลย์บอลชายหาด
worn-lair-born chai hàht

bean ถั่ว tòo-a

beansprout ถั่วงอก tòo-a ngôrk

beautiful สวย sŏo-ay

beauty salon ร้านเสริมสวย ráhn sěum
sŏo-ay

because เพราะว่า pró-wâh

bed เตียง đee-ang

bed linen ผ้าปูที่นอน pâh boo têe norn

bedding เครื่องนอน krêu-ang norn

bedroom ห้องนอน hôrng norn

bee ผึ้ง pêung

beef เนื้อวัว néu-a woo-a

beer เบียร์ bee-a

before ก่อน gòrn

beggar คนขอทาน kon kŏr tahn

behind ข้างหลัง kâhng lǎng

Belgium ประเทศเบลเยียม prà-têt
ben-yee-am

bell ระฆัง rá-kang

bell tower หอระฆัง hŏr rá-kang

below ข้างล่าง kâhng lâhng

beneath ใต้ đâi

beside ข้างๆ kâhng kâhng

best ดีที่สุด dee têe sùt

bet การพนัน gahn pá-nan

better ดีกว่า dee gwàh

between ระหว่าง rá-wàhng

bible คัมภีร์ไบเบิ้ล kam-pee bai-bêun

bicycle รถจักรยาน rót jàk-gà-yahn

big ใหญ่ yài

bigger ใหญ่กว่า yài gwàh

biggest ใหญ่ที่สุด yài tée sùt

bike chain โซ่จักรยาน sôh jàk-gà-yahn

bike lock กุญแจจักรยาน gun-jaa
jàk-gà-yahn

bike path ทางจักรยาน tahng jàk-gà-yahn

bike repair shop ร้านซ่อมจักรยาน ráhn
sôrm jàk-gà-yahn

bill (restaurant etc) บิลค์ bin

binoculars กล้อง สอง ตา glôrng sŏrng đah

bird นก nók

birth certificate ใบเกิด bai gèut

birthday วันเกิด wan gèut

biscuit ขนม kà-nŏm

bite (dog) กัด gàt

bite (insect) ต่อย đòy

bitter ขม kŏm

black สีดำ sĕe dam

bladder ถุง ปัสสาวะ tŭng Bàt-săh-wá

blanket ผ้าห่ม pâh hòm

blind ตาบอด đah bòrt

blister รอยพอง roy porng

blocked ตัน đan

blood เลือด lêu-at

blood group กลุ่มเลือด glum lêu-at

blood pressure ความดันโลหิต kwahm
    dan loh-hìt

blood test การเจาะเลือด gahn jò lêu-at

blue (light) สีฟ้า sĕe fáh

blue (dark) สีน้ำเงิน sĕe nám ngeun

board (a plane, ship etc) ขึ้น kêun

boarding house บ้านพัก bâhn pák

boarding pass บัตรขึ้นเครื่องบิน bàt kêun
    krêu-ang bin

boat เรือ reu-a

body (living) ร่างกาย râhng gai

body (dead) ศพ sòp

boiled ต้ม đôm

boiled rice ข้าวต้ม kôw đôm

bone กระดูก grà-dòok

book หนังสือ năng-sĕu

book (make a booking) จอง jorng

book shop ร้านขายหนังสือ ráhn kăi
    năng-sĕu

booked out จอง เต็มแล้ว jorng đem láa-ou

boot(s) รองเท้าบู๊ท rorng tów bút

border ชายแดน chai daan

bored เบื่อ bèu-a

boring น่าเบื่อ nâh bèu-a

borrow ยืม yeum

botanic garden สวนพฤกษาชาติ sŏo-an
    préuk-săh-châht

both ทั้งสอง táng sŏrng

bottle ขวด kòo-at

bottle opener เครื่อง เปิดขวด krêu-ang
    bèut kòo-at

bottle shop ร้านขายเหล้า ráhn kăi lôw

bottom (body) ก้น gôn

bottom (position) ข้าง ล่าง kâhng lâhng

bowl ชาม chahm

box กล่อง glòrng

boxer นักมวย nák moo-ay

boxer shorts กางเกงขาสั้น gahng-geng
    kăh sân

boxing การต่อยมวย gahn đòy moo-ay

boy เด็กชาย dèk chai

boyfriend แฟนผู้ชาย faan pôo chai

bra ยกทรง yók song

bracelet กำไลมือ gam-lai meu

brakes เบรก brèk

brandy บรั่นดี bà-ràn-dee

brave กล้าหาญ glâh-hăhn

bread ขนมปัง kà-nŏm Bang

bread rolls ขนมปังก้อน kà-nŏm Bang górn

break หัก hàk

break down เสีย sĕe-a

breakfast อาหารเช้า ah-hăhn chów

breast (body) เต้านม đôw nom

breast (poultry) อก òk

breathe หายใจ hăi jai

bribe ⓝ สินบน sĭn bon

bridge สะพาน sà-pahn

briefcase กระเป๋าเอกสาร grà-Bŏw
    èk-gà-săhn

brilliant ยอด yôrt

bring เอามา ow mah

brochure แผ่นพับโฆษณา pàan páp
    koh-sà-nah

broken หักแล้ว hàk láa-ou

broken down เสียแล้ว sĕe-a láa-ou

bronchitis โรคหลอดลมอักเสบ rôhk lòrt
    lom àk-sèp

brooch เข็มกลัด kěm glàt
brother (older) พี่ชาย pêe chai
brother (younger) น้องชาย nórng chai
brown สีน้ำตาล sěe nám đahn
bruise ⑪ รอยช้ำ roy chám
brush แปรง braang
bucket ถัง tǎng
Buddha พระพุทธเจ้า prá-pút-tá-jôw
Buddhism พุทธศาสนา pút-tá-sàht-sà-năh
Buddhist ชาวพุทธ chow pút
budget งบประมาณ ngóp bràm-mahn
buffet อาหารตั้งโต๊ะ ah-hǎhn đâng đó
bug (insect) แมลง má-laang
build ก่อสร้าง gòr sâhng
builder ช่างก่อสร้าง châhng gòr sâhng
building ตึก đèuk
bumbag กระเป๋าคาดเอว grà-bǒw kâht e-ou
bungalow บังกะโล bang-gà-loh
Burma ประเทศพม่า bràh-têt pá-mâh
burn ⑪ แผลไฟไหม้ plǎa fai mâi
burn ⑨ เผา pǒw
burnt ไหม้แล้ว mâi láa-ou
bus (city) รถเมล์ rót mair
bus (intercity) รถบัส rót bàt
bus station สถานีขนส่ง sà-thǎh-nee kǒn sòng
bus stop ป้ายรถเมล์ bâi rót mair
business ธุรกิจ tú-rá-git
business class ชั้นธุรกิจ chán tú-rá-git
business person นักธุรกิจ nák tú-rá-git
business trip เดินทางธุรกิจ deun tahng tú-rá-git
busy ยุ่ง yûng
but แต่ว่า đàa wâh
butcher คนขายเนื้อ kon kǎi néu-a
butcher's shop ร้านขายเนื้อ ráhn kǎi néu-a
butter เนย neu-i
butterfly ผีเสื้อ pěe sêu-a
button กระดุม grà-dum
buy ซื้อ séu

C

cabbage ผักกะหล่ำปลี pàk gà-làm-blee
café ร้านกาแฟ ráhn gah-faa
cake ขนม kà-nǒm
cake shop ร้านขายขนม ráhn kǎi kà-nǒm
calculator เครื่องคิดเลข krêu-ang kít lêk
calendar ปฏิทิน bà-đi-tin
call เรียก rêe-ak
Cambodia ประเทศเขมร bràh-têt kà-měn
camera กล้องถ่ายรูป glông tài rôop
camera shop ร้านขายกล้องถ่ายรูป ráhn kǎi glông tài rôop
camp พักแรม pák raam
camp site ที่ปักเต็นท์ têe bàk đén
camping ground ค่ายพักแรม kâi pák raam
camping store ร้านขายของแคมป์ปิ้ง ráhn kǎi kǒrng kaam-bîng
can (be able) เป็น ben
can (have permission) ได้ dâi
can (tin) กระป๋อง grà-bǒrng
can opener เครื่องเปิดกระป๋อง krêu-ang bèut grà-bǒrng
Canada ประเทศแคนาดา bràh-têt kaa-nah-dah
cancel ยกเลิก yók lêuk
cancer โรคมะเร็ง rôhk má-reng
candle เทียนไข tee-an kǎi
candy ลูกอม lôok om
cantaloupe แตงแคนตาลูป đaang kaan-đah-lôop
capital (provincial) อำเภอเมือง am-peu meu-ang
capsicum พริกหวาน prík wǎhn
car รถยนต์ rót yon
car hire การเช่ารถ gahn chôw rót
car owner's title ใบกรรมสิทธิ์รถยนต์ bai gam-má-sìt rót yon
car park ที่จอดรถ têe jòrt rót
car registration ทะเบียนรถ tá-bee-an rót
caravan รถคาราวาน rót kah-rah-wahn

cardiac arrest โรคหัวใจวาย rôhk hŏo·a jai wai

cards (playing) ไพ่ pâi

care (look after) ดูแล doo laa

Careful! ระวัง rá-wang

carpenter ช่างไม้ châhng mái

carrot แครอท kaa-rôrt

carry (in arms) อุ้ม ûm

carry (on back) แบก bàak

carry (in hands) หิ้ว hêw

carry (in pocket) พก pók

carry (over shoulder) สะพาย sà-pai

carton กล่อง glòrng

cash เงินสด ngeun sòt

cash (a cheque) แลก lâak

cash register เครื่องเก็บเงิน krêu·ang gèp ngeun

cashew มะม่วงหิมพานต์ má-môo·ang hĭm-má-pahn

cashier แคชเชียร์ kaa-chee·a

casino กาสิโน gah-sì-noh

cassette ม้วนเทป móo·an tép

castle ปราสาท bràh-sàht

casual work งานชั่วคราว ngahn chôo·a krow

cat แมว maa·ou

cathedral โบสถ์ bòht

Catholic คริสตัง krít-sà-đang

cauliflower ดอกกะหล่ำ dòrk gà-làm

cave ถ้ำ tâm

CD ซีดี see-dee

celebration การฉลอง gahn chà-lŏrng

cemetery สุสาน sù-săhn

cent เซ็นต์ sen

centimetre เซ็นติเมตร sen-đì-mét

centre ศูนย์กลาง sŏon glahng

ceramics กระเบื้อง grà-bêu·ang

cereal ซีเรียล see-ree·an

certificate ใบประกาศ bai brà·gàht

chain โซ่ sôh

chair เก้าอี้ gôw·êe

championships การแข่งขัน gahn kàang kăn

chance (opportunity) โอกาส oh-gàht

change ⓟ การเปลี่ยนแปลง gahn plèe·an plaang

change (coins) เงินปลีก ngeun blèek

change ⓥ เปลี่ยนแปลง blèe·an blaang

change (money) แลก lâak

changing room (in shop) ห้องเปลี่ยนเสื้อ hôrng blèe·an sêu·a

charming มีเสน่ห์ mee sà-nàir

chat up เกี้ยว gêe·o

cheap ถูก tòok

cheat คนขี้โกง kon kêe gohng

check (banking) เช็ค chék

check (bill) บิลล์ bin

check ⓥ ตรวจ đròo·at

check-in (desk) เช็คอิน chék in

checkpoint ด่านตรวจ dàhn đròo·at

cheese เนยแข็ง neu·i kăang

chef พ่อครัว pôr kroo·a

chemist ร้านขายยา ráhn kăi yah

chemist (pharmacist) เภสัชกร pair-sàt-chá-gorn

cheque (banking) เช็ค chék

cheque (bill) บิลล์ bin

cherry ลูกเชอรี่ lôok cheu-rêe

chess หมากรุก màhk rúk

chess board กระดานหมากรุก grà-dahn màhk rúk

chest (body) หน้าอก nâh òk

chestnut ลูกเกาลัด lôok gow-lát

chewing gum หมากฝรั่ง màhk fà-ràng

chicken ไก่ gài

chicken pox อีสุกอีใส ee-sùk-ee-săi

chickpea ถั่วเขียว tòo·a kĕe·o

child เด็ก dèk

child seat ที่นั่งเฉพาะเด็ก têe nâng chà-pó dèk

childminding การดูแลเด็ก gahn doo laa dèk

children เด็กๆ dèk dèk
chilli พริก prík
chilli sauce น้ำพริก nám prík
China ประเทศจีน ‖rà-têt jeen
Chinese จีน jeen
chiropractor หมอดัดสันหลัง mŏr dàt
   săn lăng
chocolate ชอกโกเลต chórk-goh-lét
choose เลือก lêu-ak
chopping board เขียง kĕe-ang
chopsticks ไม้ตะเกียบ mái đà-gèe-ap
Christian ชาวคริสต์ chow krít
Christian name ชื่อ chêu
Christmas คริสต์มาส krít-mâht
Christmas Day วันคริสต์มาส
   wan krít-màht
church โบสถ์ bòht
cigar ซิการ์ ‖ù-rèe sí-gâh
cigarette บุหรี่ ‖ù-rèe
cigarette lighter ไฟแช็ก fai cháak
cinema โรงหนัง rohng năng
circus ละครสัตว์ lá-korn sàt
citizenship สัญชาติ săn-châht
city เมือง meu-ang
city centre ใจกลางเมือง jai glahng
   meu-ang
civil rights สิทธิประชาชน sìt-tí prà-chah-
   chon
human rights สิทธิมนุษยชน sìt-tí má-nút-
   sà-yá-chon
class (category) ประเภท ‖rà-pêt
class system ระบบแบ่งชั้น rá-bòp bàang
   chán
clean ⓐ สะอาด sà-àht
clean ⓥ ทำสะอาด tam sà-àht
cleaning การทำสะอาด gahn tam sà-àht
client ลูกค้า lôok káh
cliff หน้าผา nâh păh
climb ปีน ‖een
cloakroom ห้องเก็บเสื้อ hórng gèp sêu-a
clock นาฬิกา nah-lí-gah
close ⓥ ปิด ‖it

close ⓐ ใกล้ glâi
closed ปิดแล้ว ‖it láa-ou
clothesline ราวตากผ้า row đàhk păh
clothing เสื้อผ้า sêu-a păh
clothing store ร้านขายเสื้อผ้า ráhn kăi
   sêu-a păh
cloud เมฆ mêk
cloudy ฟ้าหลุ้ม fáh klúm
clutch (car) คลัตช์ klát
coach (bus) รถทัวร์ rót too-a
coast ฝั่งทะเล fàng tá-lair
coat เสื้อคลุม sêu-a klum
cocaine โคเคน koh-ken
cockroach แมลงสาบ má-laang sàhp
cocktail ค็อกเทล kórk-ten
cocoa โกโก้ goh-gôh
coconut มะพร้าว má-prów
coconut juice น้ำมะพร้าว nám má-prów
coconut milk กะทิ gà-tí
coffee กาแฟ gah-faa
coins เหรียญ rĕe-an
cold (virus) หวัด wàt
cold เย็น yen
cold (feeling) หนาว nŏw
colleague เพื่อนงาน pêu-an ngahn
collect call โทรเก็บปลายทาง toh gèp
   ‖lai tahng
college วิทยาลัย wít-tá-yah-lai
colour สี sĕe
comb หวี wĕe
come มา mah
comedy ละครตลก lá-korn đà-lòk
comfortable สบาย sà-bai
commission ค่าธรรมเนียม kâh tam-nee-am
communications (profession) การสื่อสาร
   gahn sèu săhn
communion (Christian ceremony)
   ศีลมหาสนิท sĕen-má-hăh-sà-nìt
communist คอมมิวนิสต์ korm-mew-nít
companion เพื่อน pêu-an
company บริษัท bor-rí-sàt
compass เข็มทิศ kĕm tít

complain ร้องทุกข์ rórng túk

complaint คำร้องทุกข์ kam rórng túk

complementary (free) แถม tăam

computer คอมพิวเตอร์ korm-pew-đeu

computer game เกมส์คอมพิวเตอร์ gem korm-pew-đeu

concert การแสดง gahn sà-daang

concussion มันสมอง มกระ ทบกระเทือน man sà-mŏrng grà-tóp grà-teu-an

conditioner (hair) ยานวดผม yah nôo-at pŏm

condom ถุงยางอนามัย tŭng yahng à-nah-mai

conference การประชุม gahn bra-chum

confession การสารภาพผิด gahn săh-rá-pâhp pit

confirm (a booking) ยืนยัน yeun yan

congratulations ขอแสดงความยินดี kŏr sà-daang kwahm yin dee

conjunctivitis โรคตาแดง rohk đah daang

connection ข้อต่อ kôr đòr

connection (transport) การต่อ gahn đòr

conservative หัวเก่า hŏo-a gòw

constipation ท้องผูก tórng pòok

consulate กงสุล gong-sŭn

contact lens solution น้ำยาล้าง เลนส์สัมผัส nám yah láhng len săm-pàt

contact lenses เลนส์สัมผัส len săm-pàt

contraceptives (pills) ยาคุมกำเนิด yah kum gam-nèut

contraceptives (condoms) ถุงยางอนามัย tŭng yahng à-nah-mai

contract ใบสัญญา bai săn-yah

convenience store ร้านขายของราคาถูก ráhn kăi kŏrng cham

convent คอนแวนต์ korn-waan

cook ⓝ คนครัว kon kroo-a

cook ⓥ ทำอาหาร tam ah-hăhn

cookie ขนมคุกกี้ kà-nŏm gúk-gêe

cooking การทำอาหาร gahn tam ah-hăhn

cool เย็น yen

corkscrew เหล็กไขจุกขวด lèk kăi jùk kòo-at

corn ข้าวโพด kôw pôht

corner มุม mum

cornflakes คอร์นแฟล็กซ์ korn-flèk

corrupt ทุจริต tú-jà-rit

cost มีราคา mee rah-kah

cotton ฝ้าย fâi

cotton balls สำลี săm-lee

cotton buds ไม้สำลี mái săm-lee

cough ไอ ai

cough medicine ยาแก้ไอ yah gâa ai

count นับ náp

counter (at bar) โต๊ะบิ๊ก đó gân

country ประเทศ bra-têt

countryside ชนบท chon-ná-bot

coupon คูปอง koo-borng

court (legal) ศาล săhn

court (tennis) สนาม sà-năhm

cousin ลูกพี่ลูกน้อง lôok pêe lôok nórng

cover charge ค่าผ่านประตู kâh pàhn bra-đoo

cow วัว woo-a

crab ปู boo

cracker ขนมปังกรอบ kà-nŏm bang gròrp

crafts หัตถกรรม hàt-tà-gam

crash ⓝ ชน chon

crazy บ้า bâh

crèche ที่เลี้ยงเด็ก têe fâhk lée-ang dèk

credit เครดิต crair-dit

credit card บัตรเครดิต bàt crair-dit

crocodile จระเข้ jà-rá-kâir

crop พืชผล pêut pŏn

cross (religious) ไม้กางเขน mái gahng kĕn

crowded แออัด aa àt

cucumber แตงกวา đaang gwah

cup ถ้วย tôo-ay

cupboard ตู้ đôo

currency exchange การแลกเงิน gahn lâak ngeun

current (electricity) กระแสไฟฟ้า grà-săa fai fáh

current affairs ข่าวบ้านเมือง ง kòw báhn
  meu-ang
curry แก ง gaang
custard apple น้อยหน่า nóy nàh
custom ประเพณี ฿rà-pair-nee
customs ศุลกากร sǔn-lá-gah-gorn
cut ⓥ ตัด ฿àt
cutlery ช้อนส้อม chórn sôrm
CV ประ วัติการทำ งาน ฿rà-wàt gahn tam
  ngahn
cycle ⓥ ปั่นจักรยาน ฿àn jàk-gà-yahn
cycling การปั่นจักรยาน gahn ฿àn
  jàk-gà-yahn
cyclist คนปั่นรถจักรยาน kon ฿àn rót
  jàk-gà-yahn
cystitis ตกขาว ฿òk kõw

D

dad พ่อ pôr
daily รายวัน rai wan
dance ⓥ เต้นรำ ฿èn ram
dancing การเต้นรำ gahn ฿èn ram
dangerous อันตราย an-฿à-rai
dark มืด mêut
dark (of colour) แก่ gàa
date (a person) นัดพบ nát póp
date (appointment) การนัด gahn nát
date (day) วันที่ wan têe
date (fruit) ลูกอินทผลัม lôok in-tá-pà-lam
date of birth วันที่เกิด wan têe gèut
daughter ลูกสาว lôok sõw
dawn อรุณ à-run
day วัน wan
day after tomorrow (the) วันมะรืน wan
  má-reun
day before yesterday (the) เมื่อวานซืน
  mêu-a wahn seun
dead ตายแล้ว ฿ai láa-ou
deaf หูหนวก hõo nòo-ak
deal (cards) แจก jàak
December เดือนธันวาคม deu-an
  tan-wah-kom

decide ตัดสินใจ ฿àt sĭn jai
deep ลึก léuk
deforestation การทำลายป่า gahn tam
  lai bàh
degrees (temperature) อ งศา ong-sãh
delay การเสียเวลา gahn sẽe-a wair-lah
deliver ส่ง sòng
democracy ประชาธิปไตย ฿rà-chah-tí-
  ฿à-฿ai
demonstration การเดินขบวน gahn deun
  kà-boo-an
Denmark ประเทศเดนมาร์ก ฿rà-têt
  den-màhk
dental floss เชือกสีฟัน chêu-ak sĕe fan
dentist หมอฟัน mõr fan
deodorant ยาดับกลิ่นตัว yah ฿àp glìn
  ฿oo-a
depart (leave) ออกเดินทา ง òrk deun
  tahng
department store สรรพสินค้า sàp-pá-
  sĭn-káh
departure ขาออก kãh òrk
departure gate ประตูขาออก ฿rà-฿oo
  kãh òrk
deposit เงินมัดจำ ngeun mát jam
derailleur ที่เปลี่ยนเกียร์ têe ฿lèe-an
  gee-a
descendent ญาติ yâht
desert ทะเลทราย tá-lair sai
design แบบ ฿àap
dessert ขอ งหวาน kõrng wãhn
destination จุดหมายปลายทา ง jùt mãi
  ฿lai tahng
details รายละเอียด rai lá-èe-at
diabetes โรคเบาหวาน rôhk bow wãhn
dial tone สัญญาณโทรศัพท์ sãn-yahn
  toh-rá-sàp
diaper ผ้าอ้อม pâh ôrm
diaphragm (body) กะบั งลม gà-bang lom
diarrhoea ท้อ งเสีย tórng sẽe-a
diary บันทึกราย วัน ban-téuk rai wan
dice ลูกเต๋า lôok ฿õw

dictionary พจนานุกรม pót-jà-nah-nú-grom
die ตาย đai
diet อาหารพิเศษ ah-hǎhn pí-sèt
different ต่าง กัน đàhng gan
different from ต่าง จาก đàhng jàhk
difficult ยาก yâhk
dining car ตู้รับประทานอาหาร đôo ráp
  bra-tahn ah-hǎhn
dinner อาหารมื้อเย็น ah-hǎhn méu yen
direct ทางตรง tahng đrong
direct-dial โทรทางตรง đoh tahng đrong
direction ทิศทาง tít tahng
director (film) ผู้กำกับ pôo gam-gàp
director (company) กรรมการผู้จัดการ
  gam-má-gahn pôo jàt gahn
dirty สกปรก sòk-gà-bròk
disabled พิการ pí-gahn
disco ดิสโก้ dit-sà-goh
discount ราคาส่วนลด rah-kah sòo-an lót
discrimination การแบ่งแยก gahn bàang
  yâak
disease โรค rôhk
dish จาน jahn
disk (CD-ROM) แผ่นซีดี pàan see-dee
disk (floppy) แผ่นดิสก์ pàan dit
district เขต kèt
diving การดำน้ำ gahn dam nám
diving equipment อุปกรณ์ดำน้ำ ùp-bà-
  gorn dam nám
divorced หย่าแล้ว yàh láa-ou
dizzy เวียนหัว wee-an hǒo-a
do ทำ tam
doctor หมอ mǒr
documentary สารคดี sǎ-rá-ká-dee
dog หมา mǎh
doll ตุ๊กตา đúk-gà-đah
dollar ดอลลาร์ dorn-lah
door ประตู bra-đoo
dope (drugs) เนื้อ néu-a
double คู่ kôo
double bed เตียงคู่ đee-ang kôo
double room ห้องคู่ hôrng kôo

down ลง long
downhill ทางลง tahng long
dozen โหล lǒh
drama ละคร lá-korn
dream ฝัน fǎn
dress ⓝ กระโปรง grà-brohng
dried ตากแห้ง đàhk hâang
dried fruit ผลไม้ตากแห้ง pǒn-lá-mái
  đàhk hâang
drink ⓝ เครื่องดื่ม krêu-ang dèum
drink ⓥ ดื่ม dèum
drinking food กับแกล้ม gàp glâam
drinking water น้ำดื่ม nám dèum
drive ขับ kàp
drivers licence ใบขับขี่ bai kàp kèe
drug ยา yah
drug addiction การติดยา gahn đit yah
drug dealer ผู้ค้ายาเสพติด pôo káh yah
  sèp đit
drug trafficking การค้ายาเสพติด gahn káh
  yah sèp đit
drug user ผู้ใช้ยาเสพติด pôo chái yah
  sèp đit
drugs (illicit) ยาเสพติด yah sèp đit
drum กลอง glorng
drunk เมา mow
dry ⓐ แห้ง hâang
dry (hang out) ตากให้แห้ง đàhk hâi hâang
duck เป็ด bèt
dummy (pacifier) หัวนมเทียม hǒo-a nom
  tee-am
durian ทุเรียน tú-ree-an
DVD ดีวีดี dee-wee-dee

E

each แต่ละ đàa-lá
ear หู hǒo
early เช้า chów
earn ทำรายได้ tam rai dâi
earplugs ที่อุดหู têe ùt hǒo
earrings ตุ้มหู đûm hǒo
Earth โลก lôhk

earthquake แผ่นดินไหว pàan din wǎi

east ทิศตะวันออก tìt dà-wan òrk

Easter เทศกาลอีสเตอร์ têt-sà-gahn èet sa-đêu

easy ง่าย ngâi

eat (informal) กิน gin

eat (polite) ทาน tahn

eat (very formal) รับประทาน ráp brà-tahn

economy class ชั้นประหยัด chán brà-yàt

ecstacy (drug) ยาอี yah ee

eczema แผลเปื่อย plǎa bèu-ay

editor บรรณาธิการ ban-nah-tí-gahn

education การศึกษา gahn sèuk-sǎh

egg ไข่ kài

egg noodles บะหมี่ bà-mèe

eggplant มะเขือ má-kěu-a

election การเลือกตั้ง gahn lêu-ak đâng

electrical store ร้านขายอุปกรณ์ไฟฟ้า ráhn kǎi ùp-bà-gorn fai fáh

electricity ไฟฟ้า fai fáh

elephant ช้าง cháhng

elevator ลิฟต์ líp

email อีเมล ee-men

embarrassed อับอาย àp ai

embassy สถานทูต sà-tǎhn tôot

emergency เหตุฉุกเฉิน hèt chùk-chěrn

emotional ใจอ่อนไหว jai òrn wǎi

employee ลูกจ้าง lôok jâhng

employer นายจ้าง nai jâhng

empty ว่าง wâhng

end สิ้นสุด sîn sùt

endangered species สัตว์ใกล้จะสูญพันธุ์ sàt glâi jà sǒon pan

engaged หมั้นแล้ว mân láa-ou

engagement การหมั้น gahn mân

engine เครื่อง krêu-ang

engineer วิศวกร wít-sà-wá-gorn

engineering วิศวกรรม wít-sà-wá-gam

England ประเทศอังกฤษ brà-têt ang-grit

English อังกฤษ ang-grit

enjoy (oneself) เพลิดเพลิน plêut pleun

enough พอ por

enter เข้าไป kôw bai

entertainment guide คู่มือการบันเทิง kôo meu gahn ban-teung

entry การเข้า gahn kôw

envelope ซองจดหมาย sorng jòt-mǎi

environment สิ่งแวดล้อม sing wâat lórm

epilepsy โรคลมบ้าหมู rôhk lom bâh mǒo

equal opportunity โอกาสเท่าเทียมกัน oh-gàht tôw tee-am gan

equality ความเสมอภาค kwahm sà-měu pâhk

equipment อุปกรณ์ ùp-bà-gorn

escalator บันไดเลื่อน ban-dai lêu-an

estate agency บริษัทอสังหาริมทรัพย์ bòr-rí-sàt à-sǎng-hǎh-rí-má-sáp

euro ยูโร yú-roh

Europe ทวีปยุโรป tá-wêep yú-ròhp

evening ตอนเย็น đorn yen

every ทุก túk

everyone ทุกคน túk kon

everything ทุกสิ่ง túk sìng

exactly ตรงเป๊ะ đrong bé

example ตัวอย่าง đoo-a yàhng

excellent ยอดเยี่ยม yôrt yêe-am

excess (baggage) (น้ำหนัก) เกิน (nám nàk) geun

exchange ⓝ การแลกเปลี่ยน gahn lâak blèe-an

exchange ⓥ แลกเปลี่ยน lâak blèe-an

exchange rate อัตราการแลกเปลี่ยน àt-đrah gahn lâak blèe-an

excluded ยกเว้น yók wén

exhaust (car) ท่อไอเสีย tôr ai sěe-a

exhibition นิทรรศการ ní-tát-sà-gahn

exit ⓝ ทางออก tahng òrk

expensive แพง paang

experience ประสบการณ์ brà-sòp gahn

exploitation การเอารัดเอาเปรียบ gahn ow rát ow brèe-ap

express ด่วน dòo-an

express mail (by) ไปรษณีย์ด่วน brai-sà-nee dòo-an

extension (visa) ต่ออายุ dòr ah-yú
eye ตา đah
eye drops ยาหยอดตา yah yòrt đah
eyes ตา đah

F

fabric เนื้อผ้า néu·a pâh
face ใบหน้า bai nâh
face cloth ผ้าเช็ดหน้า pâh chét nâh
factory โรงงาน rohng ngahn
factory worker คนทำงานในโรงงาน kon tam ngahn nai rohng ngahn
fall (autumn) ฤดูใบไม้ร่วง náh bai mái rôo·ang
fall (down) ล้ม lóm
family ครอบครัว krôrp kroo·a
family name นามสกุล nahm sà·kun
famous มีชื่อเสียง mee chêu sĕe·ang
fan (machine) พัดลม pát lom
fan (sport, etc) แฟน faan
fanbelt สายพาน săi pahn
far ไกล glai
fare ค่าโดยสาร kâh doy săhn
farm ไร่นา râi nah
farmer ชาวไร่ชาวนา chow râi chow nah
fashion แฟชั่น faa-chân
fast เร็ว re·ou
fat อ้วน ôo·an
father inf พ่อ pôr
father pol บิดา bì-dah
father-in-law พ่อตา pôr đah
faucet ก๊อกน้ำ górk nám
fault (someone's) ความผิด kwahm pìt
faulty บกพร่อง a bok prôrng
fax machine เครื่องแฟกซ์ krêu·ang fâak
February เดือนกุมภาพันธ์ deu·an gum-pah-pan
feed เลี้ยงอาหาร lée·ang ah-hăhn
feel (touch) คลำ klam
feel (sense) รู้สึก róo-sèuk
feeling (physical) ความรู้สึก kwahm róo-sèuk

feelings อารมณ์ ah-rom
female หญิง yĭng
female (of animals) เพศเมีย pêt mee·a
fence รั้ว róo·a
fencing (sport) การฟันดาบ gahn fan dàhp
ferry เรือข้ามฟาก reu·a kâhm fâhk
festival งาน ngahn
fever ไข้ kâi
few น้อย nóy
fiancé(e) คู่หมั้น kôo mân
fiction เรื่องแต่ง rêu·ang đàang
fight สู้ sôo
fill เติม đeum
fillet เนื้อไม่มีก้าน néu·a mâi mee gâhn
film (cinema) ภาพยนตร์ pâhp-pá-yon
film (for camera) ฟิล์ม fim
film speed ความไวของฟิล์ม kawm wai kŏrng fim
filtered กรอง grorng
find หาเจอ hăh jeu
fine ดี dee
fine (penalty) ค่าปรับ kâh bràp
finger นิ้ว néw
finish ⓝ จุดจบ jùt jòp
finish ⓥ จบ jòp
Finland ประเทศฟินแลนด์ prà·têt fin-laan
fire ไฟ fai
fire extinguisher เครื่องดับเพลิง krêu·ang dàp pleung
firewood ฟืน feun
first ที่หนึ่ง têe nèung
first name ชื่อ chêu
first class ชั้นหนึ่ง chán nèung
first-aid kit ชุดปฐมพยาบาล chút bà·đŏm pá-yah-bahn
fish ปลา blah
fish monger คนขายปลา kon kăi plah
fish shop ร้านขายปลา ráhn kăi plah
fisherman ชาวประมง chow brà·mong
fishing การหาปลา gahn hăh plah
fishing boat เรือประมง reu·a brà·mong
flag ธง tong

flannel ผ้าขนหนู pàh kŏn nŏo
flash (camera) แฟลช flâat
flashlight ไฟฉาย fai chăi
flat แบน baan
flat (apartment) ห้องแฟลต hôrng flâat
flea หมัด màt
fleamarket ตลาดขายของเบ็ดเตล็ด đà-làht kăi kŏrng bèt đà-lèt
flight (aeroplane) เที่ยวบิน têe-o bin
floating market ตลาดน้ำ đà-làht nám
flood น้ำท่วม nám tôo-am
floor พื้น péun
floor (storey) ชั้น chán
florist คนขายดอกไม้ kon kăi dòrk mái
flour แป้ง bâang
flower ดอกไม้ dòrk mái
flu ไข้หวัด kâi wàt
fly บิน bin
foggy มีหมอก mee mòrk
follow ตาม đahm
food อาหาร ah-hăhn
food poisoning อาหารเป็นพิษ ah-hăhn ben pít
food supplies เสบียง sà-bee-ang
foot เท้า tów
football (soccer) ฟุตบอล fút-born
footpath ทางเดิน tahng deun
foreign ต่างชาติ đàhng châht
foreigner คนต่างชาติ kon đàhng châht
foreigner (Westerner) ฝรั่ง fà-ràng
forest ป่า bàh
forever ตลอดไป đà-lòrt pai
forget ลืม leum
forgive ให้อภัย hâi à-pai
fork ส้อม sôrm
fortnight ปักษ์ bàk
fortune teller หมอดู mŏr doo
foul (in football) ฟาวล์ fow
foyer ห้องโถงโรงแรม hôrng tŏhng rohng raam
fragile บอบบาง bòrp bahng
France ประเทศฝรั่งเศส brà-têt fà-ràng-sèt

free (available) ว่าง wâhng
free (gratis) ฟรี free
free (not bound) อิสระ ìt-sà-rà
freeze แช่น้ำแข็ง châa nám kăang
freezer ตู้แช่แข็ง đôo châa kăang
fresh สด sòt
Friday วันศุกร์ wan sùk
fridge ตู้เย็น đôo yen
fried ผัด pàt
fried (deep) ทอด tort
fried rice ข้าวผัด kôw pàt
friend เพื่อน pêu-an
friendly เป็นมิตร ben mít
frog กบ gòp
from จาก jàhk
frost น้ำค้างแข็ง nám káhng kăang
frozen แช่แข็ง châa kăang
fruit ผลไม้ pŏn-lá-mái
fruit juice น้ำผลไม้ nám pŏn-lá-mái
fruit picking การเก็บผลไม้ gahn gèp pŏn-lá-mái
fry ผัด pàt
fry (deep fry) ทอด tôrt
frying pan กระทะ grà-tá
full เต็ม đem
full-time เต็มเวลา đem wair-lah
fun สนุก sà-nùk
funeral งานศพ ngahn sòp
funny ตลก đà-lòk
furniture เฟอร์นิเจอร์ feu-ní-jeu
future อนาคต à-nah-kót

G

game (football) เกม gem
game (sport) เกม gem
garage อู่ซ่อมรถ òo sôrm rót
garbage ขยะ kà-yà
garbage can ถังขยะ tăng kà-yà
garden สวน sŏo-an
gardener ชาวสวน chow sŏo-an
gardening การทำสวน gahn tam sŏo-an
garlic กระเทียม grà-tee-am

gas (for cooking) ก๊าซ gáht
gas (petrol) น้ำมันเบนซิน nám-man
  ben-sin
gas cartridge ถังแก๊ซ tăng gáat
gas station ปั๊มน้ำมัน ฿ám nám-man
gastroenteritis โรคกระเพาะอักเสบ rôhk
  grà-pó ak-sèp
gate (airport, etc) ประตู ฿rà-đoo
gauze ผ้าพันแผล pâh pan plăa
gay เกย์ gair
Germany ประเทศเยอรมัน
  ฿rà-têt yeu-rá-man
get เอา ow
get off (a train, etc) ลง long
ghost ผี pĕe
gift ของขวัญ kŏrng kwăn
gig การแสดง gahn sà-daang
gin เหล้าจิน lôw jin
girl สาว sŏw
girlfriend แฟนสาว faan sŏw
give ให้ hâi
glandular fever โรคเริม rôhk reum
glass (drinking) แก้ว gâa-ou
glasses (spectacles) แว่นตา wâan đah
glove(s) ถุงมือ tŭng meu
glue กาว gow
go ไป ฿ai
go out ไปข้างนอก ฿ai kâhng nôrk
go out with ไปเที่ยวกับ ฿ai têe-o gàp
go shopping ไปซื้อของ ฿ai séu kŏrng
goal เป้าหมาย ฿ôw măi
goal (football) ประตู ฿rà-đoo
goalkeeper ผู้รักษาประตู pôo rák-săh
  ฿rà-đoo
goat แพะ paa
god (general) เทวดา tair-wá-dah
God พระเจ้า prá jôw
goggles (swimming) แว่นกันน้ำ wâan
  gan nám
gold ทองคำ torng kam
Golden Triangle สามเหลี่ยมทองคำ săhm
  lèe-am torng kam

goldsmith ช่างทอง châhng torng
golf ball ลูกกอล์ฟ lôok górp
golf course สนามกอล์ฟ sà-năhm górp
good ดี dee
goodbye ลาก่อน lah gòrn
government รัฐบาล rát-tà-bahn
gram กรัม gram
grandchild หลาน lăhn
grandfather (maternal) ตา đah
grandfather (paternal) ปู่ ฿òo
grandmother (maternal) ยาย yai
grandmother (paternal) ย่า yâh
grapes องุ่น à-ngùn
grass หญ้า yáh
grass (marijuana) กัญชา gan-chah
grateful ปลื้มใจ ฿lêum jai
grave ที่ฝังศพ têe făng sòp
gray สีเทา sĕe tow
great (fantastic) ยอด yôrt
green สีเขียว sĕe kĕe-o
green pepper พริกเขียว prík kĕe-o
greengrocer คนขายผัก kon kăi pàk
grey สีเทา sĕe tow
grocery ร้านขายของชำ ráhn kăi kŏrng
  cham
grow (a plant) ปลูก ฿lòok
grow (bigger) งอก ngôrk
grow (develop) เจริญ jà-reun
g-string จีสตริง jee sà-đring
guaranteed รับประกัน ráp ฿rà-gan
guess เดา dow
guesthouse บ้านพัก bâhn pák
guide (person) ไกด์ gai
guide dog สุนัขนำทาง คนตาบอด sù-nák
  nam tahng kon đah bòrt
guidebook คู่มือนำเที่ยว kôo meu nam
  têe-o
guided tour ทัวร์ too-a
guilty มีความผิด mee kwahm pìt
guitar กีตาร์ gee-đah
gulf อ่าว òw
gum (chewing) หมากฝรั่ง màhk fà-ràng

gun ปืน beun

gym (place) ห้องออกกำลังกาย hôrng òrk gam-lang gai

gymnastics ยิมนาสติก yim-nah-sà-dtìk

gynaecologist นรีแพทย์ ná-ree-pâat

H

hair ผม pŏm

hairbrush แปรง baang

haircut การตัดผม gahn dtàt pŏm

hairdresser ช่างตัดผม châhng dtàt pŏm

halal อาหารที่จัดทำตามหลักศาสนาอิสลาม ah-hăhn têe jàt tam dăhm làk sàht-sà-năh ìt-sà-lahm

half ครึ่ง krêung

hallucination ภาพหลอน pâhp lŏrn

ham เนื้อแฮม néu·a haam

hammer ค้อน kórn

hammock เปลญวน bplair yoo·an

hand มือ meu

handbag กระเป๋าถือพาย grà-bŏw pai

handicrafts เครื่องหัตถกรรม krêu·ang hàt-tà-gam

handkerchief ผ้าเช็ดหน้า pâh chét nâh

handlebars มือจับ meu jàp

handmade ทำด้วยมือ tam dôo·ay meu

handsome รูปหล่อ rôop lòr

happy สุข sùk

harassment การเบียดเบียน gahn bèe·at bee·an

harbour อ่าว òw

hard (not soft) แข็ง kăeng

hard (difficult) ยาก yâhk

hard-boiled ต้มแข็ง dtôm kăeng

hardware store ร้านขายอุปกรณ์ก่อสร้าง ráhn kăi ùp-bà-gorn gòr sâhng

hat หมวก mòo·ak

have มี mee

have a cold เป็นหวัด ben wàt

have fun สนุก sà-nùk

hay fever โรคภูมิแพ้ rôhk poom páa

he เขา kŏw

head หัว hŏo·a

headache ปวดหัว bòo·at hŏo·a

headlights ไฟหน้ารถ fai náh rót

health สุขภาพ sù-kà-pâhp

hear ได้ยิน dâi yin

hearing aid หูเทียม hŏo tee·am

heart หัวใจ hŏo·a jai

heart attack หัวใจวาย hŏo·a jai wai

heart condition โรคหัวใจ rôhk hŏo·a jai

heat ความร้อน kwahm rórn

heated เร่าร้อน rôw rórn

heavy หนัก nàk

Hello. สวัสดีครับ/สวัสดีค่ะ sà-wàt-dee kráp/sà-wàt-dee kâ m/f

Hello. (answering telephone) ฮัลโหล han-lŏh

helmet หมวกกันน็อก mòo·ak gan nórk

help ⓝ ความช่วยเหลือ kwahm chôo·ay lĕu·a

help ⓥ ช่วย chôo·ay

Help! ช่วยด้วย chôo·ay dôo·ay

hepatitis โรคตับอักเสบ rôhk dàp àk-sèp

her ของเขา kŏrng kŏw

herb สมุนไพร sà-mŭn-prai

herbalist คนขายสมุนไพร kon kăi sà-mŭn-prai

here ที่นี่ têe née

hermit cave ถ้ำฤๅษี tâm reu-sĕe

heroin เฮโรอีน hair-roh-een

high สูง sŏong

high school โรงเรียนมัธยม rohng ree·an mát-tá-yom

highchair เก้าอี้สูง gôw-êe sŏong

highway ทางหลวง tahng lŏo·ang

hike เดินป่า deun bàh

hiking การเดินป่า gahn deun bàh

hiking boots รองเท้าเดินป่า rorng tów deun bàh

hiking route ทางเดินป่า tahng deun bàh

hill เขา kŏw

Hindu ศาสนาฮินดู sàht-sà-năh hin-doo

hire เช่า chôw

his ของ เขา kŏrng kŏw
historical ทางประวัติศาสตร์ tahng bprà-wàt-dì-sàht
history ประวัติศาสตร์ bprà-wàt-dì-sàht
hitchhike โบกรถ bòhk rót
HIV ไวรัสเอ็ชไอวี wai-rát èt ai wee
hockey ฮอกกี้ hórk-kêe
holiday (public) วันหยุด wan yùt
holidays การพักร้อน gahn pák rórn
home บ้าน bâhn
homeless ไม่มีบ้าน mâi mee bâhn
homemaker แม่บ้าน mâe bâhn
homosexual คนรักร่วมเพศ kon rák rôo-am pêt
honey น้ำผึ้ง nám pêung
honeymoon ดื่มน้ำผึ้งพระจันทร์ dèum nám pêung prá jan
horoscope ดวงโหราศาสตร์ doo-ang hŏh-rah-sàht
horse ม้า máh
horse riding การขี่ม้า gahn kèe máh
hospital โรงพยาบาล rohng pá-yaa-bahn
hospitality การรับแขก gahn ráp kàak
hostess (bar) โฮสเตส hôht-dèt
hot ร้อน rórn
hot (spicy) เผ็ด pèt
hot springs บ่อน้ำร้อน bòr nám rórn
hot water น้ำร้อน nám rórn
hotel โรงแรม rohng raam
hour ชั่วโมง chôo-a mohng
house บ้าน bâhn
housework การบ้าน gahn bâhn
how อย่างไร yàhng rai
how much เท่าไร tôw rai
hug กอด gòrt
huge มหึมา má-hèu-mah
human resources ทรัพยากรมนุษย์ sáp-pá-yah-gorn má-nút
human rights สิทธิมนุษยชน sìt-tí má-nút-sà-yá-chon
humanities มนุษยศาสตร์ má-nút-sà-yá-sàht
hundred ร้อย róy

hungry (to be) หิว hĕw
hunting การล่าสัตว์ gahn lâh sàt
hurry (in a) รีบๆ rêep rêep
hurt ทำให้เจ็บ tam hâi jèp
hurt (to be hurt) เจ็บ jèp
husband ผัว pŏo-a

I

I ผม/ดิฉัน pŏm/dì-chăn m/f
ice น้ำแข็ง nám kăang
ice cream ไอติม ai-dim
ice hockey ฮอกกี้น้ำแข็ง hórk-gêe nám kăang
ice-cream parlour ร้านขายไอศกรีม ráhn kăi ai-sà-greem
identification หลักฐาน làk tăhn
identification card (ID) บัตรประจำตัว bàt bprà-jam doo-a
idiot ปัญญาอ่อน ban-yah òrn
if ถ้า tâh
ill ป่วย bòo-ay
immigration ตรวจคนเข้าเมือง dròo-at kon kôw meu-ang
important สำคัญ săm-kan
impossible เป็นไปไม่ได้ ben bai mâi dâi
in ใน nai
in front of ต่อหน้า dòr nâh
included รวมด้วย roo-am dôo-ay
income tax ภาษี pah-sĕe
India ประเทศอินเดีย bprà-têt in-dee-a
indicator ไฟเลี้ยว fai lée-o
indigestion อาหารไม่ย่อย ah-hăhn mâi yôy
indoor ข้างใน kâhng nai
industry อุตสาหกรรม ùt-săh-hà-gam
infection การติดเชื้อ gahn dìt chéu-a
inflammation ที่อักเสบ têe àk-sèp
influenza ไข้หวัด kâi wàt
information ข้อมูล kôr moon
ingredient ส่วนประกอบ sòo-an bprà-gòrp
inject ฉีด chèet
injection การฉีด gahn chèet

injured บาดเจ็บ bàht jèp
injury ที่บาดเจ็บ têe bàht jèp
inner tube ยางใน yahng nai
innocent บริสุทธิ์ bor-rí-sút
insect repellent ยากันแมลง yah gan má-laang
inside ข้างใน kâhng nai
instructor ผู้สอน pôo sŏrn
insurance การประกัน gahn bprà-gan
interesting น่าสนใจ nâh sŏn-jai
international ระหว่างประเทศ rá-wàhng bprà-têt
Internet อินเตอร์เนต in-đeu-nét
Internet cafe ร้านอินเตอร์เนต ráhn in-đeu-nét
interpreter ล่าม lâhm
interview การสัมภาษณ์ gahn săm-pâht
invite ชวน choo-an
Ireland ประเทศไอร์แลนด์ bprà-têt ai-laan
iron (for clothes) เตารีด đow rêet
island เกาะ gò
Israel ประเทศอิสราเอล bprà-têt ìt-sa-rah-airn
it มัน man
IT เทคโนโลยีสารสนเทศ ték-noh-loh-yee săhn sŏn-têt
Italy ประเทศอิตาลี bprà-têt ì-đah-lee
itch คัน kan
itinerary รายการ rai gahn

J

jacket เสื้อกันหนาว sêu-a gan nŏw
jail คุก kúk
jam แยม yaam
January เดือนมกราคม deu-an má-gà-rah-kom
Japan ประเทศญี่ปุ่น bprà-têt yêe-bùn
jar กระปุก grà-bùk
jaw ขากรรไกร kăh gan-grai
jealous อิจฉา ìt-chăh
jeans กางเกงยีน gahng geng yeen
jeep รถจี๊ป rót jéep
jellyfish แมงกะพรุน maang gà-prun

jet lag การปรับร่างกายกับเวลาที่แตกต่าง gahn bràp rähng gai gàp wair-lah têe đàak đàhng
jewellery เครื่องเพชรพลอย krêu-ang pét ploy
Jewish ชาวยิว chow yew
job งาน ngahn
jogging การวิ่งออกกำลัง gahn wîng òrk gam-lang
joke คำตลก kam đà-lòk
journalist นักเขียนหนังสือพิมพ์ nák kĕe-an năng-sĕu pim
journey การเดินทาง gahn deun tahng
judge ผู้พิพากษา pôo pí-pâhk-săh
juice น้ำผลไม้ nám pŏn-lá-mái
July เดือนกรกฎาคม deu-an gà-rá-gà-dah-kom
jump กระโดด grà-dòht
jumper (sweater) เสื้อถัก sêu-a tàk
jumper leads สายพ่วง săi pòo-ang
June เดือนมิถุนายน deu-an mí-tù-nah-yon
jungle ป่ารก bàh rók
junk (boat) เรือสำเภา reu-a săm-pow

K

ketchup ซอสมะเขือเทศ sôrt má-kĕu-a têt
key ลูกกุญแจ lôok gun-jaa
keyboard คีย์บอร์ด kee-bòrt
kick เตะ đè
kidney ไต đai
kilo กิโล gì-loh
kilogram กิโลกรัม gì-loh-gram
kilometre กิโลเมตร gì-loh-mét
kind (nice) ใจดี jai dee
kindergarten อนุบาล à-nú-bahn
king กษัตริย์ gà-sàt
The King ในหลวง nai lŏo-ang
kiosk ร้านเล็ก ráhn lék
kiss Ⓝ&Ⓥ จูบ jòop
kitchen ครัว kroo-a
knee หัวเข่า hŏo-a kòw
knife มีด mêet

know รู้ róo

kosher อาหารที่จัดทำตามหลักศาสนา ยิว
ah-hǎhn têe jàt tam đahm làk
sàht-sà-nǎh yew

L

labourer กรรมกร gam-má-gorn

lace ถูกไม้ lôok mái

lake ทะเลสาบ tá-lair sàhp

land ประเทศ brà-têt

landlord/landlady เจ้าของ ที่ jôw kŏrng têe

lane ซอย soy

language ภาษา pah-sǎh

Laos ประเทศลาว brà-têt low

laptop คอมพิวเตอร์แล็ปท็อป korm-pew-đeu
láap-tórp

large ใหญ่ yài

last (previous) ที่แล้ว tee láaw

last (week) ที่แล้ว tee láaw

late ช้า cháh

later ทีหลัง tee lǎng

laugh หัวเราะ hǒo·a ró

launderette โรงซักรีด rohng sák rêet

laundry (clothes) ผ้าซัก pâh sák

laundry (place) ที่ซักผ้า têe sák pâh

laundry (room) ห้องซักผ้า hôrng sák pâh

law กฎหมาย gòt-mǎi

law (study, professsion) การกฎหมาย
gahn gòt-mǎi

lawyer ทะนายความ tá-nai kwahm

laxative ยาระบาย yah rá-bai

lazy ขี้เกียจ kêe gèe·at

leader ผู้นำ pôo nam

leaf ใบไม้ bai mái

learn เรียน ree·an

leather หนัง nǎng

lecturer อาจารย์ ah-jahn

ledge เชิงผา cheung pǎh

left (direction) ซ้าย sái

left luggage กระเป๋าฝาก grà-bǒw fàhk

left luggage (office) ห้องรับฝากกระเป๋า
hôrng ráp fàhk grà-bǒw

left-wing ฝ่ายซ้าย fài sái

leg ขา kǎh

legal ทางกฎหมาย tahng gòt-mǎi

legislation นิติบัญญัติ ní-đi-ban-yàt

legume ผักถั่ว pàk tòo·a

lemonade น้ำมะนาว nám má-now

lens เลนส์ len

lentil ถั่วเขียว tòo·a kěe·o

lesbian เล็สเบียน lét-bee·an

less น้อยกว่า nóy gwàh

letter (mail) จดหมาย jòt-mǎi

lettuce ผักกาดหอม pàk gàht hǒrm

liar คนโกหก kon goh-hòk

library ห้องสมุด hôrng sà-mùt

lice เหา hǒw

licence ใบอนุญาต bai à-nú-yâht

license plate number หมายเลขทะเบียน
mǎi lêk tá-bee·an

lie (recline) นอน norn

lie (tell a lie) โกหก goh-hòk

life ชีวิต chee-wít

life jacket เสื้อชูชีพ sêu·a choo chêep

lift (elevator) ลิฟท์ líp

light (electric) ไฟ fai

light (not heavy) เบา bow

light (of colour) อ่อน òrn

light bulb หลอดไฟ lòrt fai

lighter (cigarette) ไฟแช็ก fai cháak

like ชอบ chôrp

lime มะนาว má-now

linen (material) ผ้าลินิน pâh lí-nin

linen (sheets etc) ผ้าปูที่นอน pâh boo
têe norn

lip balm ขี้ผึ้งทาริมฝีปาก kêe pêung tah
rim fěe bàhk

lips ริมฝีปาก rim fěe bàhk

lipstick ลิปสติก líp-sà-đik

liquor store ร้านขายเหล้า ráhn kǎi lôw

listen (to) ฟัง fang

little (small) น้อย nóy

little (not much) นิดหน่อย nít-nòy

live (somewhere) อยู่ yòo

liver ตับ đàp

lizard (gecko) ตุ๊กแก đúk-gaa

lizard (house) จิ้งจก jîng-jòk

lizard (monitor) ตะกวด đà-gòo-at

lobster กุ้งทะเลใหญ่ gûng tá-lair yài

local ของท้องถิ่น kŏrng tórng tìn

lock ⑥ กุญแจ gun-jaa

lock ⑥ ใส่กุญแจ sài gun-jaa

locked ใส่กุญแจแล้ว sài gun-jaa láa-ou

lollies ลูกอม lôok om

long ยาว yow

look ⑥ ดู doo

look after ดูแล doo laa

look for หา hăh

lookout ที่ชมทิวทัศน์ têe chom téw-tát

loose หลวม lŏo-am

loose change เงินปลีก ngeun ∂lèek

lose ทำหาย tam hăi

lost หาย hăi

lost property office ที่แจ้งของหาย têe
  jâang kŏrng hăi

(a) lot มาก mâhk

loud ดัง dang

love ⑥ ความรัก kwahm rák

love ⑥ รัก rák

lover คู่รัก kôo rák

low ต่ำ đàm

lubricant น้ำมันหล่อลื่น nám man lòr lêun

luck โชค chôhk

lucky โชคดี chôhk dee

luggage กระเป๋า grà-∂ŏw

luggage lockers ตู้ฝากกระเป๋า đôo fàhk
  grà-∂ŏw

luggage tag บัตรกระเป๋า bàt grà-∂ŏw

lump ก้อน gôrn

lunch อาหารกลางวัน ah-hăhn glahng wan

lung ปอด ∂òrt

luxury หรูหรา rŏo răh

M

machine เครื่อง krêu-ang

mackerel ปลาทู ∂lah too

magazine หนังสือวารสาร năng sĕu
  wah-rá-săhn

magic mushrooms เห็ดขี้ควาย hèt kêe
  kwai

mail (letters) จดหมาย jòt-măi

mail (postal system) ไปรษณีย์ ∂rai-sà-nee

mailbox ตู้ไปรษณีย์ đôo ∂rai-sà-nee

main หลัก làk

main road ทางหลวง tahng lŏo-ang

make ⑥ ทำ tam

make-up เครื่องสำอาง krêu-ang săm-ahng

mammogram เอ็กซเรย์เต้านม èk-sá-rair
  đôw nom

man ผู้ชาย pôo chai

manager ผู้จัดการ pôo jàt gahn

mandarin ส้มเขียวหวาน sôm kĕe-o wăhn

mango มะม่วง má-môo-ang

manual worker กรรมกร gam-má-gorn

many เยอะ yeu

map แผนที่ păan têe

March เดือนมีนาคม deu-an mee-nah-kom

margarine เนยเทียม neu-i tee-am

marijuana กัญชา gan-chah

marital status สถานภาพการสมรส
  sà-tăhn-ná-pâhp gahn sŏm-rót

market ตลาด đà-làht

marriage การแต่งงาน gahn đàang ngahn

married แต่งงานแล้ว đàang ngahn láa-ou

marry แต่งงาน đàang ngahn

martial arts ศิลปะการต่อสู้ป้องกันตัว sĭn-lá-
  ∂à gahn đòr sôo ∂òrng gan đoo-a

Mass (Catholic) พิธีมิสซา pí-tee mít-sah

massage ⑥ นวด nôo-at

masseur/masseuse หมอนวด mŏr nôo-at

mat เสื่อ sèu-a

match (sports) เกม gem

matches (for lighting) ไม้ขีดไฟ mái
  kèet fai

material (cloth) ผ้า pâh

mattress ฟูก fôok

May เดือนพฤษภาคม deu-an préut-sà-
  pah-kom

maybe บางที bahng tee

mayonnaise น้ำราดผักสด nám râht pàk sòt

mayor นายกเทศมนตรี nah-yók têt-sà-mon-đree

me ผม/ดิฉัน pŏm/đi-chăn m/f

meal มื้ออาหาร méu ah-hăhn

measles โรคหัด rôhk hàt

meat เนื้อ néu-a

mechanic ช่างเครื่อง châhng krêu-ang

media สื่อมวลชน sèu moo-an chon

medicine (medication) ยา yah

medicine (study, profession) การแพทย์ gahn pâat

meditation การทำสมาธิ gahn tam sà-mah-tí

meditation centre ศูนย์ภาวนา sŏon pah-wá-nah

meet พบ póp

Mekong catfish ปลาบึก đlah bèuk

melon แตง đaang

member สมาชิก sà-mah-chík

menstruation ระดู rá-doo

menu รายการอาหาร rai gahn ah-hăhn

message ข้อความฝาก kôr kwahm fàhk

metal เหล็ก lèk

metre เมตร mét

metro (sky train) รถไฟฟ้า rót fai fáh

metro station สถานีรถไฟฟ้า sà-tăh-nee rót fai fáh

microwave (oven) ตู้ไมโครเวฟ đôo mai-kroh-wép

midday เที่ยงวัน têe-ang wan

midnight เที่ยงคืน têe-ang keun

migraine โรคปวดศีรษะไมเกรน rôhk bòo-at sĕe-sà mai-gren

military การทหาร gahn tá-hăhn

military service การเป็นทหาร gahn ben tá-hăhn

milk น้ำนม nám nom

millimetre มิลลิเมตร mín-lí-mét

million ล้าน láhn

mince สับ sàp

mineral water น้ำแร่ nám râa

minivan รถตู้ rót đoo

minute นาที nah-tee

mirror กระจก grà-jòk

miscarriage การแท้ง gahn táang

miss (feel absence of) คิดถึง kít tĕung

mistake ⑩ ความผิดพลาด kwahm pit plâht

mix ผสม pà-sŏm

mobile phone โทรศัพท์มือถือ toh-rá-sàp meu tĕu

modem โมเดม moh-dem

modern ทันสมัย tan sà-măi

moisturiser น้ำยาบำรุงความชื้น nám yah bam-rung kwahm chéun

monastery วัด wát

Monday วันจันทร์ wan jan

money เงิน ngeun

monk พระ prá

monk's living quarters กุฏิ gù-đì

monsoon มรสุมหน้าฝน mor-rá-sŭm nâh fŏn

month เดือน deu-an

monument อนุสาวรีย์ à-nú-săh-wá-ree

moon พระจันทร์ prá jan

moped รถมอเตอร์ไซค์ rót mor-đeu-sai

more (than before) มากขึ้น mâhk kêun

more (than something else) มากกว่า mâhk gwàh

morning ตอนเช้า đorn chów

morning sickness แพ้ท้อง páa tórng

mosque มัสยิด mát-sà-yít

mosquito ยุง yung

mosquito coil ยาจุดกันยุง yah jùt gan yung

mosquito net มุ้ง múng

mother แม่ mâa

mother pol มารดา mahn-dah

mother-in-law (mother of husband) แม่ผัว mâa pŏo-a

mother-in-law (mother of wife) แม่ยาย mâa yai

motorbike รถมอเตอร์ไซค์ rót mor-đeu-sai

motorboat เรือยนต์ reu-a yon

motorcycle รถมอเตอร์ไซค์ rót mor-đeu-sai

motorway (tollway) ทางด่วน tahng dòo-an

mountain ภูเขา poo kŏw

mountain bike จักรยานภูเขา jàk-gà-yahn poo kŏw

mountain goat เลียงผา lee-ang pǎh

mountain path ทางภูเขา tahng poo kŏw

mountain range เทือกเขา têu-ak kŏw

mountaineering การปีนเขา gahn ḃeen kŏw

mouse หนู nŏo

mouth ปาก ḃàhk

movie ภาพยนตร pâhp-pá-yon

Mr นาย nai

Mrs นาง nahng

Miss/Ms นางสาว nahng sŏw

mud โคลน klohn

mum แม่ mâa

mumps โรคคางทูม rôhk kahng toom

murder ⓝ ฆาตกรรม kâht-đà-gam

murder ⓥ ฆ่า kâh

muscle กล้ามเนื้อ glâhm néu-a

museum พิพิธภัณฑ์ pí-pít-tá-pan

mushroom เห็ด hèt

music ดนตรี don-đree

music shop ร้านดนตรี ráhn don-đree

musician นักดนตรี nák don-đree

Muslim ชาวอิสลาม chow ìt-sà-lahm

mussel หอยแมงภู่ hŏy má-laang pôo

mute ⓐ ใบ้ ḃâi

my (for a man) ของผม kŏrng pŏm m

my (for a woman) ของดิฉัน kŏrng dì-chǎn f

N

nail clippers มีดตัดเล็บ mêet đàt lép

name ชื่อ chêu

napkin ผ้าเช็ดปาก pâh chét ḃàhk

nappy ผ้าอ้อม pâh ôrm

nappy rash ผื่น pèun

national park อุทยานแห่งชาติ ùt-tá-yahn hàang châht

nationality สัญชาติ sǎn-châht

nature ธรรมชาติ tam-má-châht

naturopathy การรักษาโรคโดยใช้วิธี ธรรมชาติ gahn rák-sǎh rôhk doy chái wí-tee tam-má-châht

nausea คลื่นไส้ klêun sâi

near ใกล้ glâi

nearby ใกล้เคียง glâi kee-ang

nearest ใกล้ที่สุด glâi têe-sùt

necessary จำเป็น jam-ben

necklace สร้อยคอ sôy kor

need ต้องการ đôrng gahn

needle (sewing) เข็ม kĕm

needle (syringe) เข็มฉีด kĕm chèet

negative ฟิล์ม fim

net ตาข่าย đah-kài

Netherlands ประเทศเนเธอร์แลนด์ ḃrà-têt nair-teu-laan

network เครือข่าย kreu-a kài

never ไม่เคย mâi keu-i

new ใหม่ mài

New Year's Day วันขึ้นปีใหม่ wan kêun ḃee mài

New Year's Eve คืนวันสิ้นปี keun wan sîn ḃee

New Zealand ประเทศนิวซีแลนด์ ḃrà-têt new see-laan

news ข่าว kòw

news stand ที่ขายหนังสือพิมพ์ têe kăi năng-sĕu pim

newsagency ร้านขายหนังสือพิมพ์ ráhn kăi năng-sĕu pim

newspaper หนังสือพิมพ์ năng-sĕu pim

next (month) หน้า nâh

next to ข้างๆ kâhng kâhng

nice (food etc) อร่อย à-ròy

nickname ชื่อเล่น chêu lên

niece หลานสาว lăhn sŏw

night คืน keun

night out เที่ยวกลางคืน têe·o glahng keun

nightclub ไนต์คลับ nai kláp

no ไม่ mâi

no vacancy ไม่มีห้องว่าง mâi mee hôrng wâhng

noisy เสียงดัง sĕe·ang dang

none ไม่มี mâi mee

non-smoking ไม่สูบบุหรี่ mâi sòop bù·rèe

noodle shop ร้านก๋วยเตี๋ยว ráhn gŏo·ay đĕe·o

noodles เส้น sen

noon เที่ยง têe·ang

north ทิศเหนือ tít nĕu·a

Norway ประเทศนอร์เวย์ ḃrà·têt nor·wair

nose จมูก jà·mòok

not ไม่ mâi

notebook สมุดบันทึก sà·mùt ban·téuk

nothing ไม่มีอะไร mâi mee à·rai

November เดือนพฤศจิกายน deu·an préut·sà·ji·gah·yon

now เดี๋ยวนี้ dĕe·o née

nuclear energy พลังงานนิวเคลียร์ pá·lang ngahn new·klee·a

nuclear testing การทดลองนิวเคลียร์ gahn tót lorng new·klee·a

nuclear waste กากนิวเคลียร์ gàhk new·klee·a

number (figure) หมายเลข măi lêk

number (quantity) จำนวน jam·noo·an

numberplate ป้ายทะเบียนรถ ḃâi tá·bee·an rót

nun แม่ชี mâa chee

nurse (man) บุรุษพยาบาล bù·rùt pá·yah·bahn

nurse (woman) นางพยาบาล nahng pá·yah·bahn

nut ถั่ว tòo·a

O

oats ข้าวโอ๊ต kòw óht

ocean มหาสมุทร má·hăh sà·mùt

October เดือนตุลาคม deu·an đù·lah·kom

off (spoiled) เสีย sĕe·a

office สำนักงาน săm·nák ngahn

office worker พนักงานสำนักงาน pá·nák ngahn săm·nák ngahn

often บ่อย bòy

oil น้ำมัน nám man

oil (motor) น้ำมันเครื่อง nám man krêu·ang

old (person) แก่ gàa

old (thing) เก่า gòw

olive มะกอก má·gòrk

olive oil น้ำมันมะกอก nám·man má·gòrk

Olympic Games กีฬาโอลิมปิก gee·lah oh·lim·ḃìk

omelette ไข่เจียว kài jee·o

on บน bon

on (not off) เปิด ḃèut

on time ตรงเวลา đrong wair·lah

once ครั้งเดียว kráng dee·o

one หนึ่ง nèung

one-way (ticket) เที่ยวเดียว têe·o dee·o

onion หัวหอม hŏo·a hŏrm

only เท่านั้น tôw nán

open ⓐ & ⓥ เปิด ḃèut

opening hours เวลาเปิด wair·lah ḃèut

opera อุปรากร ùp·ḃà·rah·gorn

opera house โรงอุปรากร rohng ùp·ḃà·rah·gorn

operation (medical) การผ่าตัด gahn pàh đàt

operator (telephone) พนักงานโทรศัพท์ pá·nák ngahn toh·rá·sàp

opinion ความเห็น kwahm hĕn

opposite ตรงกันข้าม đrong gan kâhm

optometrist หมอตรวจสายตา mŏr đròo·at săi đah

or หรือ rĕu

orange ส้ม sôm

orange (colour) สีส้ม sĕe sôm

orange juice น้ำส้ม nám sôm

orchestra วงดุริยางค์ wong đù·rí·yahng

order ⓝ ระเบียบ rá·bèe·ap

order ⓥ สั่ง sàng

ordinary ธรรมดา tam-má-dah
orgasm จุดสุดยอด jùt sùt yôrt
original ดั้งเดิม dâng deum
other อื่น èun
our ของเรา kŏrng row
out of order เสีย sĕe·a
outside ข้างนอก kâhng nôrk
ovarian cyst เนื้องอกในรังไข่ néu·a ngôrk nai rang kài
ovary รังไข่ rang kài
oven ตู้อบ đôo òp
overcoat เสื้อคลุม sêu·a klum
overdose ใช้ยาเกินขนาด chái yah geun kà-nàht
overnight แรมคืน raam keun
overseas ต่างประเทศ đàhng Ъrà-têt
owe เป็นหนี้ Ъen nêe
owner เจ้าของ jôw kŏrng
oxygen ออกซิเจน òrk-sí-jen
oyster หอยนางรม hŏy nahng rom
ozone layer ชั้นโอโซนในบรรยากาศ chán oh-sohn nai ban-yah-gàht

P

pacifier (dummy) หัวนมเทียม hŏo·a nom tee·am
package ห่อ hòr
packet (general) ห่อ hòr
paddy field นา nah
padlock แม่กุญแจ mâh gun-jaa
page หน้า nâh
pain ความปวด kwahm Ъòo·at
painful เจ็บ jèp
painkiller ยาแก้ปวด yah gâa Ъòo·at
painter ช่างทาสี châhng tah sĕe
painting (a work) ภาพเขียน pâhp kĕe·an
painting (the art) การเขียนภาพ gahn kĕe·an pâhp
pair (couple) คู่ kôo
Pakistan ประเทศปากีสถาน Ъrà-têt Ъah-gee-sà-tähn
palace วัง wang

pan กระทะ grà-tá
pandanus leaf ใบเตย bai đeu·i
pants (trousers) กางเกง gahng-geng
panty liners ผ้าอนามัย pâh à-nah-mai
pantyhose ถุงน่อง tŭng nôrng
pap smear ตรวจภายใน đròo·at pai nai
paper กระดาษ grà-dàht
paperwork เอกสาร èk-gà-săhn
paraplegic คนอัมพาต kon am-má-pâht
parcel ห่อ hòr
parents พ่อแม่ pôr mâa
park สวนสาธารณะ sŏo·an săh-tah-rá-ná
park (a car) จอด jòrt
parliament รัฐสภา rát-tà-sà-pah
part (component) ชิ้นส่วน chín sòo·an
part-time ไม่เต็มเวลา mâi đem wair-lah
party (night out) งานเลี้ยง ngahn lée·ang
party (politics) พรรค pák
pass ผ่าน pàhn
passenger ผู้โดยสาร pôo doy săhn
passport หนังสือเดินทาง năng-sĕu deun tahng
passport number หมายเลขหนังสือเดินทาง măi lêk năng-sĕu deun tahng
past อดีต à-dèet
pasta เส้น sên
pastry ขนม kà-nŏm
path ทาง tahng
pay ⊙ จ่าย jài
payment การจ่าย gahn jài
pea ถั่วลันเตา tòo·a lan-dow
peace สันติภาพ săn-đi-pâhp
peak (mountain) ยอดเขา yôrt kŏw
peanut ถั่วลิสง tòo·a lí-sŏng
pear ลูกแพร์ lôok paa
pedal บันไดรถจักรยาน ban-dai rót jàk-gà-yahn
pedestrian คนเดินเท้า kon deun tów
pedicab รถสามล้อ rót săhm lór
pedicab (motorised) รถตุ๊กๆ rót đúk đúk
pen (ballpoint) ปากกา (ลูกลื่น) pàhk-gah (lôok lêun)

english-thai

P

223

pencil ดินสอ din-sŏr

penis อ วัยวะชาติ ong-ká-chàht

penknife มีดพับ mêet páp

pensioner คนกินเงินบำนาญ kon gin ngeun bam-nahn

people คน kon

pepper พริกไทย prík tai

pepper (bell) พริก prík

per (day) ต่อ đòr

per cent เปอร์เซ็นต์ ฺbeu-sen

perfect สมบูรณ์ sŏm-boon

performance งานแสดง ngahn sà-daang

perfume น้ำหอม nám hŏrm

period pain ปวดระดู ฺbòo-at rá-doo

permission อนุญาต à-nú-yâht

permit ใบอนุญาต bai à-nú-yâht

person คน kon

petition หนังสือร้องเรียน nǎng-sĕu rórng ree-an

petrol เบนซิน ben-sin

petrol station ปั๊มน้ำมัน ฺbám nám-man

pharmacist เภสัชกร pair-sàt-chá-gorn

pharmacy ร้านขายยา ráhn kǎi yah

phone book สมุดโทรศัพท์ sà-mùt toh-rá-sàp

phone box ตู้โทรศัพท์ đôo toh-rá-sàp

phone card บัตรโทรศัพท์ bàt toh-rá-sàp

photo ภาพถ่าย pâhp tài

photographer ช่างถ่ายภาพ châhng tài pâhp

photography การถ่ายภาพ gahn tài pâhp

phrasebook คู่มือสนทนา kôo meu sŏn-tá-nah

pickaxe พลั่ว plôo-a

pickles ของดอง kŏrng dorng

pickpocket ⓝ ขโมยล้วงกระเป๋า kà-moy lóo-ang grà-ฺbŏw

picnic ปิกนิก ฺbìk-ník

pie ขนมพาย kà-nŏm pai

piece ชิ้น chín

pier ท่าเรือ tâh reu-a

pig หมู mŏo

pill เม็ดยา mét yah

Pill (the) ยาคุมกำเนิด yah kum gam-nèut

pillow หมอน mŏrn

pillowcase ปลอกหมอน ฺblòrk mŏrn

pineapple สับปะรด sàp-ฺbà-rót

pink สีชมพู sĕe chom-poo

pipe (smoking) กล้องสูบยา glôrng sòop yah

pistachio พิสตาชิโอ pí-sà-đah-chí-oh

place ⓝ สถานที่ sà-tǎhn-têe

place of birth สถานที่เกิด sà-tǎhn-têe gèut

plane (aeroplane) เครื่องบิน krêu-ang bin

planet ดาวเคราะห์ dow kró

plant พืช pêut

plastic พลาสติก plah-sà-đìk

plate จาน jahn

plateau ที่ราบสูง têe râhp sŏong

platform ชานชาลา chahn chah-lah

play (cards) เล่น lên

play (guitar) เล่น lên

play (theatre) ละคร lá-korn

plug (bath) จุก jùk

plug (electricity) ปลั๊ก ฺblák

poached ทอดน้ำ tôrt nám

pocket (shirt, jacket) กระเป๋าเสื้อ grà-ฺbŏw sêu-a

pocket (pants) กระเป๋ากางเกง grà-ฺbŏw gahng geng

pocket knife มีดพับ mêet páp

poetry คำกลอน kam glorn

point ⓝ จุด jùt

point ⓥ ชี้ chée

poisonous มีพิษ mee pít

police ตำรวจ đam-ròo-at

police officer นายตำรวจ nai đam-ròo-at

police station สถานีตำรวจ sà-tǎh-nee đam-ròo-at

policy นโยบาย ná-yoh-bai

polite สุภาพ sù-pâhp

politician นักการเมือง nák gahn meu-ang

politics การเมือง gahn meu-ang

pollen เกสรดอกไม้ gair-sŏrn dòrk mái

pollution มลภาวะ mon-lá-pah-wá
pool (game) สนุกเกอร์ sà-núk-geu
pool (swimming) สระว่ายน้ำ sà wâi nám
poor จน jon
poppy ดอกฝิ่น dòrk fin
popular เป็นที่นิยม ben tée ní-yom
pork เนื้อหมู néu-a mŏo
pork sausage ไส้กรอกหมู sâi-gròrk mŏo
port (sea) ท่าเรือ tâh reu-a
porter คนขนของ kon kŏn kŏrng
positive (optimistic) มองในแง่ดี morng nai ngâa dee
positive (certain) แน่นอน nâa norn
possible เป็นไปได้ ben bai dâi
post code รหัสไปรษณีย์ rá-hàt brai-sà-nee
post office ที่ทำการไปรษณีย์ têe tam gahn brai-sà-nee
postage ค่าส่ง kâh sòng
postcard ไปรษณียบัตร brai-sà-nee-yá-bàt
poster ภาพโปสเตอร์ pâhp boh-sà-đeu
pot (ceramics) หม้อดิน môr din
pot (dope) กัญชา gan-chah
potato มันฝรั่ง man fà-ràng
pottery การปั้นหม้อ gahn bân môr
pound (money, weight) ปอนด์ born
poverty ความยากจน kwahm yâhk jon
powder แป้ง bpông
power อำนาจ am-nâht
prawn กุ้ง gûng
prayer บทสวดมนต์ bòt sòo-at mon
prayer book หนังสือสวดมนต์ năng-sĕu sòo-at mon
prefer นิยม ní-yom
pregnancy test kit ชุดตรวจการตั้งท้อง chút đròo-at gahn đâng tórng
pregnant ตั้งครรภ์ đâng kan
premenstrual tension ความเครียดก่อนเป็นระดู kwahm krêe-at gòrn ben rá-doo
prepare เตรียม đree-am
prescription ใบสั่งยา bai sàng yah
present (gift) ของขวัญ kŏrng kwăn

present (time) ปัจจุบัน bàt-jù-ban
present ⓥ มอบ môrp
president ประธานาธิบดี brà-tah-nah-tí-bà-dee
pressure ความดัน kwahm dan
pretty สวย sŏo-ay
price ราคา rah-kah
priest บาทหลวง bàht lŏo-ang
prime minister นายกรัฐมนตรี nah-yók rát-tà-mon-đree
printer (computer) เครื่องพิมพ์ krêu-ang pim
prison คุก kúk
prisoner นักโทษ nák tôht
private ส่วนตัว sòo-an đoo-a
produce ⓥ ผลิต pà-lìt
profit กำไร gam-rai
program โครงการ krohng gahn
program (computer) โปรแกรม broh-graam
projector เครื่องฉายภาพ krêu-ang chăi pâhp
promise สัญญา săn-yah
prostitute โสเภณี sŏh-pair-nee
protect ป้องกัน bôrng gan
protected (species) (สัตว์) สงวน (sàt) sà-ngŏo-an
protest ⓝ การประท้วง gahn brà-tóo-ang
protest ⓥ ประท้วง brà-tóo-ang
province จังหวัด jang-wàt
provincial capital อำเภอเมือง am-peu meu-ang
provisions เสบียง sà-bee-ang
pub (bar) ผับ pàp
public gardens สวนสาธารณะ sŏo-an săh-tah-rá-ná
public relations การประชาสัมพันธ์ gahn brà-chah săm-pan
public telephone โทรศัพท์สาธารณะ toh-rá-sàp săh-tah-rá-ná
public toilet สุขาสาธารณะ sù-kăh săh-tah-rá-ná

publishing การพิมพ์ gahn pim
pull ดึง deung
pump สูบ sòop
pumpkin ฟักทอง fák torng
puncture ยาง แตกๆ yahng đàak
pure บริสุทธิ์ bor-rí-sùt
purple สีม่วง sĕe môo·ang
purse กระเป๋าเงิน grà-bŏw ngeun
push ผลัก plùk
put on ใส่ sài

Q

quadriplegic คนอัมพาต kon am-má-pâht
qualifications คุณวุฒิ kun-ná-wút
quality คุณภาพ kun-ná-pâhp
quarantine ด่านกักโรค dàhn gàk rôhk
quarter หนึ่งส่วนสี่ nèung sòo·an sèe
queen พระราชินี prá rah-chí-nee
question คำถาม kam tăhm
queue คิว kew
quick เร็ว re·ou
quiet เงียบ ngêe·ap
quit (a job) ลาออก lah òrk
quit (a habit) เลิก lêuk

R

rabbit กระต่าย grà-đài
race (sport) การแข่ง gahn kàang
racetrack สนามแข่ง sà-năhm kàang
racing bike จักรยานแข่ง jàk-gà-yahn kàang
racism ลัทธิแบ่งผิว lát-tí bàang pĕw
racquet ไม้ตี mái đee
radiator (car) หม้อน้ำ môr nám
radio วิทยุ wít-tá-yú
radish (blank)
railway station สถานีรถไฟ sà-tăh-nee rót fai
rain ฝน fŏn
raincoat เสื้อกันฝน sêu·a gan fŏn
rainy season หน้าฝน nâh fŏn

raisin ลูกเกด lôok gèt
rally การชุมนุม gahn chum-num
rape ⓝ การข่มขืน gahn kòm kĕun
rape ⓥ ข่มขืน kòm kĕun
rare (food) ไม่สุกมาก mâi sùk mâhk
rare (uncommon) หายาก hăh yâhk
rash ผื่น pèun
rat หนู nŏo
rave งานเต้นรำ ngahn đên ram
raw ดิบ dìp
razor มีดโกน mêet gohn
razor blade ใบมีดโกน bai mêet gohn
read อ่าน àhn
reading การอ่าน gahn àhn
ready พร้อม prórm
real estate agent คนขายอสังหาริมทรัพย์ kon kăi à-săng-hăh-rim-má-sáp
realistic สมจริง sŏm jing
rear (seat etc) หลัง lăng
reason เหตุ hèt
receipt ใบเสร็จ bai sèt
recently เร็วๆ นี้ re·ou re·ou née
recommend แนะนำ náa nam
record (sound) อัดเสียง àt sĕe·ang
recording การบันทึก gahn ban-téuk
recyclable รีไซเคิลได้ ree-sai-keun dâi
recycle รีไซเคิล ree-sai-keun
red สีแดง sĕe daang
red pepper พริกแดงๆ prík daang
referee กรรมการผู้ตัดสิน gam-má-gahn pôo đàt sĭn
reference ที่อ้างอิง têe âhng ing
reflexology การนวดเส้น gahn nôo·at sên
refrigerator ตู้เย็น đôo yen
refugee คนอพยพ kon òp-pá-yop
refund เงินคืน ngeun keun
refuse ปฏิเสธ pà-đì-sèt
regional พื้นเมือง péun meu·ang
registered mail (post by)
ไปรษณีย์ลงทะเบียน Ďrai-sà-nee long tá-bee·an
rehydration salts เกลือแร่ gleu·a râa

relationship ความสัมพันธ์ kwahm săm-pan

relax ผ่อนคลาย pòrn klai

relic วัตถุโบราณ wát-tù boh-rahn

religion ศาสนา sàht-sà-năh

religious ทางศาสนา tahng sàht-sà-năh

remote ห่างไกล hàhng glai

remote control รีโมท ree-môht

rent เช่า chôw

repair ซ่อม sôrm

republic สาธารณรัฐ săh-tah-rá-ná-rát

reservation (booking) การจอง gahn jorng

rest พัก pák

restaurant ร้านอาหาร ráhn ah-hăhn

resume (CV) ประวัติการทำงาน brà-wàt
   gahn tam ngahn

retired ปลดเกษียณ blòt gà-sĕe-an

return (ticket) ไปกลับ bai glàp

return (come back) กลับ glàp

review คำวิจารณ์ kam wí-jahn

rhythm จังหวะ jang-wà

rib ซี่โครง sêe krohng

rice ข้าว kôw

rice field นา nah

rich (wealthy) รวย roo-ay

ride ⓝ เที่ยว têe-o

ride ⓥ ขี่ kèe

right (correct) ถูก tòok

right (direction) ขวา kwăh

right-wing ฝ่ายขวา fài kwăh

ring (on finger) แหวน wăan

ring (phone) โทร toh

rip-off การโกง gahn gohng

risk ⓝ ความเสี่ยง kwahm sèe-ang

risk ⓥ เสี่ยง sèe-ang

river แม่น้ำ mâa nám

road ถนน tà-nŏn

road map แผนที่ถนน păan têe tà-nŏn

rob ขโมย kà-moy

rock หิน hĭn

rock (music) ดนตรีร็อค don-dree rórk

rock climbing การปีนหน้าผา gahn been
   nâh păh

rock group วงดนตรีร็อค wong don-dree
   rórk

rockmelon แตงหวาน đaang wăhn

roll (bread) ขนมปังก้อน kà-nŏm bang
   gôrn

rollerblading การเล่นโรลเลอร์เบลด gahn
   lên rohn-leu-blèt

romantic โรแมนติค roh-maan-đik

roof หลังคา lăng-kah

room ห้อง hôrng

room number หมายเลขห้อง măi lêk hôrng

rope เชือก chêu-ak

round กลม glom

roundabout วงเวียน wong wee-an

route สาย săi

rowing การพายเรือ gahn pai reu-a

rubbish ขยะ kà-yà

rubella โรคหัดเยอรมัน rôhk hàt
   yeu-rá-man

rug เสื่อ sèu-a

rugby รักบี้ rák-bêe

ruins ซากโบราณสถาน sâhk boh-rahn-ná
   sà-tăhn

rule กฎ gòt

rum เหล้ารัม lôw ram

run ⓥ วิ่ง wîng

running การวิ่ง gahn wîng

runny nose น้ำมูกไหล nám môok lăi

S

sad เศร้า sôw

saddle อานม้า ahn máh

safe ⓝ ตู้เซฟ đôo sép

safe ⓐ ปลอดภัย blòrt pai

safe sex เพศสัมพันธ์แบบปลอดภัย pêt
   săm-pan bàap blòrt pai

saint (Christian) นักบุญ nák bun

saint (Buddhist) พระอรหันต์ prá à-rá-hăn

salad ผักสดรวม pàk sòt roo-am

salami ไส้กรอก sâi gròrk

salary เงินเดือน ngeun deu-an

sale ลดราคา lót rah-kah

sales tax ภาษีมูลค่าเพิ่ม pah-sĕe moon
  kâh pêum
salmon ปลาแซลมอน ɓlah saan-morn
salt เกลือ gleu·a
same เหมือน mĕu·an
sampan เรือสำปั้น reu·a săm-ɓân
sand ทราย sai
sandal รองเท้าแตะ rorng tów đaa
sanitary napkin ผ้าอนามัย pâh à-nah-mai
sardine ปลาซาร์ดีน ɓlah sah-deen
Saturday วันเสาร์ wan sŏw
sauce น้ำซอส nám sórt
saucepan หม้อ môr
sauna ซาวน่า sow-nâh
sausage ไส้กรอก sâi gròrk
say ว่า wâh
scalp หนังศีรษะ năng sĕe-sà
scarf ผ้าพันคอ pâh pan kor
school โรงเรียน rohng ree-an
science วิทยาศาสตร์ wít-tá-yah-sàht
scientist นักวิทยาศาสตร์ nák wít-tá-
  yah-sàht
scissors กรรไกร gan-grai
score ⓥ คะแนน ká-naan
scoreboard กระดานบอกคะแนน grà-dahn
  ɓòrk ká-naan
Scotland ประเทศสก็อตแลนด์ ɓrà-tét
  sà-gòrt-laan
scrambled กวน goo·an
sculpture (moulded) รูปปั้น rôop ɓân
sculpture (cut) รูปสลัก rôop sà-làk
sea ทะเล tá-lair
sea gypsies ชาวน้ำ chow nám
seafood อาหารทะเล ah-hăhn tá-lair
seasick เมาคลื่น mow klêun
seaside ริมทะเล rim tá-lair
season หน้า nâh
seat (place) ที่นั่ง têe nâng
seatbelt เข็มขัดนิรภัย kĕm kàt ní-rá-pai
second (of time) วินาที wí-nah-tee
second (place) ที่สอง têe sŏrng
second class ชั้นสอง chán sŏrng

second-hand มือสอง meu sŏrng
second-hand shop ร้านขายของมือสอง
  ráhn kăi kŏrng meu sŏrng
secretary เลขา lair-kăh
see เห็น hĕn
self-employed ทำธุรกิจส่วนตัว tam tú-rá-
  git sòo·an đoo·a
selfish เห็นแก่ตัว hĕn gàa đoo·a
sell ขาย kăi
send ส่ง sòng
sensible มีเหตุผล mee hèt pŏn
sensual น่าใคร่ nâh krâi
separate ต่างหาก đàhng hàhk
September เดือนกันยายน deu·an
  gan-yah-yon
serious (earnest) เอาจริงเอาจัง ow jing
  ow jang
serious (important) สำคัญ săm-kan
service การบริการ gahn bor-rí-gahn
service charge ค่าบริการ kâh bor-rí-gahn
service station ปั๊มน้ำมัน ɓám nám-man
serviette ผ้าเช็ดปาก pâh chét ɓàhk
several หลาย lăi
sew เย็บ yép
sex (gender) เพศ pêt
sex (the act) การร่วมเพศ gahn rôo·am pêt
sexism เหนียม pêt ní-yom
sexy เซ็กซ์ซี่ sek-sêe
shade ร่ม rôm
shadow เงา ngow
shampoo น้ำยาสระผม nám yah sà pŏm
shape รูปทรง rôop song
share (a dorm etc) รวมกันใช้ rôo·am
  gan chái
share (with) แบ่ง bàang
shave โกน gohn
shaving cream ครีมโกนหนวด kreem
  gohn nòo·at
she เขา kŏw
sheep แกะ gàa
sheet (bed) ผ้าปูนอน pâh ɓoo norn
shelf ชั้น chán

shingles (illness) โรคงูสวัด rôhk ngoo
   sà-wàt
ship เรือ reu·a
shirt เสื้อเชิ้ต sêu·a chéut
shoe รองเท้า rorng tów
shoe shop ร้านขายรองเท้า ráhn kǎi
   rórng tów
shoes รองเท้า rorng tów
shoot ยิง ying
shop ⓝ ร้าน ráhn
shop ⓥ ซื้อของ séu kǒrng
shophouses ห้องแถว hôrng tǎa·ou
shopping การซื้อของ gahn séu kǒrng
shopping centre สรรพสินค้า sàp-pá-sǐn-káh
short (height) เตี้ย ɗêe·a
short (length) สั้น sân
shortage ความขาดแคลน kwahm kàht klaan
shorts กางเกงขาสั้น gahng-geng kǎh sân
shoulder ไหล่ lài
shout ตะโกน ɗà-gohn
show ⓝ งานแสดง ngahn sà-daang
show ⓥ แสดง sà-daang
shower ฝักบัว fàk boo·a
shrimp กุ้ง gûng
shrine (Buddhist) แท่นพระ tâan prá
shut ปิด ɓìt
shy อาย ai
sick ป่วย ɓòo·ay
side ข้าง kâhng
side street ซอย soy
sign ป้าย ɓâi
signature ลายเซ็น lai sen
silk ผ้าไหม pâh mǎi
silver เงิน ngeun
similar คล้ายๆ klái klái
simple ง่าย ngâi
since (May) ตั้งแต่ ɗâng ɗàa
sing ร้องเพลง rórng pleng
Singapore ประเทศสิงคโปร์ ɓrà-têt
   sǐng-ká-ɓoh
singer นักร้อง nák rórng
single (person) โสด sòht

single room ห้องเดี่ยว hôrng dèe·o
singlet เสื้อกล้าม sêu·a glâhm
sister (older) พี่สาว pêe sǒw
sister (younger) น้องสาว nórng sǒw
sit นั่ง nâng
size (general) ขนาด kà-nàht
skate เล่นสเก็ต lên sà-gèt
skateboarding การเล่นกระดานสเก็ต gahn
   lên grà-dahn sà-gèt
ski เล่นสกี lên sà-gee
skiing การเล่นสกี gahn lên sà-gee
skimmed milk นมพร่องนมเนย nom
   prôrng nom neu·i
skin ผิวหนัง pěw nǎng
skirt กระโปรง grà-ɓrohng
skull กะโหลกศีรษะ gà-lòhk sěe-sà
sky ท้องฟ้า tórng fáh
sleep ⓥ นอน norn
sleeping bag ถุงนอน tǔng norn
sleeping berth ที่นอนในตู้นอน têe norn
   nai ɗôo norn
sleeping car ตู้นอน ɗôo norn
sleeping pills ยานอนหลับ yah norn làp
sleepy ง่วงนอน ngôo·ang norn
slice ชิ้น chín
slide (film) ฟิล์มสไลด์ fim sà-lái
slow ช้า cháh
slowly อย่างช้า yàhng cháh
small เล็ก lék
smaller เล็กกว่า lék gwàh
smallest เล็กที่สุด lék têe sùt
smell ⓝ กลิ่น glin
smile ⓥ ยิ้ม yím
smoke ⓥ ควัน kwan
snack ⓝ อาหารว่าง ah-hǎhn wâhng
snail หอย hǒy
snake งู ngoo
snorkelling การดำน้ำใช้ท่อหายใจ gahn
   dam nám chái tôr hǎi jai
snow ⓝ หิมะ hì-má
snow pea ถั่วลันเตา tòo·a lan-ɗow
soap สบู่ sà-ɓòo

soap opera ละครโทรทัศน์ lá-korn toh-rá-tát

soccer ฟุตบอล fút-born

social welfare การประชาสงเคราะห์ gahn brà-chah sŏng-kró

socialist คนถือลัทธิสังคมนิยม kon tĕu lát-tí săng-kom ní-yom

sock(s) ถุงเท้า tŭng tów

soft drink น้ำอัดลม nám àt lom

soft-boiled ลวก lôo-ak

soldier ทหาร tá-hăhn

someone คนใดคนหนึ่ง kon dai kon nèung

something สิ่งใดสิ่งหนึ่ง sing dai sìng nèung

sometimes บางครั้ง bahng kráng

son ลูกชาย lôok chai

song เพลง pleng

soon เร็ว ๆ นี้ re·ou re·ou née

sore เจ็บ jèp

soup น้ำซุป nám súp

south ทิศใต้ tít đâi

souvenir ของที่ระลึก kŏrng têe rá-léuk

souvenir shop ร้านขายของที่ระลึก ráhn kăi kŏrng têe rá-léuk

soy milk นมถั่วเหลือง nom tòo-a lĕu-ang

soy sauce ซอสซีอิ๊ว sórt see-éw

space ที่ว่าง têe wâhng

Spain ประเทศสเปน ̀brà-têt sà-̀ben

sparkling wine เหล้าองุ่นสปาร์คลิ่ง lôw à-ngùn sà-̀bah-kling

speak พูด pôot

special พิเศษ pí-sèt

specialist ผู้เชี่ยวชาญเฉพาะทาง pôo chêe-o chahn chá-pó tahng

speed ความเร็ว kwahm re·ou

speed limit กำหนดความเร็ว gam-nòt kwahm re·ou

speedometer เครื่องวัดความเร็ว krêu·ang wát kwahm re·ou

spider แมงมุม má-laang mum

spinach ผักโขม pàk kŏhm

spirit shrine ศาลเจ้า săhn jôw

spoiled เสีย sĕe-a

spoke ซี่ล้อรถ sêe lór rót

spoon ช้อน chórn

sport กีฬา gee-lah

sports store ร้านขายอุปกรณ์กีฬา ráhn kăi ùp-̀bà-gorn gee-lah

sportsperson นักกีฬา nák gee-lah

sprain ความแคล็ด kwahm klét

spring (coil) ขดลวดสปริง kòt lôo-at sà-̀bring

spring (season) หน้าใบไม้ผลิ nâh bai mái plì

squid ปลาหมึก ̀blah mèuk

stadium สนามกีฬา sà-năhm gee-lah

stairway บันได ban-dai

stale ไม่สด mâi sòt

stamp แสตมป์ sà-̀đaam

star ดาว dow

(four-) star (สี่) ดาว (sèe) dow

start (beginning) จุดเริ่ม jùt rêum

start เริ่ม rêum

start (a car) สตาร์ท sà-̀đáht

station สถานี sà-tăh-nee

stationer's (shop) ร้านขายอุปกรณ์เขียน ráhn kăi ùp-̀bà-gorn kĕe-an

statue รูปหล่อ rôop lòr

stay (at a hotel) พัก pák

stay (in one place) หยุดอยู่ yùt yùt

steak (beef) เนื้อสะเต๊ะ néu-a sà-đé

steal ขโมย kà-moy

steep ชัน chan

step ขั้น kân

stereo สเตริโอ sà-đair-ree-o

sticky rice ข้าวเหนียว kôw nĕe-o

still water น้ำเปล่า nám ̀blòw

stock (food) ซุปก้อน súp gôrn

stockings ถุงน่อง tŭng nôrng

stolen ขโมยแล้ว kà-moy láa-ou

stomach ท้อง tórng

stomachache (to have a) เจ็บท้อง jèp tórng

stone หิน hĭn

stoned (drugged) เมา mow

stop (bus, tram, etc) ป้าย ̀bâi

stop (cease) หยุด yùt
stop (prevent) ห้าม hâhm
Stop! หยุด yùt
storm พายุ pah-yú
story นิทาน ní-tahn
stove เตาอบ ɗow òp
straight ตรง ɗrong
strange แปลก ɓlàak
stranger คนแปลกหน้า kon ɓlàak nâh
strawberry ลูกสตรอว์เบอร์รี่ lôok sà-ɗror-beu-rêe
stream ห้วย hôo-ay
street ถนน tà-nŏn
street market ตลาดนัด ɗà-làht nát
strike ⑩ สไตรค์ sà-ɗrái
string เชือก chêu-ak
stroke (health) เส้นเลือดในสมองแตก sên lêu-at nai sà-mŏrng ɗàak
stroller รถเข็นเด็ก rót kĕn dèk
strong แข็งแรง kăang raang
stubborn ดื้อ dêu
student นักศึกษา nák sèuk-săh
studio (for recording) ห้องอัดเสียง hôrng àt sĕe-ang
stupa พระสถูป prá sà-tòop
stupid โง่ ngôh
style ทรง song
subtitles คำบรรยาย kam ban-yai
suburb เทศบาล tèt-sà-bahn
subway (train) รถไฟใต้ดิน rót fai ɗâi din
sugar น้ำตาล nám ɗahn
suitcase กระเป๋าเดินทาง grà-ɓŏw deun tahng
sultana องุ่นแห้ง à-ngùn hâang
summer หน้าร้อน nâh rórn
sun พระอาทิตย์ prá ah-tít
sunblock ครีมกันแดด kreem gan dàat
sunburn ผิวเกรียมแดด pĕw gree-am dàat
Sunday วันอาทิตย์ wan ah-tít
sunglasses แว่นกันแดด wâen gan dàat
sunny ฟ้าใส fáh săi
sunrise พระอาทิตย์ขึ้น ɗà-wan kêun

sunset ตะวันตก ɗà-wan ɗòk
sunstroke โรคแพ้แดด rôhk páa dàat
supermarket ซูเปอร์มาร์เก็ต soo-ɓeu-mah-gèt
superstition ความเชื่อเรื่องผีเรื่องสาง kwahm chêu-a rêu-ang pĕe rêu-ang săhng
supporter (politics) ผู้สนับสนุน pôo sà-nàp sà-nŭn
supporter (sport) แฟน faan
surf เล่นโต้คลื่น lên ɗôh klêun
surface mail ไปรษณีย์ทางธรรมดา ɓrai-sà-nee tahng tam-má-dah
surfboard กระดานโต้คลื่น grà-dahn ɗôh klêun
surfing การเล่นโต้คลื่น gahn lên ɗôh klêun
surname นามสกุล nahm sà-gun
surprise ความประหลาดใจ kwahm ɓrà-làht jai
swamp หนอง nŏrng
sweater เสื้อถัก sêu-a tàk
Sweden ประเทศสวีเดน ɓrà-têt sà-wee-den
sweet หวาน wăhn
sweet & sour เปรี้ยวหวาน ɓrêe-o wăhn
sweets ของหวาน kŏrng wăhn
swelling ความบวม kwahm boo-am
swim ⓥ ว่ายน้ำ wâi nám
swimming (sport) การว่ายน้ำ gahn wâi nám
swimming pool สระว่ายน้ำ sà wâi nám
swimsuit ชุดว่ายน้ำ chút wâi nám
Switzerland ประเทศสวิตเซอร์แลนด์ ɓrà-têt sà-wít-seu-laan
synagogue สุเหร่ายิว sù-ròw yew
synthetic สังเคราะห์ săng-kró
syringe เข็มฉีดยา kĕm chèet yah

T

table โต๊ะ ɗó
table tennis ปิงปอง ɓing ɓorng
tablecloth ผ้าปูโต๊ะ pâh ɓoo ɗó
tail หาง hăhng

tailor ช่างตัดเสื้อ cháhng đàt sêu·a
take เอาไป ow ðai
take a photo ถ่ายรูป tài rôop
talk พูด pôot
tall สูง sŏong
tampon แทมพอน taam-porn
tanning lotion ครีมอาบแดด kreem àhp dàat
tap ก๊อกน้ำ górk nám
tap water น้ำประปา nám ðrà-ðah
tasty อร่อย à-ròy
tax ภาษี pah-sĕe
taxi รถแท็กซี่ rót táak-sêe
taxi stand ที่จอดรถแท็กซี่ têe jòrt rót táak-sêe
tea น้ำชา nám chah
tea (leaves) ใบชา bai chah
teacher อาจารย์ ah-jahn
team ทีม teem
teaspoon ช้อนชา chórn chah
technique เทคนิค ték-ník
teeth ฟัน fan
telegram โทรเลข toh-rá-lêk
telephone ⓝ โทรศัพท์ toh-rá-sàp
telephone ⓥ โทร toh
telephone box ตู้โทรศัพท์ đôo toh-rá-sàp
telephone centre ศูนย์โทรศัพท์ sŏon toh-rá-sàp
telescope กล้องส่องทางไกล glôrng sòrng tahng glai
television โทรทัศน์ toh-rá-tát
tell บอก ðòrk
temperature (fever) ไข้ kâi
temperature (weather) อุณหภูมิ un-hà-poom
temple วัด wát
temple fair งานวัด ngahn wát
tennis เทนนิส ten-nít
tennis court สนามเทนนิส sà-năhm ten-nít
tent เต็นท์ đén
tent peg หลักปักเต็นท์ làk bàk đén
terrible แย่ yâa

test การสอบ gahn sòrp
Thai ไทย tai
Thailand ประเทศไทย ðrà-têt tai
thank ขอบใจ kòrp jai
Thank you. ขอบคุณ kòrp kun
that (one) (อัน) นั้น (an) nán
theatre โรงละคร rohng lá-korn
their ของเขา kŏrng kŏw
there ที่นั่น têe nán
therefore ฉะนั้น chà-nán
thermometer ปรอท ðà-ròrt
they เขา kŏw
thick หนา năh
thief ขโมย kà-moy
thin (general) บาง bahng
thin (of a person) ผอม pŏrm
think คิด kít
third ที่สาม têe săhm
thirsty (to be) หิวน้ำ hĕw nám
this (month etc) (เดือน) นี้ (deu·an) née
thread เส้นด้าย sên dâi
throat คอหอย kor hŏy
thrush (health) เชื้อรา chéu·a rah
thunderstorm พายุฟ้าร้อง pah-yú fáh rórng
Thursday วันพฤหัสบดี wan pá-réu-hàt
ticket ตั๋ว đŏo·a
ticket collector คนเก็บตั๋ว kon gèp đŏo·a
ticket machine เครื่องบริการตั๋ว krêu·ang bor-rí-gahn đŏo·a
ticket office ช่องขายตั๋ว chôrng kăi đŏo·a
tide น้ำขึ้นน้ำลง nám kêun nám long
tight แน่น nâan
time เวลา wair-lah
time difference ความต่างของเวลา kwahm đàhng kŏrng wair-lah
timetable ตารางเวลา đah-rahng wair-lah
tin (can) กระป๋อง grà-ðŏrng
tin opener เครื่องเปิดกระป๋อง krêu·ang ðèut grà-ðŏrng
tiny เล็กนิดเดียว lék nít dee·o
tip (gratuity) เงินทิป ngeun típ

tired เหนื่อย nèu·ay

tissues กระดาษทิชชู่ grà·dàht tít·chôo

to ถึง tĕung

toast ขนมปังปิ้ง kà·nŏm bang bîng

toaster เครื่องปิ้งขนมปัง krêu·ang bîng kà·nŏm bang

tobacco ยาเส้น yah sên

tobacconist คนขายยาสูบ kon kăi yah sòop

today วันนี้ wan née

toe นิ้วเท้า néw tów

tofu เต้าหู้ dôw·hôo

together ด้วยกัน dôo·ay gan

toilet ส้วม sôo·am

toilet paper กระดาษห้องน้ำ grà·dàht hôrng nám

tomato มะเขือเทศ má·kĕu·a têt

tomato sauce ซอสมะเขือเทศ sórt má·kĕu·a têt

tomorrow พรุ่งนี้ prúng née

tomorrow afternoon พรุ่งนี้บ่าย prúng née bài

tomorrow evening พรุ่งนี้เย็น prúng née yen

tomorrow morning พรุ่งนี้เช้า prúng née chów

tonight คืนนี้ keun née

too (expensive etc) เกินไป geun bai

tooth ฟัน fan

toothache ปวดฟัน bòo·at fan

toothbrush แปรงสีฟัน braang sĕe fan

toothpaste ยาสีฟัน yah sĕe fan

toothpick ไม้จิ้มฟัน mái jîm fan

torch (flashlight) ไฟฉาย fai chăi

touch แตะ dàa

tour ⓝ ทัวร์ too·a

tourist นักท่องเที่ยว nák tôrng têe·o

tourist office สำนักงานท่องเที่ยว săm·nák ngahn tôrng têe·o

towards ไปถึง bai tĕung

towel ผ้าเช็ดตัว pâh chét đoo·a

tower หอสูง hŏr sŏong

toxic waste มูลมีพิศ moon mee pít

toy ของเล่นเด็ก kŏrng lên dèk

toy shop ร้านขายของเล่นเด็ก ráhn kăi kŏrng lên dèk

track (path) ทาง tahng

track (sport) ทาง tahng

trade อาชีพ ah·chêep

tradesperson ช่าง châhng

traffic จราจร jà·rah·jorn

traffic light ไฟจราจร fai jà·rah·jorn

trail ทางเดิน tahng deun

train รถไฟ rót fai

train station สถานีรถไฟ sà·tăh·nee rót fai

transsexual กะเทย gà·teu·i

transit lounge ห้องพักสำหรับคนเดินทางผ่าน hôrng pák săm·ràp kon deun tahng pàhn

translate แปล blaa

transport ⓝ การขนส่ง gahn kŏn sòng

transvestite กะเทย gà·teu·i

travel ⓥ เดินทาง deun tahng

travel agency บริษัทท่องเที่ยว bor·rí·sàt tôrng têe·o

travel sickness (car) เมารถ mow rót

travel sickness (boat) เมาคลื่น mow klêun

travel sickness (air) เมาเครื่อง mow krêu·ang

travellers cheque เช็คเดินทาง chék deun tahng

tree ต้นไม้ đôn mái

trip (journey) เที่ยว têe·o

trolley รถเข็น rót kĕn

trousers กางเกง gahng·geng

truck รถบรรทุก rót ban·túk

trust ไว้ใจ wái jai

try (try out) ลอง lorng

try (attempt) พยายาม pá·yah·yahm

T-shirt เสื้อยืด sêu·a yêut

tube (tyre) ยางใน yahng nai

Tuesday วันอังคาร wan ang·kahn

tumour เนื้องอก néu·a ngôrk

tuna ปลาทูน่า blah too·nah

tune ทำนองเพลง tam·norng pleng

turkey ไก่งวง gài ngoo-ang
turn เลี้ยว lée-o
TV โทรทัศน์ toh-rá-tát
tweezers แหนบ nàap
twin beds สองเตียง sŏrng đee-ang
twins แฝด fàat
two สอง sŏrng
type ชนิด chá-nít
typical ธรรมดา tam-má-dah
tyre ยางรถ yahng rót

U

ultrasound อุลตราซาวนด์ un-đrah-sow
umbrella ร่ม rôm
uncomfortable ไม่สบาย mâi sà-bai
underneath ใต้ đâi
understand เข้าใจ kôw jai
underwear กางเกงใน gahng-geng nai
unemployed ตกงาน đòk ngahn
unfair ไม่ยุติธรรม mâi yút-đi-tam
uniform เสื้อแบบ sêu-a bàap
universe มหาจักรวาล má-hăh-jàk-gà-wahn
university มหาวิทยาลัย má-hăh-wít-tá-yah-lai
unleaded ไร้สารตะกั่ว rái săhn đà-gòo-a
unsafe ไม่ปลอดภัย mâi blòrt pai
until (Friday, etc) จนถึง jon tĕung
unusual แปลก bplàak
up ขึ้น kêun
uphill ทางขึ้น tahng kêun
urgent ด่วน dòo-an
urinary infection ท่อปัสสาวะอักเสบ tòr bàt-săh-wá àk-sèp
USA สหรัฐอเมริกา sà-hà-rát à-mair-rí-gah
useful มีประโยชน์ mee brà-yòht

V

vacancy ห้องว่าง hôrng wâhng
vacant ว่าง wâhng
vacation เที่ยวพักผ่อน têe-o pák pòrn
vaccination ฉีดวัคซีน chèet wák-seen

vagina ช่องคลอด chôrng klôrt
validate ทำให้ถูกต้อง tam hâi tòok đôrng
valley หุบเขา hùp kŏw
valuable มีค่า mee kâh
value (price) ราคา rah-kah
van รถตู้ rót đôo
veal เนื้อลูกวัว néu-a lôok woo-a
vegetable ผัก pàk
vegetarian คนกินเจ kon gin jair
vein เส้นเลือด sên lêu-at
venereal disease กามโรค gahm-má-rôhk
venue สถานที่ sà-tăhn têe
very มาก mâhk
video recorder กล้องถ่ายวีดีโอ glôrng tài wee-dee-oh
video tape เทปวีดีโอ tép wee-dee-oh
view ⑩ ทิวทัศน์ tew tát
village หมู่บ้าน mòo bâhn
villager ชาวบ้าน chow bâhn
vine (not grape) เถาวัลย์ tŏw-wan
vinegar น้ำส้ม nám sôm
vineyard ไร่องุ่น rài à-ngùn
virus ไวรัส wai-rát
visa วีซ่า wee-sâh
visit ⑨ เยี่ยม yêe-am
vitamins วิตามิน wí-đah-min
vodka เหล้าวอดก้า lôw wôrt-gáh
voice เสียง sĕe-ang
volleyball (sport) วอลเลย์บอล worn-lair-born
volume (sound) ความดัง kwahm dang
volume (capacity) ปริมาตร bà-rí-mâht
vomit อ้วก ôo-ak
vote ลงคะแนนเสียง long ká-naan sĕe-ang

W

wage ค่าแรง kâh raang
wait (for) รอ ror
waiter คนเดินโต๊ะ kon deun đó
waiting room ห้องพักรอ hôrng pák ror
wake someone up ปลุก blùk
wake up ตื่น đèun

walk เดิน deun

wall (outer) กำแพง gam-paang

want อยาก yàhk

war สงคราม sŏng-krahm

wardrobe ตู้เสื้อผ้า đôo sêu·a pâh

warm อุ่น ùn

warn เตือน đeu·an

wash (oneself) ล้าง láhng

wash (something) ล้าง láhng

wash (clothes) ซัก sák

wash cloth (flannel) ผ้าขนหนู pâh kŏn nŏo

washing machine เครื่องซักผ้า krêu·ang sák pâh

watch ⓝ นาฬิกา nah-lí-gah

watch ⓥ ดู doo

water น้ำ nám

water bottle ขวดน้ำ kòo·at nám

waterfall น้ำตก nám đòk

watermelon แตงโม đaang moh

waterproof ชุดกันน้ำ chút gan nám

waterskiing สกีน้ำ sà-gee nám

wave ⓝ คลื่น klêun

way ทาง tahng

we เรา row

weak อ่อน òrn

wealthy รวย roo·ay

wear ใส่ sài

weather อากาศ ah-gàht

wedding งานแต่ง ngahn đàang

wedding cake ขนมฉลองงานแต่งงาน kà-nŏm chà-lŏrng wan đàang ngahn

wedding present ของขวัญแต่งงาน kŏrng kwăn đàang ngahn

Wednesday วันพุธ wan pút

week อาทิตย์ ah-tít

(this) week อาทิตย์ (นี้) ah-tít (née)

weekend วันเสาร์อาทิตย์ wan sŏw ah-tít

weigh ชั่ง châng

weight น้ำหนัก nám-nàk

weights จานน้ำหนัก jahn nám-nàk

welcome ต้อนรับ đôrn ráp

welfare (well-being) ความผาสุก kwahm păh-sùk

well ดี dee

west ทิศตะวันตก tít đà-wan đòk

Western ฝรั่ง fà-ràng

Westerner ฝรั่ง fà-ràng

wet เปียก bèe·ak

what อะไร à-rai

wheel ล้อ lór

wheelchair รถเข็น rót kĕn

when เมื่อไร mêu·a rai

where ที่ไหน têe năi

which อันไหน an năi

whisky เหล้าวิสกี้ lôw wit-sà-gêe

white สีขาว sĕe kŏw

who ใคร krai

wholemeal bread ขนมปังทำด้วยแป้งข้าวสาลีที่ไม่ได้เอารำออก kà-nŏm bang tam dôo·ay bâang kôw săh-lee têe mâi dâi ow ram òrk

why ทำไม tam mai

wide กว้าง gwâhng

wife เมีย mee·a

win ชนะ chá-ná

wind ลม lom

window หน้าต่าง nâh đàhng

windscreen กระจกหน้ารถ grà-jòk nâh rót

windsurfing การเล่นกระดานโต้ลม gahn lên grà-dahn đôh lom

wine เหล้าไวน์ lôw wai

wings ปีก bèek

winner ผู้ชนะ pôo chá-ná

winter หน้าหนาว nâh nŏw

wire ลวด lôo·at

wish ⓥ ปรารถนา bràh-tà-năh

with กับ gàp

within (an hour) ภายใน pai nai

without ไม่มี mâi mee

wok กระทะ grà-tá

woman ผู้หญิง pôo yĭng

wonderful ดีเยี่ยม dee yêe·am

wood ไม้ mái

wool ขนแกะ kŏn gàa
word ศัพท์ sàp
work ⓝ งาน ngahn
work ⓥ ทำงาน tam ngahn
work experience ประสบการณ์ในการทำงาน
brà-sòp gahn nai gahn tam ngahn
work permit ใบแรงงาน bai raang ngahn
workout การออกกำลังกาย gahn òrk
gam-lang gai
workshop ห้องทำงาน hôrng tam ngahn
world โลก lôhk
World Cup บอลโลก born lôhk
worms (intestinal) พยาธิ pá-yáht
worried กังวล gang-won
worship บูชา boo-chah
wraparound (for men) ผ้าขะม้า
pâh kà-máh
wraparound (for women) ผ้าถุง pâh tŭng
wrist ข้อมือ kôr meu
write เขียน kĕe·an
writer นักเขียน nák kĕe·an
wrong ผิด pìt

Y

year ปี bee
(this) year ปี (นี้) bee (née)
yellow สีเหลือง sĕe lĕu·ang
yes ใช่ châi
(not) yet ยัง yang
yesterday เมื่อวาน mêu·a wahn
yoga โยคะ yoh-ká
yogurt โยเกิร์ต yoh-gèut
you inf เธอ teu
you pl pol คุณ kun
young หนุ่ม nùm
your ของคุณ kŏrng kun
youth hostel บ้านเยาวชน bâhn yow-
wá-chon

Z

zip/zipper ซิป síp
zodiac สิบสองราศี sìp-sŏrng rah-sĕe
zoo สวนสัตว์ sŏo·an sàt

If you're having trouble understanding Thai, or if a Thai-speaking person wants to communicate with you in English, point to the text below. This gives directions on how to to look up words in Thai and show you the English translation.

ใช้พจนานุกรมไทย–อังกฤษนี้เพื่อช่วยชาวต่างชาติคนนี้เข้าใจง่าย ที่คุณอยากจะพูด ค้นหาศัพท์จากรายการคำศัพท์ภาษาไทย แล้วชี้ให้เห็นคำศัพท์ภาษาอังกฤษที่ตรงกับศัพท์นั้น

ก

ก งสุล gong-sŭn **consulate**

กรรไกร gan-grai **scissors**

กระจก grà-jòk **mirror**

กระดาษ grà-dàht **paper**

กระดาษทิชชู่ grà-dàht tít-chôo **tissues**

กระดาษห้องน้ำ grà-dàht hôrng nám **toilet paper**

กระดุม grà-dum **button**

กระป๋อง grà-bŏrng **can • tin**

กระเป๋า grà-bŏw **baggage • luggage**

กระเป๋าเงิน grà-bŏw ngeun **purse**

กระเป๋าเดินทาง grà-bŏw deun tahng **suitcase**

กระโปรง grà-brohng **dress • skirt**

กระแสไฟฟ้า grà-săa fai fáh **current (electricity)**

กรัม gram **gram**

กรุงเทพ grung têp **Bangkok**

กล้องถ่ายรูป glôrng tài rôop **camera**

กล้องถ่ายวีดีโอ glôrng tài wee-dee-oh **video recorder**

กลับ glàp **return (come back)**

กลิ่น glin **smell**

กลุ่มเลือด glum lêu-at **blood group**

กษัตริย์ gà-sàt **king**

ก๊อกน้ำ górk nám **tap**

กับแกล้ม gàp glâam **drinking food**

กางเกง gahng-geng **pants • trousers**

กางเกงขาสั้น gahng-geng kăh sân **shorts**

กางเกงใน gahng geng nai **underwear**

กางเกงยีน gahng geng yeen **jeans**

ก๊าซ gáht **gas (for cooking)**

กาแฟ gah-faa **coffee**

การกฎหมาย gahn gòt-măi **law (study, professsion)**

การเขียนภาพ gahn kĕe-an pâhp **painting (the art)**

การจอง gahn jorng **reservation (booking)**

การจ่าย gahn jài **payment**

การช้าเวลา gahn cháh wair-lah **delay**

การเช่ารถ gahn chôw rót **car hire**

การดูแลเด็ก gahn doo laa dèk **childminding**

การต่อ gahn dòr **connection (transport)**

การตัดผม gahn đàt pŏm **haircut**

การเต้นรำ gahn đên ram **dancing**

การถ่ายภาพ gahn tài pâhp **photography**

การทำสะอาด gahn tam sà-àht **cleaning**

การนัด gahn nát **appointment**

การบริการ gahn bor-rí-gahn **service**

การประกัน gahn bràa-gan **insurance**

การประชุม gahn bràa-chum **conference**

การปรับร่างกายกับเวลาที่แตกต่าง gahn bràp râhng gai gàp wair-lah têe đàak đàhng **jet lag**

การพักร้อน gahn pák rórn **holidays**

การแพ้ gahn páa **allergy**

การแพทย์ gahn pâat **medicine (study, profession)**

การร่วมเพศ gahn rôo·am pêt **sex (the act)**

การเล่นสกี gahn lên sà·gee **skiing**

การแลกเงิน gahn lâak ngeun **currency exchange**

การสัมภาษณ์ gahn sǎm·pâht **interview**

การแสดง gahn sà·daang **concert**

การต่อยมวย gahn đòy moo·ay **boxing**

กำหนดความเร็ว gam·nòt kwahm re·ou **speed limit**

กิน gin **eat** inf

กิโลกรัม gì·loh·gram **kilogram**

กิโลเมตร gì·loh·mêt **kilometre**

เกม gem **match (sports)**

เกย์ gair **gay**

เก่า gòw **old (thing)**

เก้าอี้ gôw·êe **chair**

เกาะ gò **island**

เกินไป geun ปai **too (expensive etc)**

แก่ gàa **dark (of colour)**

แก่ gàa **old (person)**

แก้ว gâa·ou **glass (drinking)**

โกน gohn **shave**

ใกล้ glâi **close • near**

ใกล้เคียง glâi kee·ang **nearby**

ใกล้ที่สุด glâi têe·sùt **nearest**

ไก่ gài **chicken**

ไกด์ gai **guide (person)**

ข

ขนแกะ kǒn gàa **wool**

ขนมปัง kà·nǒm ปang **bread**

ขนมปังปิ้ง kà·nǒm ปang ปîng **toast**

ขนาด kà·nàht **size (general)**

ขม kǒm **bitter**

ขโมยแล้ว kà·moy láa·ou **stolen**

ขยะ kà·yà **garbage**

ขวด kòo·at **bottle**

ขวา kwǎh **right (direction)**

ข้อความฝาก kôr kwahm fàhk **message**

ของขวัญ kǒrng kwǎn **present (gift)**

ของเขา kǒrng kǒw **his • her**

ของดิฉัน kǒrng dì·chǎn **my (for a woman)**

ของท้องถิ่น kǒrng tórng tìn **local**

ของที่ระลึก kǒrng têe rá·léuk **souvenir**

ของผม kǒrng pǒm **my (for a man)**

ของเรา kǒrng row **our**

ของหวาน kǒrng wǎhn **dessert**

ข้อต่อ kôr đòr **connection**

ข้อเท้า kôr tów **ankle**

ขอบคุณ kòrp kun **thank you**

ข้อมูล kôr moon **information**

ขอแสดงความยินดี kôr sà·daang kwahm yin dee **congratulations**

ขับ kàp **drive**

ขา kǎh **leg**

ขากรรไกร kǎh gan·grai **jaw**

ขาเข้า kǎh kôw **arrivals**

ข้างนอก kâhng nôrk **outside**

ข้างใน kâhng nai **inside**

ข้างหลัง kâhng lǎng **behind**

ข้างๆ kâhng kâhng **beside**

ข่าว kòw **news**

ขาวดำ kǒw dam **B&W (film)**

ขาออก kǎh òrk **departures**

ขึ้น kêun **board (a plane, ship etc)**

ขึ้น kêun **up**

เข็ม kěm **needle (sewing)**

เข็มขัดนิรภัย kěm kàt ní·rá·pai **seatbelt**

เข็มฉีด kěm chèet **needle (syringe)**

เขา kǒw **he, she, they**

แข็ง kǎang **hard (not soft)**

แขน kǎan **arm**

ไข้ kâi **fever**

ไข้หวัด kâi wàt **influenza • flu**

ค

คนกินเงินบำนาญ kon gin ngeun bam·nahn **pensioner**

คนกินเจ kon gin jair **vegetarian**

คนขายผัก kon kǎi pàk **greengrocer**

คนครัว kon kroo·a **cook**

คนเดินโต๊ะ kon deun đó **waiter**

คนต่างชาติ kon đàhng châht **foreigner**
คนรักร่วมเพศ kon rák rôo·am pét
  homosexual
ครอบครัว krôrp kroo·a **family**
คริสต์มาส krít-mâht **Christmas**
ครีมกันแดด kreem gan dàat **sunblock**
ครีมโกนหนวด kreem gohn nòo·at
  shaving cream
ครีมทาหลังโกนหนวด kreem tah lăng gohn
  nòo·at **aftershave**
ครีมอาบแดด kreem àhp dàat **tanning
  lotion**
คลื่นไส้ klêun sâi **nausea**
ควัน kwan **smoke**
ความเคล็ด kwahm klét **sprain**
ความต่างของเวลา kwahm đàhng kŏrng
  wair-lah **time difference**
ความปวด kwahm ปòo·at **pain**
ความร้อน kwahm rórn **heat**
ความรัก kwahm rák **love**
ความไวของฟิล์ม kawhm wai kŏrng fim
  film speed
ค็อกเทล kórk-ten **cocktail**
คอมพิวเตอร์ korm-pew-đeu **computer**
คอมพิวเตอร์แล็ปท็อป korm-pew-đeu láap-
  tórp **laptop**
คอหอย kor hŏy **throat**
คัน kan **itch**
ค่าเข้า kâh kôw **admission (price)**
ค่าธรรมเนียม kâh tam-nee-am
  commission
ค่าบริการ kâh bor-ri-gahn **service charge**
ค่าปรับ kâh ปràp **fine (penalty)**
ค่าผ่านประตู kâh pàhn ปrà-đoo **cover
  charge**
ค่ายพักแรม kâi pák raam **camping ground**
คำตลก kam đà-lòk **joke**
คำบรรยาย kam ban-yai **subtitles**
คำร้องทุกข์ kam rórng túk **complaint**
คืน keun **night**
คืนนี้ keun née **tonight**
คืนวันสิ้นปี keun wan sîn ปee **New Year's
  Eve**
คุก kúk **jail**

คุณ kun **you** pl pol
คู่มือน่าเที่ยว kôo meu nam têe-o
  guidebook
คู่มือสนทนา kôo meu sŏn-tá-nah
  phrasebook
เครดิต crair-dit **credit**
เครือข่าย kreu-a kài **network**
เครื่องเก็บเงิน krêu-ang gèp ngeun **cash
  register**
เครื่องคิดเลข krêu-ang kit lêk **calculator**
เครื่องซักผ้า krêu-ang sák pâh **washing
  machine**
เครื่องดื่ม krêu-ang dèum **drink**
เครื่องนอน krêu-ang norn **bedding**
เครื่องบริการตั๋ว
  krêu-ang bor-rí-gahn đŏo-a
  ticket machine
เครื่องบิน krêu-ang bin **aeroplane**
เครื่องปิ้งขนมปัง
  krêu-ang bîng kà-nŏm bang **toaster**
เครื่องเปิดกระป๋อง
  krêu-ang ปèut grà-ปŏrng
  can opener • tin opener
เครื่องเปิดขวด krêu-ang ปèut kòo-at
  bottle opener
เครื่องพิมพ์ krêu-ang pim **printer
  (computer)**
เครื่องเพชรพลอย krêu-ang pét ploy
  jewellery
เครื่องสำอาง krêu-ang săm-ahng **make-up**
เครื่องหัตถกรรม krêu-ang hàt-tà-gam
  handicrafts
แคเชียร์ kaa-chee-a **cashier**
ใคร krai **who**

ง

งบประมาณ ngóp ปrà-mahn **budget**
งาน ngahn **festival**
งาน ngahn **job**
งานเต้นรำ ngahn đên ram **rave • dance
  party**
งานเลี้ยง ngahn lée-ang **party
  (celebration)**

งานแสดง ngahn sà-daang **show**
เงิน ngeun **money**
เงิน ngeun **silver**
เงินคืน ngeun keun **refund**
เงินทิป ngeun típ **tip (gratuity)**
เงินปลีก ngeun blèek **change (coins)**
เงินมัดจำ ngeun mát jam **deposit**
เงินสด ngeun sòt **cash**
เงียบ ngêe·ap **quiet**

จ

จดหมาย jòt-mǎi **letter • mail**
จนถึง jon tĕung **until (Friday, etc)**
จมูก jà-mòok **nose**
จอง jorng **book (make a booking)**
จอด jòrt **park (a car)**
จาน jahn **dish**
จาน jahn **plate**
จีสตริง jee sà-đring **g-string**
จุ๊ก júk **plug (bath)**
จูบ jòop **kiss**
เจ็บ jèp **painful**
เจ็บท้อง jèp tórng **stomachache (to have a)**
ใจกลางเมือง jai glahng meu·ang **city centre**

ฉ

ฉะนั้น chà-nán **therefore**
ฉีดวัคซีน chèet wák-seen **vaccination**

ช

ชนบท chon-ná-bot **countryside**
ช่วยด้วย chôo·ay dôo·ay **Help!**
ช็อกโกเลต chórk-goh-lét **chocolate**
ช่องขายตั๋ว chôrng kǎi đǒo·a **ticket office**
ช้อน chórn **spoon**
ช้อนชา chórn chah **teaspoon**
ช้อนส้อม chórn sôrm **cutlery**

ชอบ chôrp **like**
ชั้นธุรกิจ chán tú-rá-git **business class**
ชั้นสอง chán sǒrng **second class**
ชั่วโมง chôo·a mohng **hour**
ช้า cháh **late**
ช่างตัดผม châhng đàt pǒm **hairdresser**
ช่างตัดเสื้อ châhng đàt sêu·a **tailor**
ช่างถ่ายภาพ châhng tài pâhp **photographer**
ช่างทาสี châhng tah sěe **painter**
ชานชาลา chahn chah-lah **platform**
ชาม chahm **bowl**
ชายแดน chai daan **border**
ชายหาด chai hàht **beach**
ชาวยิว chow yew **Jewish**
ชาวไร่ชาวนา chow rài chow nah **farmer**
ชิ้น chín **slice**
ชี้ chée **point**
ชื่อ chêu **name**
ชุดว่ายน้ำ chút wâi nám **swimsuit**
เช็ค chék **cheque • check**
เช็คเดินทาง chék deun tahng **travellers cheque**
เช็คอิน chék in **check-in (desk)**
เช่า chôw **hire • rent**
เชือกสีฟัน chêu·ak sěe fan **dental floss**
ใช่ chái **yes**

ซ

ซ่อม sôrm **repair**
ซัก sák **wash (clothes)**
ซากโบราณสถาน sâhk boh-rahn-ná sà-tǎhn **ruins**
ซ้าย sái **left (direction)**
ซิป síp **zip/zipper**
ซีดี see-dee **CD**
ซื้อ séu **buy**
ซื้อของ séu kǒrng **shop**
ซูเปอร์มาร์เก็ต soo-beu-mah-gèt **supermarket**
เซนติเมตร sen-đi-mét **centimetre**

ค

คนตรี don-ðree **music**
คนตรีร็อค don-ðree rórk **rock (music)**
ด่วน ðòo·an **urgent**
ด้วยกัน ðôo·ay gan **together**
ดอกไม้ ðòrk mái **flower**
ดอลลาร์ ðorn-lah **dollar**
ดัง dang **loud**
ดินสอ din-sŏr **pencil**
ดี dee **good**
ดีกว่า dee gwàh **better**
ดีที่สุด dee têe sùt **best**
ดื่ม ðèum **drink**
ดื่มน้ำผึ้งพระจันทร์ ðèum nám pêung prá
    jan **honeymoon**
เด็ก ðèk **child**
เด็กชาย ðèk chai **boy**
เด็กๆ ðèk ðèk **children**
เดิน deun **walk**
เดินทางธุรกิจ deun tahng tú-rá-git
    business trip
เดินป่า deun bàh **hike**
เดียว ðèe·o **alone**
เดี๋ยวนี้ ðĕe·o née **now**
เดือน deu·an **month**
ได้ยิน ðâi yin **hear**

ต

ตรงเวลา ðrong wair-lah **on time**
ตรวจคนเข้าเมือง ðròo·at kon kôw
    meu·ang **immigration**
ตลาด ða-làht **market**
ตลาดนัด ða-làht nát **street market**
ตลาดน้ำ ða-làht nám **floating market**
ต่อ ðòr **per (day)**
ตอนเช้า ðorn chów **morning**
ตอนบ่าย ðorn bài **afternoon**
ตะวันขึ้น ða-wan kêun **sunrise**
ตะวันตก ða-wan ðòk **sunset**
ตั้งครรภ์ ðâng kan **pregnant**
ตัด ðàt **cut**
ตัน ðan **blocked**

ตั๋ว ðŏo·a **ticket**
ตา ðah **grandfather (maternal)**
ต่างกัน ðàhng gan **different**
ต่างจาก ðàhng jàhk **different from**
ต่างชาติ ðàhng châht **foreign**
ต่างประเทศ ðàhng brà-têt **overseas**
ตารางเวลา ðah-rahng wair-lah **timetable**
ตำรวจ ðam-ròo·at **police**
ตึก ðèuk **building**
ตื่น ðèun **wake up**
ตู้เซฟ ðôo sép **safe**
ตู้โทรศัพท์ ðôo toh-rá-sàp **phone box**
ตู้โทรศัพท์ ðôo toh-rá-sàp **telephone box**
ตู้นอน ðôo norn **sleeping car**
ตู้ไปรษณีย์ ðôo brai-sà-nee **mailbox**
ตู้ฝากกระเป๋า ðôo fàhk grà-bŏw **luggage
    lockers**
ตู้ไมโครเวฟ ðôo mai-kroh-wép
    microwave (oven)
ตู้เย็น ðôo yen **refrigerator**
ตู้รับประทานอาหาร ðôo ráp brà-tahn ah-
    hăhn **dining car**
ตู้เอทีเอ็ม ðôo air te em **automated teller
    machine (ATM)**
เต้นรำ ðên ram **dance**
เต้าหู้ ðôw-hôo **tofu**
เตี้ย ðêe·a **short (height)**
เตียง ðee·ang **bed**
เตียงคู่ ðee·ang kôo **double bed**
แต่งงานแล้ว ðàang ngahn láa·ou **married**
ใต้ ðâi **beneath**

ถ

ถนน tà-nŏn **road**
ถนน tà-nŏn **street**
ถ้วย tôo·ay **cup**
ถังแก๊ส tăng gáat **gas cartridge**
ถังขยะ tăng kà-yà **garbage can**
ถ้า tâh **if**
ถ่านไฟฉาย tàhn fai chăi **battery
    (flashlight)**
ถ่ายรูป tài rôop **take a photo**
ถึง tĕung **to**

ถุง ถุง tŭng **bag**

ถุง น่อ ง tŭng nôrng **pantyhose**

ถุง น่อ ง tŭng nôrng **stockings**

ถุง นอน tŭng norn **sleeping bag**

ถุง ยา งอนา มัย tŭng yahng à-nah-mai **condom**

ถูก tòok **cheap**

แถม tăam **complementary (free)**

ท

ทอง คำ torng kam **gold**

ท้อ ง tórng **stomach**

ท้อ งผูก tórng pòok **constipation**

ท้อ งเสีย tórng sĕe·a **diarrhoea**

ทะ นายความ tá-nai kwahm **lawyer**

ทะเบียนรถ tá-bee·an rót **car registration**

ทะเล tá-lair **sea**

ทะเลสาบ tá-lair sàhp **lake**

ทั้ งสอ ง táng sŏrng **both**

ทั้ งหมด táng mòt **all**

ทันสมัย tan sà-măi **modern**

ทัวร์ too·a **tour · guided tour**

ทาง tahng **path**

ทาง ด่วน tahng dòo·an **motorway (tollway)**

ทางเดิน tahng deun **aisle (on plane)**

ทางตร ง tahng drong **direct**

ทางหล วง tahng lŏo·ang **highway**

ทาน tahn **eat (polite)**

ทาร ก tah-rók **baby**

ทำด้วยมือ tam dôo·ay meu **handmade**

ทำไม tam mai **why**

ทำสะ อาด tam sà-àht **clean**

ทำให้เจ็บ tam hâi jèp **hurt (to hurt someone)**

ทำให้ถูกต้อ ง tam hâi tòok dôrng **validate**

ทำอาหาร tam ah-hăhn **cook**

ทิวทัศน์ tew tát **view**

ทิศตะ วันตก tít đà-wan đòk **west**

ทิศใต้ tít đâi **south**

ทิศทาง tít tahng **direction**

ทิศเหนือ tít nĕu·a **north**

ที่ têe **at**

ที่ขายขนมป ง têe kăi kà-nŏm ฿ang **bakery**

ที่เขี่ยบุหรี่ têe kèe·a bù-rèe **ashtray**

ที่จอดรถแท็กซี่ têe jòrt rót táak-sêe **taxi stand**

ที่แจ้งของ หาย têe jáang kŏrng hăi **lost property office**

ที่ซักผ้า têe sák pâh **laundry (place)**

ที่ทำการไปรษณีย์ têe tam gahn ฿rai-sà-nee **post office**

ที่นอนในตู้นอน têe norn nai đôo norn **sleeping berth**

ที่นั่ ง têe nâng **seat (place)**

ที่นั่ งเฉพาะเด็ก têe nâng chà-pó dèk **child seat**

ที่นั่น têe nán **there**

ที่นี่ têe née **here**

ที่ฝากเลี้ยงเด็ก têe fàhk lée·ang dèk **creche**

ที่พัก têe pák **accommodation**

ที่รับกระเป๋า têe ráp grà-bŏw **baggage claim**

ที่แล้ว tee láaw **last (previous)**

ที่หลัง tee lăng **later**

ที่ไหน têe năi **where**

ที่อยู่ têe yòo **address**

เทคโนโลยีสารสนเทศ ték-noh-loh-yee săhn sŏn-tét **IT**

เทนนิส ten-nít **tennis**

เทปวีดีโอ têp wee-dee-oh **video tape**

เท้า tów **foot**

เที่ย งคืน têe·ang keun **midnight**

เที่ย งวัน têe·ang wan **midday**

เที่ยวกลา งคืน têe·o glahng keun **night out**

เที่ยวเดียว têe·o dee·o **one-way (ticket)**

เที่ยวบิน têe·o bin **flight (aeroplane)**

เที่ยวพักผ่อน têe·o pák pòrn **vacation**

แทมพอน taam-porn **tampon**

โทร toh **telephone**

โทรเก็บปลายทาง toh gèp ฿lai tahng **collect call**

โทรทัศน์ toh-rá-tát **television**

โทรทัศน์ toh-rá-tát **TV**

โทรทาง ตร ง toh tahng drong **direct-dial**

โทรเลข toh-rá-lêk **telegram**

โทรศัพท์ toh-rá-sàp **telephone**

โทรศัพท์มือถือ toh-rá-sàp meu tĕu **mobile phone**
โทรศัพท์สาธารณะ toh-rá-sàp săh-tah-rá-ná **public telephone**

ธ

ธนบัตร tá-ná-bàt **banknote**
ธนาคาร tá-nah-kahn **bank**
ธุรกิจ tú-rá-git **business**
เธอ teu **you** inf

น

นวด nôo-at **massage**
น้องชาย nórng chai **brother (younger)**
นอน norn **sleep**
นักวิทยาศาสตร์ nák wít-tá-yah-sàht **scientist**
นักศึกษา nák sèuk-săh **student**
นักแสดง nák sà-daang **actor**
(อัน) นั้น (an) nán **that (one)**
(อัน) นี้ (an) née **this (one)**
น้ำ nám **water**
น้ำแข็ง nám kăang **ice**
นาง nahng **Mrs**
นางพยาบาล nahng pá-yah-bahn **nurse (woman)**
นางสาว nahng sŏw **Miss/Ms**
นาที nah-tee **minute**
น่าเบื่อ nâh bèu-a **boring**
นามสกุล nahm sà-kun **family name • surn**
นาย nai **Mr**
นาฬิกา nah-lí-gah **watch**
นาฬิกาปลุก nah-lí-gah blùk **alarm clock**
น้ำซุป nám súp **soup**
น้ำนม nám nom **milk**
น้ำผลไม้ nám pŏn-lá-mái **juice**
น้ำมัน nám man **oil**
น้ำมันเครื่อง nám man krêu-ang **oil (motor)**
น้ำมันเบนซิน nám-man ben-sin **gas (petrol)**
น้ำมันหล่อลื่น nám man lòr lêun **lubricant**

น้ำแร่ nám râa **mineral water**
น้ำหอม nám hŏrm **perfume**
นิ้วเท้า néw tów **toe**
เนยแข็ง neu-i kăang **cheese**
เนื้อ néu-a **meat**
แนะนำ náa-nam **recommend**
ใน nai **in**
ในหลวง nai lŏo-ang **the King**

บ

บน bon **on**
บริษัท bor-rí-sàt **company**
บริษัทท่องเที่ยว bor-rí-sàt tôrng têe-o **travel agency**
บอบบาง bòrp bahng **fragile**
บัญชี ban-chee **account**
บัญชีธนาคาร ban-chee tá-nah-kahn **bank account**
บัตรขึ้นเครื่องบิน bàt kêun krêu-ang bin **boarding pass**
บัตรเครดิต bàt crair-dìt **credit card**
บัตรโทรศัพท์ bàt toh-rá-sàp **phone card**
บันได ban-dai **stairway**
บันทึกรายวัน ban-téuk rai wan **diary**
บ้าน bâhn **home • house**
บ้านพัก bâhn pák **boarding house**
บ้านเยาวชน bâhn yow-wá-chon **youth hostel**
บาร์ bah **bar**
บิล bin **bill (restaurant etc)**
บิล bin **check (bill)**
บุรุษพยาบาล bù-rùt pá-yah-bahn **nurse (man)**
บุหรี่ bù-rèe **cigarette**
บุหรี่ซิการ์ bù-rèe sí-gàh **cigar**
เบนซิน ben-sin **petrol**
เบรก brèk **brakes**
เบา bow **light (not heavy)**
เบียร์ bee-a **beer**
แบ่ง bàang **share (with)**
โบสถ์ bòht **cathedral**
โบสถ์ bòht **church**

ใบกรรมสิทธิ์รถยนต์ bai gam-má-sìt rót
  yon car owner's title
ใบขับขี่ bai kàp kèe drivers licence
ใบมีดโกน bai mêet gohn razor blade
ใบสั่งยา bai sàng yah prescription
ใบเสร็จ bai sèt receipt
ใบหน้า bai nâh face

ป

ปรอท ฺbà-ròrt thermometer
ประตู ฺbrà-doo door
ประตู ฺbrà-đoo gate (airport, etc)
ประเทศแคนาดา ฺbrà-têt kaa-nah-dah
  Canada
ประเทศนิวซีแลนด์ ฺbrà-têt new see-laan
  New Zealand
ประเทศเนเธอร์แลนด์ ฺbrà-têt nair-teu-laan
  Netherlands
ประเทศฝรั่งเศส ฺbrà-têt fà-ràng-sèt France
ประเทศสก็อตแลนด์ ฺbrà-têt sà-gòrt-laan
  Scotland
ประเทศออสเตรเลีย
  ฺbrà-têt or-sà-drair-lee-a Australia
ประเพณี ฺbrà-pair-nee custom
ปรับอากาศ ฺbràp ah-gàht air-conditioned
ปราสาท ฺbrah-sàht castle
ปลอกหมอน ฺblòrk mŏrn pillowcase
ปลั๊ก ฺblák plug (electricity)
ปลุก ฺblùk wake someone up
ปวดฟัน ฺbòo-at fan toothache
ปวดหัว ฺbòo-at hŏo-a headache
ป่วย ฺbòo-ay sick • ill
ปอนด์ ฺborn pound (money, weight)
ปัญญาอ่อน ฺban-yah òrn idiot
ปั๊มน้ำมัน ฺbám nám-man petrol station
ปั๊มน้ำมัน ฺbám nám-man service station
ปาก ฺbàhk mouth
ปากกา (ลูกลื่น) ฺbàhk-gah (lôok lêun) pen
  (ballpoint)
ปาเต๊ะ ฺbah-đé batik
ป้ายรถเมล์ ฺbâi rót mair bus stop
ป่ารก ฺbàh rók jungle

ปิกนิก ฺbìk-ník picnic
ปิด ฺbìt close • shut
ปิดแล้ว ฺbìt láa-ou closed
ปี ฺbee year
ปู่ ฺbòo grandfather (paternal)
เป้ ฺbâir backpack
เป็นไปไม่ได้ ฺben bai mâi dâi impossible
เปลี่ยนแปลง ฺblèe-an ฺblaang change
  (general)
แปรง ฺbraang brush
แปรงสีฟัน ฺbraang sĕe fan toothbrush
แปล ฺblaa translate
ไป ฺbai go
ไปกลับ bai glàp return (ticket)
ไปข้างนอก ฺbai kâhng nôrk go out
ไปซื้อของ ฺbai séu kŏrng go shopping
ไปเที่ยวกับ ฺbai têe-o gàp go out with
ไปรษณีย์ ฺbrai-sà-nee mail (postal
  system)
ไปรษณีย์ทางธรรมดา ฺbrai-sà-nee tahng
  tam-má-dah surface mail
ไปรษณียบัตร ฺbrai-sà-nee-yà-bàt postcard
ไปรษณีย์ลงทะเบียน ฺbrai-sà-nee long tá-
  bee-an registered mail (post by)
ไปรษณีย์อากาศ prai-sà-nee ah-gàht
  airmail

ผ

ผม ฺpŏm hair
ผม/ดิฉัน ฺpŏm/di-chăn m/f I • me
ผลไม้ ฺpŏn-lá-mái fruit
ผัก ฺpàk vegetable
ผับ ฺpàp pub (bar)
ผ้าเช็ดตัว ฺpâh chét đoo-a towel
ผ้าเช็ดปาก ฺpâh chét ฺbàhk napkin
ผ้าซัก ฺpâh sák laundry (clothes)
ผ้าปูที่นอน ฺpâh ฺboo têe norn bed linen
ผ้าพันคอ ฺpâh pan kor scarf
ผ้าพันแผล ฺpâh pan plăa bandage
ผ้าลินิน ฺpâh lí-nin linen (material)
ผ้าห่ม ฺpâh hòm blanket
ผ้าไหม ฺpâh măi silk

ผ้าอนามัย pâh à-nah-mai **panty liners**

ผ้าอนามัย pâh à-nah-mai **sanitary napkin**

ผ้าอ้อม pâh ôrm **diaper**

ผ้าอ้อม pâh ôrm **nappy**

ผิวเกรียมแดด pĕw gree-am dàat **sunburn**

ผู้จัดการ pôo jàt gahn **manager**

ผู้ชาย pôo chai **man**

ผู้โดยสาร pôo doy săhn **passenger**

ผู้หญิง pôo yĭng **woman**

เผ็ด pèt **hot (spicy)**

เผา pŏw **burn**

แผ่นซีดี pàan see-dee **disk (CD-ROM)**

แผ่นดิสก์ pàan dìt **disk (floppy)**

แผนที่ pàan têe **map**

แผ่นพับโฆษณา pàan páp koh-sà-nah **brochure**

แผลไฟไหม้ plăa fai mâi **burn**

ฝ

ฝน fŏn **rain**

ฝรั่ง fà-ràng **foreigner (Westerner)**

ฝักบัว fàk boo-a **shower**

ฝ้าย fâi **cotton**

พ

พจนานุกรม pót-jà-nah-nú-grom **dictionary**

พระอาทิตย์ prá ah-tít **sun**

พริกเขียว prík kĕe-o **green pepper**

พรุ่งนี้ prúng née **tomorrow**

พรุ่งนี้เช้า prúng née chów **tomorrow morning**

พรุ่งนี้บ่าย prúng née bài **tomorrow afternoon**

พรุ่งนี้เย็น prúng née yen **tomorrow evening**

พ่อครัว pôr kroo-a **chef**

พ่อแม่ pôr mâa **parents**

พิกัดน้ำหนักกระเป๋า pí-gàt nám nàk grà-bŏw **baggage allowance**

พิการ pí-gahn **disabled**

พิพิธภัณฑ์ pí-pít-tá-pan **museum**

พี่ชาย pêe chai **brother (older)**

พี่เลี้ยงเด็ก pêe lée-ang dèk **babysitter**

พูด pôot **speak**

เพศ pêt **sex (gender)**

เพศสัมพันธ์แบบปลอดภัย pêt săm-pan bàap blòrt pai **safe sex**

เพื่อน pêu-an **companion**

เพื่อน pêu-an **friend**

เพื่อนงาน pêu-an ngahn **colleague**

ฟ

ฟรี free **free (gratis)**

ฟัง fang **listen (to)**

ฟิล์ม fim **film (for camera)**

ฟิล์มสไลด์ fim sà-lái **slide (film)**

ฟุตบอล fút-born **football (soccer)**

ฟูก fôok **mattress**

แฟนผู้ชาย faan pôo chai **boyfriend**

แฟนสาว faan sŏw **girlfriend**

แฟลช flâat **flash (camera)**

ไฟ fai **light (electric)**

ไฟฉาย fai chăi **torch (flashlight)**

ไฟแช็ก fai cháak **cigarette lighter**

ไฟหน้ารถ fai nâh rót **headlights**

ภ

ภาพเขียน pâhp kĕe-an **painting (a work)**

ภาพถ่าย pâhp tài **photo**

ภาพยนตร์ pâhp-pá-yon **film • movie**

ภาษา pah-săh **language**

ภาษีสนามบิน pah-sĕe sà-năhm bin **airport tax**

ภูเขา poo kŏw **mountain**

เภสัชกร pair-sàt-chá-gorn **pharmacist**

ม

ม้วนเทป móo-an têp **cassette**

มหาวิทยาลัย má-hăh-wít-tá-yah-lai **university**

มะม่วงหิมพานต์ má-môo-ang hĭm-má-pahn **cashew**

มันสมอง กระทบกระเทือน man sà-mŏrng grà-tóp grà-teu·an **concussion**

มากกว่า mâhk gwàh **more (than something else)**

มากขึ้น mâhk kêun **more (than before)**

มิลลิเมตร min-lí-mét **millimetre**

มีค่า mee kâh **valuable**

มีด mêet **knife**

มีดโกน mêet gohn **razor**

มีดตัดเล็บ mêet dàt lép **nail clippers**

มีดพับ mêet páp **penknife**

มีราคา mee rah-kah **cost**

มืด mêut **dark**

มือ meu **hand**

มือจับ meu jàp **handlebars**

มื้ออาหาร méu ah-hăhn **meal**

เม็ดยา mét yah **pill**

เมตร mét **metre**

เมล็ดอามันด์ má-lét ah-man **almond**

เมา mow **drunk**

เมาคลื่น mow klêun **travel sickness (boat)**

เมาเครื่อง mow krêu·ang **travel sickness (air)**

เมารถ mow rót **travel sickness (car)**

เมีย mee·a **wife**

เมือง meu·ang **city**

เมื่อไร mêu·a rai **when**

เมื่อวาน mêu·a wahn **yesterday**

เมื่อวานซืน mêu·a wahn seun **day before yesterday**

แม่กุญแจ mâe gun-jaa **padlock**

แม่น้ำ mâa nám **river**

แม่ผัว mâa pŏo·a **mother-in-law (mother of husband)**

แม่ยาย mâa yai **mother-in-law (mother of wife)**

โมเดม moh-dem **modem**

ไม่ mâi **no**

ไม้ขีดไฟ mái kèet fai **matches (for lighting)**

ไม่มี mâi mee **without**

ไม่มีห้อง ว่าง mâi mee hôrng wâhng **no vacancy**

ไม่มีอะไร mâi mee à-rai **nothing**

ไม่สบาย mâi sà-bai **uncomfortable**

ไม่สูบบุหรี่ mâi sòop bù-rèe **non-smoking**

ยกทรง yók song **bra**

ยกเลิก yók lêuk **cancel**

ยอด yôrt **great (fantastic)**

ยา yah **drug**

ยา yah **medicine (medication)**

ย่า yâh **grandmother (paternal)**

ยาก yâhk **hard (difficult)**

ยากันแมลง yah gan má-laeng **insect repellent**

ยาแก้ปวด yah gâe ปๆๆ·at **painkiller**

ยาแก้ไอ yah gâe ai **cough medicine**

ยาคุมกำเนิด yah kum gam-nèut **contraceptives (pills)**

ยาฆ่าเชื้อ yah kâh chéu·a **antiseptic**

ยาดับกลิ่นตัว yah dàp glìn ดๆๆ·a **deodorant**

ยานวดผม yah nôo·at pŏm **conditioner (hair)**

ยาปฏิชีวนะ yah pà-đi-chee-wá-ná **antibiotics**

ยาย yai **grandmother (maternal)**

ยาระบาย yah rá-bai **laxative**

ยาว yow **long**

ยาสีฟัน yah sĕe fan **toothpaste**

ยาเสพติด yah sèp ดิt **drugs (illicit)**

ยาแอสไพริน yah àat-sà-pai-rin **aspirin**

ยืนยัน yeun yan **confirm (a booking)**

ยุ่ง yûng **busy**

เย็น yen **cool • cold**

แย่ yâa **awful**

รถเข็น rót kĕn **trolley**

รถเข็น rót kĕn **wheelchair**

รถเข็นเด็ก rót kĕn dèk **stroller**

รถจักรยาน rót jàk-gà-yahn **bicycle**

รถแท็กซี่ rót táak-sèe **taxi**

รถบัส rót bàt **bus (intercity)**
รถพยาบาล rót pá-yah-bahn **ambulance**
รถไฟ rót fai **train**
รถมอเตอร์ไซค์ rót mor-đeu-sai **motorcycle**
รถเมล์ rót mair **bus (city)**
รถยนต์ rót yon **car**
ร่ม rôm **shade • umbrella**
ร่วมกันใช้ rôo-am gan chái **share (a dorm etc)**
รหัสไปรษณีย์ rá-hàt brai-sà-nee **post code**
รอ ror **wait (for)**
รองเท้า rorng tów **shoe**
รองเท้าบู๊ท rorng tów bút **boot**
ร้อน rórn **hot**
รอยพอง roy porng **blister**
ระวัง rá-wang **Careful!**
รัก rák **love**
รัฐบาล rát-tà-bahn **government**
รับประกัน ráp brà-gan **guaranteed**
รับประทาน ráp brà-tahn **eat (very formal)**
ราคา rah-kah **price**
ราคาส่วนลด rah-kah sòo-an lót **discount**
ร้าน ráhn **shop**
ร้านกาแฟ ráhn gah-faa **cafe**
ร้านขายขนม ráhn kǎi kà-nǒm **cake shop**
ร้านขายของชำ ráhn kǎi kǒrng cham **convenience store**
ร้านขายของที่ระลึก ráhn kǎi kǒrng têe rá-léuk **souvenir shop**
ร้านขายเนื้อ ráhn kǎi néu-a **butcher's shop**
ร้านขายยา ráhn kǎi yah **pharmacy**
ร้านขายรองเท้า ráhn kǎi rorng tów **shoe shop**
ร้านขายเสื้อผ้า ráhn kǎi sêu-a pâh **clothing store**
ร้านขายหนังสือพิมพ์ ráhn kǎi nǎng-sěu pim **newsagency**
ร้านขายเหล้า ráhn kǎi lôw **liquor store**
ร้านขายอุปกรณ์กีฬา ráhn kǎi ùp-bà-gorn gee-lah **sports store**
ร้านขายอุปกรณ์เขียน ráhn kǎi ùp-bà-gorn kěe-an **stationer's (shop)**

ร้านดนตรี ráhn don-đree **music shop**
ร้านเสริมสวย ráhn sěum sǒo-ay **beauty salon**
ร้านอาหาร ráhn ah-hǎhn **restaurant**
ร้านอินเตอร์เนต ráhn in-đeu-nét **Internet cafe**
รายการ rai gahn **itinerary**
รายการอาหาร rai gahn ah-hǎhn **menu**
รายวัน rai wan **daily**
รีโมท ree-môht **remote control**
รูปหล่อ rôop lòr **handsome**
เรือ reu-a **boat**
เรือข้ามฟาก reu-a kâhm fâhk **ferry**
เรือสำเภา reu-a sǎm-pow **junk (boat)**
แรมคืน raam keun **overnight**
โรคกระเพาะอักเสบ rôhk grà-pó àk-sèp **gastroenteritis**
โรคตับอักเสบ rôhk đàp àk-sèp **hepatitis**
โรคเบาหวาน rôhk bow wǎhn **diabetes**
โรคหัวใจ rôhk hǒo-a jai **heart condition**
โรงซักรีด rohng sák rêet **launderette**
โรงพยาบาล rohng pá-yaa-bahn **hospital**
โรงแรม rohng raam **hotel**
โรงละคร rohng lá-korn **theatre**
โรงหนัง rohng nǎng **cinema**
โรแมนติค roh-maan-đìk **romantic**
ไร่นา rài nah **farm**

ถ

ลอง lorng **try (try out)**
ละคร lá-korn **play (theatre)**
ลาก่อน lah gòrn **goodbye**
ล้าง láhng **wash (something)**
ล่าม lâhm **interpreter**
ลิปสติก líp-sà-đìk **lipstick**
ลิฟต์ líp **lift (elevator)**
ลูกค้า lôok káh **client**
ลูกชาย lôok chai **son**
ลูกสาว lôok sǒw **daughter**
เล็ก lék **small**
เล็กกว่า lék gwàh **smaller**
เล็กที่สุด lék têe sùt **smallest**
เลนส์ len **lens**

เลนส์สัมผัส len săm-pàt **contact lenses**
เลว le-ou **bad**
เล็สเบียน lét-bee-an **lesbian**
เลือด lêu-at **blood**
แลก lâak **cash (a cheque)** • **change (money)**
แลก lâak
และ láa **and**

ว

วงคนตรี wong don-đree **band (music)**
ว่าง wâhng **palace**
วัตถุโบราณ wát-tù boh-rahn **antique**
วัน wan **day**
วันเกิด wan gèut **birthday**
วันขึ้นปีใหม่ wan kêun bee mài **New Year's Day**
วันที่ wan têe **date (day)**
วันที่เกิด wan têe gèut **date of birth**
วันนี้ wan née **today**
วันมะรืน wan má-reun **day after tomorrow**
วันเสาร์อาทิตย์ wan sŏw ah-tít **weekend**
ว่าง wâhng **free (available)**
ว่าง wâhng **vacant**
ว่ายน้ำ wâi nám **swim**
วิทยาศาสตร์ wit-tá-yah-sàht **science**
วิทยุ wit-tá-yú **radio**
วีซ่า wee-sâh **visa**
เวลาเปิด wair-lah bèut **opening hours**
แว่นกันแดด wâen gan dàat **sunglasses**
แว่นตา wâen đah **glasses (spectacles)**
ไวรัสเอ็ชไอวี wai-rát èt ai wee **HIV**

ศ

ศาสนาฮินดู sàht-sà-nâh hin-doo **Hindu**
ศิลปะ sĭn-lá-bà **art**
ศิลปิน sĭn-lá-bin **artist**
ศุลกากร sŭn-lá-gah-gorn **customs**
ศูนย์กลาง sŏon glahng **centre**

ส

สกปรก sòk-gà-bròk **dirty**
ส่ง sòng **deliver**
สไตรค์ sà-đrai **strike**
สถานี sà-tăh-nee **station**
สถานีขนส่ง sà-thăh-nee kŏn sòng **bus station**
สถานีตำรวจ sà-tăh-nee đam-ròo-at **police station**
สถานีรถไฟ sà-tăh-nee rót fai **railway station**
สถานีรถไฟ sà-tăh-nee rót fai **train station**
สถานีรถไฟฟ้า sà-tăh-nee rót fai fáh **metro station**
สนามเทนนิส sà-năhm ten-nít **tennis court**
สนามบิน sà-năhm bin **airport**
สบาย sà-bai **comfortable**
สบู่ sà-bòo **soap**
สมุดโทรศัพท์ sà-mùt toh-rá-sàp **phone book**
สมุดบันทึก sà-mùt ban-téuk **notebook**
สรรพสินค้า sàp-pá-sĭn-káh **department store**
สรรพสินค้า sàp-pá-sĭn-káh **shopping centre**
สร้อยคอ sôy kor **necklace**
สระว่ายน้ำ sà wâi nám **swimming pool**
สวน sŏo-an **garden**
สวนสัตว์ sŏo-an sàt **zoo**
สวนสาธารณะ sŏo-an săh-tah-rá-ná **park**
ส้วม sôo-am **toilet**
สวย sŏo-ay **beautiful**
สวัสดีครับ/สวัสดีค่ะ sà-wàt-dee kráp/ sà-wàt-dee kà m/f **Hello.**
สหรัฐอเมริกา sà-hà-rát à-mair-rí-gah **USA**
สอง sŏrng **two**
สองเตียง sŏrng đee-ang **twin beds**
สะพาน sà-pahn **bridge**
สะอาด sà-àht **clean**
สัญญาณโทรศัพท์ săn-yahn toh-rá-sàp **dial tone**
สามเหลี่ยมทองคำ săhm lèe-am torng kam **Golden Triangle**
สายการบิน săi gahn bin **airline**

สายพ่วง sǎi pôo·ang **jumper leads**
สำคัญ sǎm-kan **important**
สำนักงานท่องเที่ยว sǎm-nák ngahn tôrng
    têe·o **tourist office**
สำลี sǎm-lee **cotton balls**
สี sěe **colour**
สีขาว sěe kǒw **white**
สีเขียว sěe kěe·o **green**
สีชมพู sěe chom-poo **pink**
สีดำ sěe dam **black**
สีแดง sěe daang **red**
สีน้ำเงิน sěe nám ngeun **blue (dark)**
สีน้ำตาล sěe nám đahn **brown**
สีฟ้า sěe fáh **blue (light)**
สีส้ม sěe sôm **orange (colour)**
สีเหลือง sěe lěu·ang **yellow**
สุข sùk **happy**
สุขภาพ sù-kà-pâhp **health**
สุขาธารณะ sù-kǎh sǎh-tah-rá-ná
    public toilet
สุสาน sù-sǎhn **cemetery**
เสีย sěe·a **off (spoiled)**
เสีย sěe·a **out of order**
เสียงดัง sěe·ang dang **noisy**
เสียแล้ว sěe·a láa-ou **broken down**
เสื้อกันฝน sêu·a gan fǒn **raincoat**
เสื้อกันหนาว sêu·a gan nǒw **jacket**
เสื้อคลุม sêu·a klum **coat**
เสื้อชูชีพ sêu·a choo chêep **life jacket**
เสื้อเชิ้ต sêu·a chéut **shirt**
เสื้อถัก sêu·a đàk **jumper • sweater**
เสื้อผ้า sêu·a pâh **clothing**
เสื้อยืด sêu·a yêut **T-shirt**
แสตมป์ sà-đáam **stamp**
โสด sòht **single (person)**
โสเภณี sõh-pair-nee **prostitute**
ใส่กุญแจ sài gun-jaa **lock**
ใส่กุญแจแล้ว sài gun-jaa láa-ou **locked**

ห

หนัก nàk **heavy**
หนัง nǎng **leather**
หนังสือ nǎng-sěu **book**

หนังสือเดินทาง nǎng-sěu deun tahng
    passport
หนังสือพิมพ์ nǎng-sěu pim **newspaper**
หน้า nâh **next (month)**
หน้า nâh **season**
หน้าต่าง nâh đàhng **window**
หน้าใบไม้ผลิ nâh bai mái pli **spring (season)**
หน้าฝน nâh fǒn **rainy season**
หน้าร้อน nâh rórn **summer**
หนาว nǒw **cold (sensation)**
หน้าหนาว nâh nǒw **winter**
หน้าอก nâh òk **chest (body)**
หนึ่ง nèung **one**
หมอ mǒr **doctor**
หมอน mǒrn **pillow**
หมอนวด mǒr nôo·at **masseur/masseuse**
หม้อแบตเตอรี่ mǒr bàat-đeu-rêe
    battery (car)
หม้อแปลง mǒr blaang **adaptor**
หมอฟัน mǒr fan **dentist**
หมา mǎh **dog**
หมายเลขหนังสือเดินทาง mǎi lêk nǎng-sěu
    deun tahng **passport number**
หมายเลขห้อง mǎi lêk hôrng **room number**
หย่าแล้ว yàh láa-ou **divorced**
หยุด yùt **Stop!**
หรูหรา rǒo-ràh **luxury**
หลัง lǎng **after**
หลัง lǎng **back (body)**
หลัง lǎng **rear (seat etc)**
หลาน lǎhn **grandchild**
หวาน wǎhn **sweet**
หวี wěe **comb**
ห่อ hòr **package**
ห้อง hôrng **room**
ห้องเก็บเสื้อ hôrng gèp sêu·a **cloakroom**
ห้องคอนโด hôrng korn-doh **apartment**
ห้องคู่ hôrng kôo **double room**
ห้องเดี่ยว hôrng dèe·o **single room**
ห้องนอน hôrng norn **bedroom**
ห้องน้ำ hôrng nám **bathroom**
ห้องเปลี่ยนเสื้อ hôrng blèe-an sêu·a
    changing room (in shop)
ห้องพักรอ hôrng pák ror **waiting room**

ห้องพักสำหรับคนเดินทางผ่าน hôrng pák sǎm-ràp kon deun tahng pàhn **transit lounge**

ห้องรับฝากกระเป๋า hôrng ráp fàhk grá-bǒw **left luggage (office)**

ห้องว่าง hôrng wâhng **vacancy**

ห้องสมุด hôrng sà-mùt **library**

ห้องแสดงภาพ hôrng sà-daang pâhp **art gallery**

หักแล้ว hàk láa-ou **broken**

หัตถกรรม hàt-tà-gam **crafts**

หัว hǒo-a **head**

หัวใจ hǒo-a jai **heart**

หัวใจวาย hǒo-a jai wai **heart attack**

หัวนมเทียม hǒo-a nom tee-am **dummy • pacifier**

หาย hǎi **lost**

หายาก hǎh yâhk **rare (uncommon)**

หิวน้ำ hěw nám **thirsty (to be)**

หูเทียม hǒo tee-am **hearing aid**

เหนื่อย nèu-ay **tired**

เหรียญ rěe-an **coins**

เหล็กไขจุกขวด lèk kǎi jùk kòo-at **corkscrew**

เหล้า lôw **alcohol**

เหล้าไวน์ lôw wai **wine**

แห้ง hâang **dry**

แหนบ nàap **tweezers**

แหวน wǎan **ring (on finger)**

ใหญ่ yài **big**

ใหญ่กว่า yài gwàh **bigger**

ใหม่ mài **new**

ไหล่ lài **shoulder**

อ

องคชาติ ong-ká-châht **penis**

อย่างช้า yàhng cháh **slowly**

อร่อย à-ròy **tasty**

อรุณ à-run **dawn**

อ้วน ôo-an **fat**

ออกเดินทาง òrk deun tahng **depart (leave)**

อ่อน òrn **light (of colour)**

อันตราย an-dà-rai **dangerous**

อาบน้ำ àhng nám **bath**

อาจารย์ ah-jahn **teacher**

อาทิตย์ ah-tít **week**

อารมณ์ ah-rom **feelings**

อาหาร ah-hǎhn **food**

อาหารกลางวัน ah-hǎhn glahng wan **lunch**

อาหารเช้า ah-hǎhn chów **breakfast**

อาหารตั้งโต๊ะ ah-hǎhn đâng đó **buffet**

อาหารทารก ah-hǎhn tah-rók **baby food**

อาหารที่จัดทำตามหลักศาสนายิว ah-hǎhn têe jàt tam đahm làk sàht-sà-nǎh yew **kosher**

อาหารที่จัดทำตามหลักศาสนาอิสลาม ah-hǎhn têe jàt tam đahm làk sàht-sà-nǎh ìt-sà-lahm **halal**

อาหารมื้อเย็น ah-hǎhn méu yen **dinner**

อาหารไม่ย่อย ah-hǎhn mâi yôy **indigestion**

อาหารว่าง ah-hǎhn wâhng **snack**

อินเตอร์เนต in-đeu-nét **Internet**

อีก (อัน) หนึ่ง èek (an) nèung **another**

อุณหภูมิ un-hà-poom **temperature (weather)**

อุ่น ùn **warm**

อุบัติเหตุ ù-bàt-đi-hèt **accident**

เอกสาร èk-gà-sǎhn **paperwork**

ไอ ai **cough**

ไอติม ai-đim **ice cream**

ฮ

เฮโรอีน hair-roh-een **heroin**

A

B

C

D

E

F

G

H

I